D1785496

YOU ARE MORE THAN
JUST YOUR SUN SIGN

An Insightful, Intuitive, and Practical Interpretation

Joan Zodianz

ZODIANZ

ZODIANZ | Anaheim, CA 92801
Copyright © 2021 Joan Zodianz. All rights reserved.

www.zodianz.com

You Are More Than Just Your Sun Sign
An Insightful, Intuitive, and Practical Interpretation

Self-Published in 2021

Written, illustrated, and designed by Joan Zodianz
Final Edit by Lyric Dodson

All rights reserved, including the right of reproduction or distribution in whole or in part in any form or by any graphic, electronic, or any mechanical means. No part of this book may be used or reproduced (online or offline) without written permission from the publisher.

ISBN 978-0-578-85830-2

Library of Congress Control Number: 2021902809

I dedicate this book to the following:

To all minorities who have a dream worth fighting for;
to all my true supporters whom I call friends and family;
and to my guide, Archangel Gabriel, because without
my Angel, I would be at a loss of words.

As you do with the Sun and the Moon,
accept and master both the light and dark
energies within yourself.

Love,
Joan Zodianz

COZMIC CONTENTS

PREFACE ....

READING THIS BOOK 1

HOW THIS BOOK HELPS YOU 3
WHAT THIS BOOK WILL NOT DO....................3
SUGGESTIVE WAY OF LEARNING....................4
ASTROLOGY BASICS 5

UNDERSTANDING HOROSCOPES..........7

MACRO AND MICRO INSIGHTS....................9
STANDARD TIME 10
TRADITIONAL DATES VS. SOLAR CALENDARS ...11
YOUR NATAL/BIRTH CHART 12

HOW TO READ AN EPHEMERIS 13

PLANETS 15

EVOLUTION OF PLANETS 18
PLANETARY CHEAT SHEET 19
LUMINARIES: SUN AND MOON 20
INNER PLANETS (INTERNAL)...................20
OUTER PLANETS (EXTERNAL) 20
RETROGRADE (Rx) VERSUS DIRECT (D)..........21
ORBITAL/RETROGRADE CHEAT SHEET 22
SUN...23
MOON 24
MERCURY 25
VENUS 27
MARS 29
JUPITER 31
SATURN.......................................33
URANUS 35
NEPTUNE.....................................37
PLUTO 39

HEMISPHERES AND QUADRANTS.......41

ASCENDANT & DESCENDANT 42
MIDHEAVEN & IMUM COELI 44

HOUSE SYSTEMS 47

EQUAL HOUSING SYSTEMS 49
UNEQUAL HOUSING SYSTEMS 51

HOUSES EXPLAINED 53

HOUSES CHEAT SHEET 53
BOTTOM (INTERNAL) HEMISPHERE...............54
TOP (EXTERNAL) HEMISPHERE...................56

HOUSE LANDLORDS 59

HOUSE LANDLORDS CHEAT SHEET...............59
HOUSE DOMINANCE............................62
1ST HOUSE OF SELF (SELF-AWARENESS) 63
2ND HOUSE OF POSSESSIONS 64
3RD HOUSE OF COMMUNICATION 65
4TH HOUSE OF HOME...........................66
5TH HOUSE OF CREATIVITY 67
6TH HOUSE OF SERVICE & HEALTH...............68
7TH HOUSE OF LOVE & PARTNERSHIP 69
8TH HOUSE OF REGENERATION &
TRANSFORMATION...............................70
9TH HOUSE OF MENTAL EXPLORATION 71
10TH HOUSE OF CAREER 72
11TH HOUSE OF HOPE AND FRIENDSHIPS 73
12TH HOUSE OF SELF-UNDOING..................74

ASPECTS 77

ORBS & DEGREES 77
ASPECT CHEAT SHEET 78
ASPECT MEANINGS 79
CONJUNCTION (MARRIED) 79
SEXTILE (DATING)...........................79
SQUARE (DIVORCED) 80
TRINE (PROFESSIONAL) 80
OPPOSITION (COMPLICATED) 81

ELEMENTS 83

COMPATIBLE ELEMENTS...........................84
FIRE SIGNS (SPIRIT).........................85

Earth Signs (Body) 86
Air Signs (Mind) 87
Water Signs (Heart) 88

MODALITIES **89**

Cardinal Signs 90
Fixed Signs 91
Mutable Signs 92

ZODIAC SIGNS IN DETAIL **93**

Zodiac Cheat Sheet 94

ARIES **95**

Aries Sun 96
Unevolved Aries – Wild Barbarian 101
Evolved Aries – Wise General.............. 102
Aries Moon 103
Aries Energy in Other Placements 104
    Aries Ascendant (Rising) 104
    Aries Midheaven (MC) 104
    Aries Mercury 105
    Aries Venus 105
    Aries Mars............................... 106
    Aries Jupiter 106
    Aries Saturn 107
    Aries Uranus 107
    Aries Neptune 108
    Aries Pluto.............................. 108

TAURUS **109**

Taurus Sun 110
Unevolved Taurus – Stubborn Dictator
.... 115
Evolved Taurus – Life Mentor 116
Taurus Moon 117
Taurus Energy in Other Placements 118
    Taurus Ascendant (Rising) 118
    Taurus Midheaven (MC) 118
    Taurus Mercury 119

Taurus Venus...................... 119
Taurus Mars 120
Taurus Jupiter........................ 120
Taurus Saturn 121
Taurus Uranus 121
Taurus Neptune........................ 122
Taurus Pluto 122

GEMINI **123**

Gemini Sun 124
Unevolved Gemini – Chaotic Gossiper .. 129
Evolved Gemini – Creative Composer ... 130
Gemini Moon 131
Gemini Energy in Other Placements 132
    Gemini Ascendant (Rising) 132
    Gemini Midheaven (MC) 132
    Gemini Mercury....................... 133
    Gemini Venus 133
    Gemini Mars............................ 134
    Gemini Jupiter 134
    Gemini Saturn 135
    Gemini Uranus........................ 135
    Gemini Neptune 136
    Gemini Pluto........................... 136

CANCER...................................... **137**

Cancer Sun....................................... 138
Unevolved Cancer – Emotional Wreck 143
Evolved Cancer – Emotional Master ... 144
Cancer Moon 145
Cancer Energy in Other Placements..... 146
    Cancer Ascendant (Rising)........ 146
    Cancer Midheaven (MC)........... 146
    Cancer Mercury 147
    Cancer Venus........................... 147
    Cancer Mars 148
    Cancer Jupiter......................... 148
    Cancer Saturn 149
    Cancer Uranus 149

Cancer Neptune *150*
Cancer Pluto *150*

LEO **151**

LEO SUN 152
UNEVOLVED LEO – DRAMATIC DIVA/DIVO ... 157
EVOLVED LEO – PASSIONATE VISIONARY 158
LEO MOON 159
LEO ENERGY IN OTHER PLACEMENTS 160
    Leo Ascendant (Rising) *160*
    Leo Midheaven (MC) *160*
    Leo Mercury *161*
    Leo Venus *161*
    Leo Mars *162*
    Leo Jupiter *162*
    Leo Saturn *163*
    Leo Uranus *163*
    Leo Neptune *164*
    Leo Pluto *164*

VIRGO **165**

VIRGO SUN 166
UNEVOLVED VIRGO – ANXIOUS CRITICIZER .. 171
EVOLVED VIRGO – TACTFUL ARCHITECT 172
VIRGO MOON 173
VIRGO ENERGY IN OTHER PLACEMENTS 174
    Virgo Ascendant (Rising) *174*
    Virgo Midheaven (MC) *174*
    Virgo Mercury *175*
    Virgo Venus *175*
    Virgo Mars *176*
    Virgo Jupiter *176*
    Virgo Saturn *177*
    Virgo Uranus *177*
    Virgo Neptune *178*
    Virgo Pluto *178*

LIBRA **179**

LIBRA SUN 180

UNEVOLVED LIBRA – VAIN CON ARTIST 185
EVOLVED LIBRA – CAPTIVATING INNOVATOR 186
LIBRA MOON 187
LIBRA ENERGY IN OTHER PLACEMENTS 188
    Libra Ascendant (Rising) *188*
    Libra Midheaven (MC) *188*
    Libra Mercury *189*
    Libra Venus *189*
    Libra Mars *190*
    Libra Jupiter *190*
    Libra Saturn *191*
    Libra Uranus *191*
    Libra Neptune *192*
    Libra Pluto *192*

SCORPIO **193**

SCORPIO SUN 194
UNEVOLVED SCORPIO – VENGEFUL
MANIPULATOR 199
EVOLVED SCORPIO – INTUITIVE PSYCHIC 200
SCORPIO MOON 201
SCORPIO ENERGY IN OTHER PLACEMENTS ... 202
    Scorpio Ascendant (Rising) *202*
    Scorpio Midheaven (MC) *202*
    Scorpio Mercury *203*
    Scorpio Venus *203*
    Scorpio Mars *204*
    Scorpio Jupiter *204*
    Scorpio Saturn *205*
    Scorpio Uranus *205*
    Scorpio Neptune *206*
    Scorpio Pluto *206*

SAGITTARIUS **207**

SAGITTARIUS SUN 208
UNEVOLVED SAGITTARIUS – RECKLESS GAMBLER
.... 213
EVOLVED SAGITTARIUS – ENLIGHTENED
TRAVELER 214

SAGITTARIUS MOON 215
SAGITTARIUS ENERGY IN OTHER PLACEMENTS
.... 216

    Sagittarius Ascendant (Rising).. 216
    Sagittarius Midheaven (MC)..... 216
    Sagittarius Mercury 217
    Sagittarius Venus 217
    Sagittarius Mars 218
    Sagittarius Jupiter 218
    Sagittarius Saturn 219
    Sagittarius Uranus 219
    Sagittarius Neptune 220
    Sagittarius Pluto 220

CAPRICORN...................................... **221**

CAPRICORN SUN 222
UNEVOLVED CAPRICORN – ABUSIVE CAPITALIST
.... 227
EVOLVED CAPRICORN – RESOURCEFUL PROVIDER
.... 228
CAPRICORN MOON................................. 229
CAPRICORN ENERGY IN OTHER PLACEMENTS 230
    Capricorn Ascendant (Rising).... 230
    Capricorn Midheaven (MC)....... 230
    Capricorn Mercury 231
    Capricorn Venus 231
    Capricorn Mars 232
    Capricorn Jupiter 232
    Capricorn Saturn 233
    Capricorn Uranus 233
    Capricorn Neptune 234
    Capricorn Pluto 234

AQUARIUS **235**

AQUARIUS SUN..................................... 236
UNEVOLVED AQUARIUS – OPINIONATED REBEL
.... 241
EVOLVED AQUARIUS – WORLD ADVOCATE.. 242
AQUARIUS MOON 243

AQUARIUS ENERGY IN OTHER PLACEMENTS . 244
    Aquarius Ascendant (Rising) 244
    Aquarius Midheaven (MC) 244
    Aquarius Mercury 245
    Aquarius Venus 245
    Aquarius Mars 246
    Aquarius Jupiter 246
    Aquarius Saturn........................ 247
    Aquarius Uranus....................... 247
    Aquarius Neptune 248
    Aquarius Pluto.......................... 248

PISCES **249**

PISCES SUN.. 250
UNEVOLVED PISCES – PETTY SIREN............. 255
EVOLVED PISCES – COMPASSIONATE MERMAID
.... 256
PISCES MOON 257
PISCES ENERGY IN OTHER PLACEMENTS 258
    Pisces Ascendant (Rising) 258
    Pisces Midheaven (MC) 258
    Pisces Mercury 259
    Pisces Venus 259
    Pisces Mars............................... 260
    Pisces Jupiter 260
    Pisces Saturn 261
    Pisces Uranus 261
    Pisces Neptune 262
    Pisces Pluto.............................. 262

CUSPS **263**

ARIES – TAURUS CUSP 264
TAURUS – GEMINI CUSP 264
GEMINI – CANCER CUSP 265
CANCER – LEO CUSP................................ 265
LEO – VIRGO CUSP.................................. 266
VIRGO – LIBRA CUSP 266
LIBRA – SCORPIO CUSP 267
SCORPIO – SAGITTARIUS CUSP................... 267

SAGITTARIUS – CAPRICORN CUSP 268
CAPRICORN – AQUARIUS CUSP 268
AQUARIUS – PISCES CUSP 269
PISCES – ARIES CUSP 269

DECANATES 271

ARIES DECANATES 273
TAURUS DECANATES 274
GEMINI DECANATES 275
CANCER DECANATES 276
LEO DECANATES......................................277
VIRGO DECANATES 278
LIBRA DECANATES 279
SCORPIO DECANATES 280
SAGITTARIUS DECANATES 281
CAPRICORN DECANATES 282

AQUARIUS DECANATES 283
PISCES DECANATES 284

POLAR OPPOSITES...........................285

ARIES & LIBRA 286
TAURUS & SCORPIO 287
GEMINI & SAGITTARIUS 288
CANCER & CAPRICORN 289
LEO & AQUARIUS 290
VIRGO & PISCES 291

NATAL CHART FORMULA 293

SAMPLE FORMULA 295

ACKNOWLEDGEMENT 299

SPIRITUAL RESOURCES 303

PREFACE

Hello Cozmic Clan,

My name is Joan Zodianz. I'm Filipino American, currently 34 years old, and a Sun in Sagittarius on the cusp of Scorpio. I'm also a professional astrologer, tarot reader, spiritual teacher, and Angel medium. I have been developing my spiritual gifts since I was 16 years old, perhaps even younger.

Throughout the years, I have done my very best to learn and expand my knowledge beyond the traditional foundation of astrology we all have grown to love. I wrote this book because I wanted to teach people a more practical and intuitive way of interpreting astrology, and I love how it can help our mental, emotional, and spiritual well-being.

To me, astrology is the art of learning and mastering your own energy and the language of universal energy. Therefore, it's important to understand how to adapt this knowledge into our everyday lives.

Please understand that you are more than just your Sun sign. You are a kaleidoscope of cosmic placements and complex aspects, which make us all unique, so learn astrology to gain in-depth self-awareness and universal energy awareness. It's in this way you will be able to accept and appreciate diverse energies in yourself and in others.

Love always,

. . . you are more than just your Sun sign.

You are a kaleidoscope of cosmic placements and complex aspects, which makes us all unique . . .

READING THIS BOOK

You, like many, are probably wondering what the stars can reveal about your inner strengths and weaknesses. Most people start by learning their Sun sign then never really get into their other placements. Then, there are actual students who want to expand their knowledge, so they dive deeper into the rabbit hole. Regardless of where you fit, astrology can help you understand yourself and others in more depth.

Learning **how to read a horoscope** is challenging for a beginner, but the best way to learn is to break it down piece by piece, aspect by aspect. There is no better way of reading and learning a horoscope than by starting with your own natal/birth chart.

The zodiac signs, houses, and aspects are all co-dependent on planets, so if you're looking for a place to start, then it's advised to start by gaining a deep understanding of how astrological planets and luminaries work both independently and with each other. Learning the deeper meaning of planets and zodiac signs can provide you with as much information as you need to come up with stronger interpretations moving forward.

When reading the planets, connect them with the houses and zodiac signs they're aligned to. Next, read the meaning of the house the planet is in. Afterward, read the meaning of the zodiac sign within that house. Do this for each planet until you gain a basic understanding of what each of them means. From there, it's advised to read everything as a whole and how it relates to the event, the person, or you.

When you feel comfortable, you should then learn the meaning of aspects, which is more advanced astrology. There are many books that cover aspects in full detail; however, this book will not cover all of them as that can be its own book. However, you don't always have to know aspects either.

✸☆☾

Example (Sun – Moon Vibration): My Sun is Sagittarius (mutable fire) on the cusp of Scorpio in the 10th House of Career. My Moon is Virgo (mutable earth) in the 8th House of Regeneration. Traditional astrology states this pairing creates a square aspect. You can read the square aspect as tension between the Sun and Moon, and you can also read it as the zodiac signs and elements being incompatible; both create tension between the Sun and Moon.

From my experience, I find that both ways work wonderfully. The method you choose to use is dependent on if you're more intuitive and free-flowing or more logical and analytical. At the end of the day, you'll have your own experiences that will show you which one you are.

Since astrology is complex and there is much to learn, don't get frustrated if the information you find is overwhelming. You don't have to understand it all today, so be kind to yourself. Even the best astrologers have dedicated years to educating themselves and grasping the meaning of astrology.

It's good to keep in mind that every astrologer possesses their own unique interpretation, although most will have a strong understanding of the same basic foundations. The point is to collect as much information as you can so you can develop your own insights and interpretations and become an amazing astrologer in your own right!

Always follow your intuition and don't stop learning!

As humanity evolves, so does astrology. You don't have to always go by the book because time permits us to change our perspectives. That's the wonderful thing about life: we are constantly moving, just like the planets. Remember, always follow your intuition and don't stop learning!

☼ ☆ ☾

HOW THIS BOOK HELPS YOU

This book will help you gain an intuitive and practical understanding of astrology by breaking down the following: horoscope and planets in macro and micro perspectives, patterns in astrology, and evolution between houses, elements, modalities, and signs.

For we are all born in darkness before we reach the light.

This book *will not* coddle your feelings. You will learn the good, the bad, the ugly, and the beautiful for each planet and each zodiac sign. This book will share all sides of astrology, embracing both light and dark energies, for we are all born in darkness before we reach the light.

WHAT THIS BOOK WILL NOT DO

Due to the complexity and uniqueness of horoscopes, it is impossible for this book, or any book, to interpret a horoscope completely. Books can only interpret things in parts. As such, this book will not teach you everything in astrology, and it will not teach everything from a historical perspective. It will share as much information as possible in as much detail as possible for you to gain an informed interpretation using your own intuition and wisdom.

Books can only interpret things in parts.

Learning astrology takes time, education, experience, and lots of patience and kindness toward yourself and your learning capabilities. Don't try to rush the journey. Read as much as you can from multiple sources, and enjoy it at a pace that gives you peace.

✵☆☾

SUGGESTIVE WAY OF LEARNING

★ **Generate your birth/natal chart** through Zodianz.com
★ **Read Planets:** Learn about the planets and understand the difference between the internal and external planets
★ **Read Houses:** Learn the meaning of each house and their "landlords"
★ **Read Zodiac Signs:** Learn the energy of each zodiac sign
★ **Read Aspects:** Check the relationship (the energy) between your planets
★ **Use the Natal Chart Formula** featured at the end of this book

AUTHOR NOTES

Nobody is perfect, and we all have good and bad sides that we eventually learn to embrace and acknowledge. My intent for this book is to help you see all sides of yourself. It's with this knowledge that you'll able to understand and redefine who you are as a person. When we confront and overcome our weaknesses, we then learn how to strengthen them.

Astrology has helped shape who I am today, and I am always learning something new about myself and astrology. I hope this book helps someone do the same. So be kind and realistic with who you are and who you envision yourself to be. It's the first step to true spiritual enlightenment.

☼ ☆ ☾

ASTROLOGY BASICS

Astrology is more about planets and luminaries than actual constellations. It's the study of how the movement of the planets and luminaries affect our energies from a societal (macro) and individual (micro) perspective. The movements of luminaries and planets are casted in what we call a horoscope.

Here are patterns you should remember:

★ **Four elements:** fire, earth, air, water
★ **Three modalities:** cardinal, fixed, mutable
★ **Masculine positive (Yang) energies:** fire and air
★ **Feminine negative (Yin) energies:** earth and water
★ **12 zodiac signs:** Aries, Taurus, Gemini, Cancer, Leo, Virgo, Libra, Scorpio, Sagittarius, Capricorn, Aquarius, and Pisces
★ **12 houses:** self, possessions, communication, home, creativity, service, partnership, regeneration, mental exploration, career, hopes, and self-undoing
★ **10 ruling "planets":** Sun and Moon (the luminaries), Mercury, Venus, Mars, Jupiter, Saturn, Uranus, Neptune, and Pluto (some zodiac signs share planets)
★ Horoscopes represent a **24-hour day** and a **360° chart**
★ **Three decanates, aka decans, per zodiac sign,** associated with a ruling planet from their elemental sibling
★ **Aspects** describe the relationship and energy between planets, which influences our personality and energy
★ **Synastry** describes the relationship/compatibility between two natal charts, usually for lovers but it can be used for any type of relationship
★ Zodiac signs evolve from the sign behind them. Therefore, **cusps are important** because these denote transitional phases between signs.

☼ ☆ ☾

☼ ☆ ☾

UNDERSTANDING HOROSCOPES

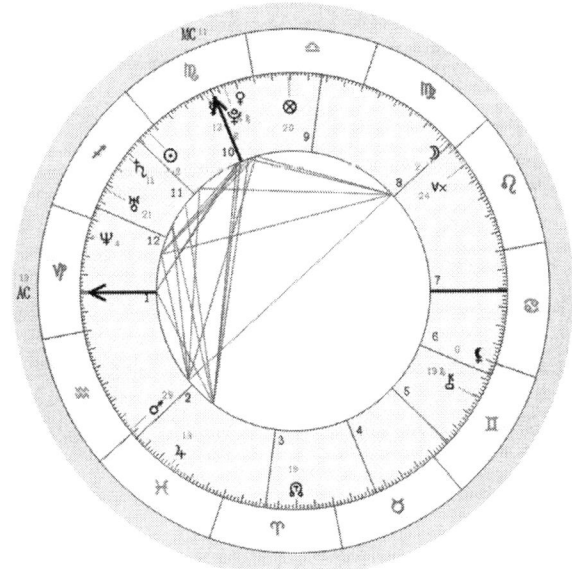

Sample Birth Chart:
Generated on Zodianz.com
Placidus - Unequal Housing System - Tropical

A horoscope is a 360° chart of the planets, houses, and zodiac signs casted on a specific day, month, year, time zone, and location. In the middle of the chart is Earth in relation to our solar system.

In a horoscope, you will find multiple aspects (denoted by the crossing lines) within the planets. These chart the relationships between planets. Along the border of the horoscope are the 12 zodiac signs, which remain stationary (fixed, non-moving) with an even 30° each.

You will notice multiple glyphs (symbols) that represent zodiac signs, planets, quadrants, and nodes. The arrows point to the Ascendant (Rising/AC) and Midheaven (MC) signs. Lastly, the 12 numbers along the border of the Earth represent the 12 houses, which divide the chart into 12 sections.

You must understand that there are hundreds, if not thousands, of unique combinations when reading charts. With so many celestial factors to consider and interpret, it's rare to see identical charts. The accuracy of horoscopes is also dependent on a mixture of different energies. With that in mind, it's best to utilize your intuition and knowledge to the best of your ability.

As you advance through astrology, you will learn the aspects between planets, houses, and zodiac signs in any horoscope, which will provide in-depth insights into universal energies. This, in turn, allows you to harness predictive energy for yourself and others.

KEY NOTES

Important pattern of numbers in astrology: 360, 30, 12, and 10

★ 360 is the number of degrees in a horoscope
★ 30 is the total number of degrees in a zodiac sign
★ 12 is the number of zodiac signs and houses
★ 10 is the number of degrees per cusp and decanate (decan)

REMEMBER THE FOLLOWING

To read a horoscope accurately, you must know the following:

★ Planets: Provide insights into our energy and how it works universally
★ Zodiac Signs: Offer deeper insights into our personal energy and how it works with the planets
★ Houses: Shows us how our energy works on Earth
★ Aspects: Depicts the energetic relationship between planets

☼ ☆ ☾

Macro and Micro Insights

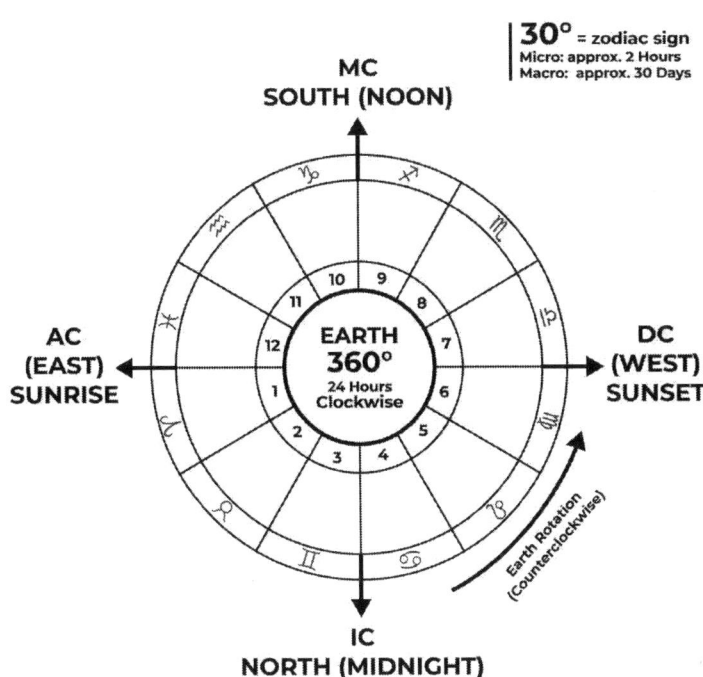

It's best to see the horoscope from **a macro and micro level.** A macro level approach shows a map of every planet's annual rotation, including Earth, which follows the orbital path of the Sun. The micro level shows a map of Earth's daily time (24 hours) based on a specific time zone.

From a macro level: You will notice that the horoscope is split into four hemispheres and governed by four quadrants: North (IC – Imum Coeli), South (MC – Medium Coeli), East (AC — Ascendant), and West (DC — Descendant). You will also notice that the 12 zodiac signs and houses move counterclockwise, which follows the Earth's rotation on its axis; whereas time continues to move clockwise (note sunrise, noon, sunset, and midnight). This follows the Earth's orbital path of the Sun.

☀☆☾

STANDARD TIME

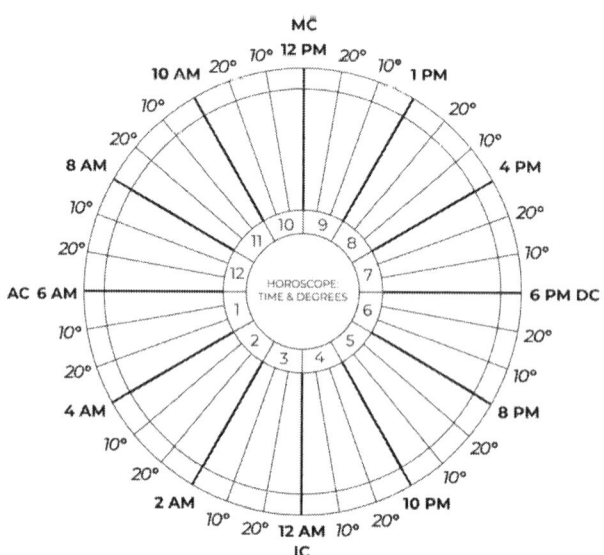

From a micro level: Time is fixed at 24 hours, and the horoscope represents a 24-hour day. That means 24 hours/12 signs = two hours (120 minutes) per zodiac sign. Every zodiac sign is 30°, which calculates as 120 minutes/30 degrees = approximately four minutes per degree.

When you are reading a horoscope, especially when using an unequal housing system, accuracy of time is imperative. Since our Sun moves through each zodiac sign every two hours at four minutes per degree, an inaccurate time can lead to inaccurate horoscopes.

Based on this knowledge, as well as other celestial factors, astronomers can estimate planetary positions and rotations based on time zones. So unless you're a mathematician specializing in astrophysics, calculations can be confusing and challenging. Fortunately, there are plenty of resources for astrologers, such as an ephemeris or computer-generated horoscope.

TRADITIONAL DATES VS. SOLAR CALENDARS

First, you must be aware that there are two types of international calendars: solar and lunar. A solar year consists of 365 days, whereas the lunar year consists of 354 days. In western astrology, we primarily utilize the solar calendar for most astrological events. However, it's important to know the lunar year if you are going to cast moonscopes.

Keep in mind that there are annual **traditional dates** (approximate fixed dates) of zodiac seasons per month just like there are fixed monthly dates on our calendars. However, these zodiac dates are not annually accurate because the orbital path of the Sun changes every year.

For more accuracy on specific planetary placements for the solar year, you must refer to an ephemeris book or computer-generated ephemeris (available online through many astrology websites). For now, let's simplify.

We know the following statements are true:

★ 12 months, 30/31 days per month, totaling 365 days
★ A horoscope is 360° (degrees of a complete circle)
★ There are 12 zodiac signs at 30° each

Let's Put It All Together: 365 divided by 12 months is approximately 30 days ($360/12 = 30.41$), which is approximately how long the Sun stays in each zodiac sign ($360°/30° = 12$ signs). Meaning, each zodiac sign's season lasts 30 days in their respective month following the orbital path of the Sun.

It is only an approximate time because our orbital path around the Sun is not a perfect circle; therefore, dates for zodiac signs may shift a couple days off the traditional dates each year. This is a huge reason why zodiac cusps are an important astrological factor and should be included into personal horoscopes.

YOUR NATAL/BIRTH CHART

A natal/birth chart is what makes every person unique. It's your personal horoscope that is casted on your birthday based on the date, time, and location of your birth. It's also the most accurate way of finding your astrological placements, as well as the energies you possess.

Important: For most housing systems, you will not see your houses or Ascendant (rising) sign without knowing the time of your birth. To get your birth time, check your birth certificate. If you don't have a birth certificate available, ask your parents or a family member who was at your birth for an estimated time.

YOUR PLACEMENTS

Generate your natal chart using your birth information at zodianz.com, then list your zodiac signs and houses aligned to the Sun, Moon, and planets within your natal/birth chart. This will help you remember your energies.

PLANET	GLYPHS	HOW IT RELATES	ZODIAC SIGN	HOUSE
Sun	☉	I am a/an....		
Moon	☽	With emotions of...		
Mercury	☿	I think like a/an...		
Venus	♀	I love like a/an....		
Mars	♂	With energy of...		
Jupiter	♃	With luck of a/an...		
Saturn	♄	I have the discipline of		
Uranus	♅	With originality of a/an...		
Neptune	♆	I have the spirit of a/an...		
Pluto	♇	I'll transform like a/an...		

HOW TO READ AN EPHEMERIS

LONGITUDE - UNIVERSAL TIME (MONTH / YEAR)						
DAY	☉	☽ 0 hr	☽ noon	☿	♀	♂
10 SU	19 ♉ 49 06	24 24 21	01 ♑ 21 27	25 ♉ 54.5	21 ♊ 38.0	27 ♒ 49.4
11 M	20 46 04	08 ♑ 11 43	14 55 11	28 03.2	21 44.4	28 30.5
12 TU	21 44 00	21 32 04	28 02 39	00 ♊ 10.8	21 48.5	29 11.6
13 W	22 41 55	04 ♒ 27 20	10 ♒ 46 36	02 17.0	21 R 50.3	29 52.7
14 TH	23 39 49	17 00 59	23 11 02	04 21.6	21 49.8	00 ♓ 33.7
15 F	24 37 41	29 17 19	05 ♓ 20 27	06 24.3	21 46.9	01 14.6
16 SA	25 35 32	11 ♓ 21 01	17 19 33	08 24.8	21 D 41.6	01 55.5

Sample Ephemeris: does not include all planets

For educational purposes, we will use randomly generated numbers for the table above. The table also does not include all planets. However, in a real ephemeris table, you will see all planetary glyphs, which can also include asteroids and nodes. The descriptions below provide the same meanings for all planets in an ephemeris.

An ephemeris is a well-calculated monthly and yearly log of all past, present, and future astronomical and celestial paths for planets, luminaries, and other celestial astronomical objects, such as asteroids. There can be more astrological data included depending on the source.

When reading an ephemeris, notice the following:

★ Glyphs, which represent luminaries, the planets, and zodiac signs
★ The degrees of planetary movement (ranging from 0°–29°)
★ Planetary positions in longitude or latitude (ex: 54.5)
★ Time frames to denote the day of the month and time of the Moon
★ Phases of planetary positions in zodiac signs and retrogrades

Notice there are several columns categorized by Day, Sun, Moon (midnight and noon), and other planets in glyph format. In the first column, labeled "Day," the numbers indicate the days of the week and month.

✵✧☾

Under the luminaries and planets, you will see numbers that provide the position of the planet in longitudinal degrees, (latitudinal degrees are rarely included). Between some of those numbers, you will see zodiac glyphs, which indicate the transition from one zodiac sign to another. The numbers on the left are what you want to focus on, as they point out the exact degree of where a planet is under a specific zodiac sign.

As stated before, every zodiac sign is 30°. The numbers on the left range from 0°–29°. When it reaches 30°, the number will change back to 0° because the planet has moved into the cusp of the next zodiac sign. When you see "R" in a table, it represents that a retrograde (planet has changed its orbital path to move backward) has begun. When you see "D" in a table, it represents that a retrograde has stationed direct (planet has changed its orbital path to move forward).

Most ephemeris books will also have a table for Moon phases, such as the dates and positions of a New Moon in transition to a Full Moon. This will help you if you want to follow the path of the Moon and provide moonscopes. There are also more tables that can be included in your book, and fortunately, most books will help provide a guide to each of their meanings.

If you really want to predict astrological events, it's strongly advised to buy an ephemeris and learn how to read it. You will have the solar system in your hands if you do. This way, you can predict worldly horoscopes, even personal horoscopes, more accurately.

✺ ☆ ☾

PLANETS

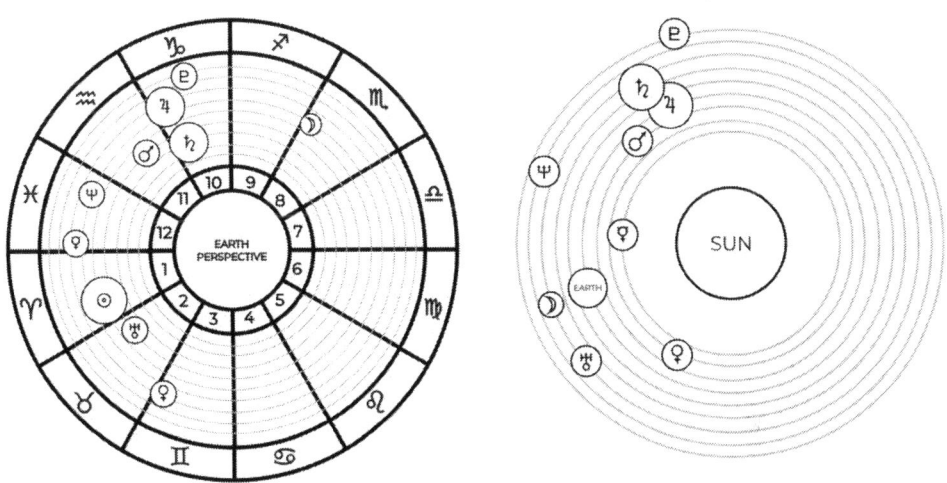

Astrology Perspective   Astronomy Perspective

Look at the pictures above and note the differences. From the astronomy perspective (right), one cannot calculate horoscopes correctly. The reason for this is because the zodiac signs are fixed in relation to the Sun and not the Earth (the Sun is in the center).

From the astrology perspective (left), we can calculate horoscopes more accurately because it's fixed in relation to the Earth's perspective. We can see which planets and luminaries are aligned with a zodiac sign during a specific time and day. We can then break the information down into macro and micro perspectives and interpret horoscopes on a personal (individual) or public (societal) level.

MACRO

When reading horoscopes on a global level, envision yourself as Earth itself. As an astrologer, you're in charge of knowing and interpreting universal energy, not just for you but for everyone on Earth. Every planet in our solar

✸☆☾

system works through its own orbital path, yet somehow all planets work as one in tandem with the Sun. If one planet strays from its path, it will affect the orbital paths of every planet thereafter.

Seeing this on a universal scale makes us feel small, but all planets are important to the life of the solar system, as well as all the life-forms on this planet and the next.

MICRO

When reading your own natal chart, envision yourself as the Sun with a solar system of your own planets. Your Sun sign is the center of you, just like the Sun is the center of our solar system. Your planetary signs revolve around your Sun sign and influences who you are as a person, creating the bulk of your energy.

If it was a soup, the Sun would be the broth, and the rest of your planets would be the ingredients that heighten the flavor. Every piece in your solar system works together to create energetic balance: life and death, good and evil, and every energy in between.

Your Sun and Moon signs will be the most important to know because they are not actual planets. Your other planetary signs are co-dependent on aspects with your Sun and Moon signs because they revolve around them.

Your planets are then split between inner planets (internal energies) versus outer planets (external energies). The closer they are to you, the more impact they will have. The further they are from you, the less impact they will have, though this doesn't make them any less important.

IMPORTANT

To read any horoscope fully and accurately, you will have to gain a strong understanding of astrology, such as planetary aspects, compatibility between signs, and a deeper meaning of the houses.

☀ ☆ ☾

KEY NOTES

★ **Macro level:** worldly predictions, cosmic events, and general zodiac horoscopes for society
★ **Micro level:** personal predictions, natal/birth charts (personal energy), and love compatibility (synastry)

AUTHOR NOTES

Learning about planets should be your top priority. Knowing a little, or a lot, about astronomy will help you understand how planets orbit the Sun. The movements of planets are the very foundation of astrology. If you are not aware of how they move or when, you will have a challenging time fully understanding how astrology even works.

To learn more about planets, I studied various birth charts of celebrities, friends, and relatives then compared them to my own interpretations or theories. I encourage you to do the same.

✱☆☾

EVOLUTION OF PLANETS

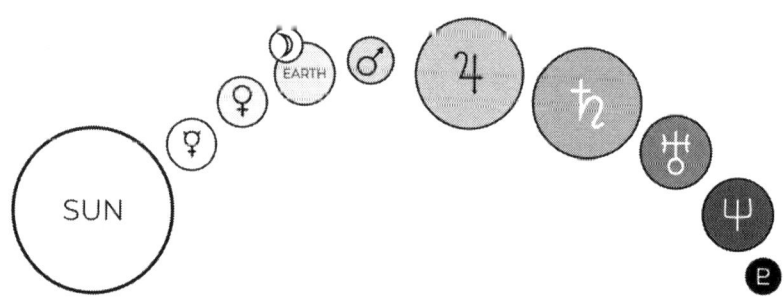

As with everything else in life, there is an evolution between the planets from the Sun all the way to Pluto. The light of each planet gradually fades into the darkness of the universe. This symbolizes how our energy works as a society and as an individual. The planets closest to the Sun have more power and impact on our personal lives than the planets that are furthest away from the Sun. However, this doesn't make the outer planets less important.

From the Sun (luminary), we are born into the physical realm; and as we reach Pluto, the last planet, we transition into the spiritual realm to die. As morbid as it sounds, it's how our energy works. The planets and luminaries are then split into two categories: inner/internal and outer/external, and every planet possesses their own type of energy and specialty. With the internal planets, the Sun shines on planets that impact our personalities. It's how we function as an individual. The darkness of the external planets helps us utilize our personality and inner strengths to overcome events within the physical realm. It's how we shine our light in dark spaces.

With that said, we exist to discover what our purpose is and how we, as individuals, can utilize our unique light to shine in our own right. Learning the meaning of astrological planets can help you gain the insights needed to maneuver the ever-changing flow of energy from our solar system.

☀☆☽

PLANETARY CHEAT SHEET

PLANET	GLYPH	EST. TIME IN EACH SIGN	CHARACTERISTICS
Sun	☉	30 Days	**Macro:** Dictates the time of zodiac seasons, the base energy of the month **Micro:** True self or the outer self, the core of your energy, where most of your energy lies
Moon	☽	2.5 Days	**Macro:** The fluctuating moods and emotions of society, things hidden from society **Micro:** Inner emotions and habits, how you see yourself, your hidden self/dark side
Mercury	☿	15–60 Days	**Macro:** Public communication, technology, ideas, innovation, speed, and intellect **Micro:** Mentality, beliefs, values, intellect, how you communicate and learn, how you receive messages
Venus	♀	24–120 Days	**Macro:** Love, relationships, unity as a society **Micro:** Love, pleasure, and all types of relationships in your inner and outer circles
Mars	♂	57–180 Days	**Macro:** Energy and aggression based on the actions we take as a society **Micro:** Physical energy and aggression, sexual energy, how you like to act
Jupiter	♃	1 Year	**Macro:** Fortune, philosophy, expansion **Micro:** Luck, blessings, fortune, and expansion, how you will/want to/why you expand
Saturn	♄	2.5 Years	**Macro:** Responsibilities as a society, hierarchy, government, rebellion, and peace **Micro:** Boundaries, discipline, responsibilities, and limitations
Uranus	♅	7 Years	**Macro:** Mental and emotional evolution, humanity's perspective on spiritual evolution **Micro:** Change and originality, how you like to evolve mentally and emotionally
Neptune	♆	13.5 Years	**Macro:** Creativity, spirituality, and religion **Micro:** Spirituality, imagination, intuition, mysteriousness, illusions/delusions
Pluto	♇	20 Years	**Macro:** Societal transformations and evolutions **Micro:** Death, transformation, regeneration (life meaning, soul's purpose, karma)

LUMINARIES: SUN AND MOON

Your Sun and Moon are your main "planets." In astrology, we call them "luminaries," but astrologers often categorize them as planets to easily digest the information provided.

Your Sun sign is your solar system's star (your center of energy), and your Moon sign is your orbiting satellite (your second most influential and co-dependent source of energy). Together, coupled with other planetary aspects, they offer the most insight into our personalities.

INNER PLANETS (INTERNAL)

If you didn't already guess, time, speed, and position are essential factors in astrology. The closer a planet is to Earth, the faster it revolves around the Sun, which has a significant impact in our personal lives.

Mercury, Venus, and Mars are considered our inner/internal planets. Just like the Sun and Moon, they influence our sense of self in more detail. They each have their own specialty and create energy that dictates how we may think, feel, or act in certain situations.

When these planets are retrograde (Rx), they impact us more than the outer (external) planets. Mercury influences our mentality, Venus influences love and relationships, and Mars influences our physical aggression and energy. These can be read individually and still make some sense, whereas outer/external planets are more accurate when read in an aspect.

OUTER PLANETS (EXTERNAL)

The further a planet is away from the Sun, the slower it revolves around it and the less impact and influence it has in our personal lives. Jupiter, Saturn, Uranus, Neptune, and Pluto are considered the outer/external planets.

☼ ☆ ☾

Though their energies can be read individually for worldly horoscopes, they cannot necessarily be read the same for personal horoscopes. Outer planets rely heavily on aspects, especially ones with the inner planets. This provides more accurate horoscopes based on an individual's birth/natal chart.

External planets affect more of our direct environment (worldly changes), which can tell us where we're headed in life, how our energies react with environmental changes, where and how our spirit flows with time and space, as well as predictive insights. Because of these factors, they are heavily co-dependent on the internal planets for in-depth insights and accuracy.

RETROGRADE (RX) VERSUS DIRECT (D)

℞

Keep in mind that all planets, even Earth, are not perfect circles, and they do not orbit the Sun in a perfect circle either. Every planet possesses its own unique orbital path and planetary rotation around the Sun. When a planet is retrograde (Rx), it means a planet's orbit around the Sun has slowed or changed, therefore giving the illusion of it going backward because other planets are still moving at their natural speed (direct).

The Sun and Moon cannot be retrograde, but internal and external planets can. When a planet is retrograde (Rx), it means certain energies are backward, delayed, and/or slow or slowing down. There is a sense of greater change and confrontation, which can impact humanity as a whole and trickle down in our communities to affect us individually.

When we look at retrogrades, we must look at the placement of the planet and the zodiac sign it sits in. In a retrograde position, we gain insight into the darker side (the shadow side) of that specific zodiac sign. Afterward, we must consider the aspects of this Rx placement with other planets. This will provide us with further insights into how it affects us.

☀ ✫ ☾

Many people are afraid of retrogrades because of the stigma they carry. However, retrogrades exist to challenge and change our emotional, mental, and spiritual evolution. Retrogrades also symbolize the end of a phase or journey (good or bad) in your life or the beginning of a new one. Therefore, it's best to embrace the changes that need to happen in your life path. The more you resist it, the more intense the retrograde will be.

The more you resist it, the more intense the retrograde will be.

Important: Retrogrades are not the only factors that create tension or evolution. If certain energies or aspects create planetary friction, then an evolution will take place regardless of a retrograde. There is also more of an impact when a retrograde matches a person's planetary placement. However, no evolution is as intense or impactful than multiple retrogrades taking place simultaneously.

ORBITAL/RETROGRADE CHEAT SHEET

PLANET GLYPHS	PLANET	APPROX. ORBITAL PATH IN EARTH DAYS / YEARS	APPROX. DAYS A PLANET IS IN RETROGRADE EACH YEAR
☿	MERCURY	88 DAYS	21+ DAYS
♀	VENUS	225 DAYS	41 DAYS
♂	MARS	1.8 YEARS	72+ DAYS
♃	JUPITER	12 YEARS	121 DAYS
♄	SATURN	30 YEARS	138 DAYS
♅	URANUS	84 YEARS	151 DAYS
♆	NEPTUNE	165 YEARS	158 DAYS
♇	PLUTO	248 YEARS	183 DAYS

☀ ☆ ☾

SUN

RULING PLANET OF LEO

MACRO (SOCIETAL)

The Sun determines the solar return for every zodiac sign, which lasts approximately one month (30 days) each. Whatever sign the Sun is in creates the base of universal energy for that month. Planets are co-dependent on the Sun, as it is the core of our energy and has the biggest impact on our daily lives. Depending on the house the Sun falls in, the Sun can highlight a "glow-up" or a "blow up" for a certain zodiac sign. The Sun can then be used to cast predictive monthly horoscopes for all zodiac signs, or it can be used to simply appreciate the sign of the month.

MICRO (PERSONAL)

The Sun is the most important planet in your natal chart. It's your true self and the persona you show people. It's the base and molding of you; therefore, it provides the bulk of your personality. Birthday months are also a huge bonus to your personal energy, as this was the time when you were born into the physical realm (the brightest light you have to share).

The Moon and planets are co-dependent on the Sun, revolving around it, giving your Sun sign different properties, and either heightening, adding to, or lessening its traits. People may not resonate with their Sun sign because they may have a more dominant sign in other planets or an overall weak Sun (little to no aspects with the Sun).

Think of It This Way: The Sun is the broth, and the Moon and other planets are ingredients. They are adding to the recipe of you.

☼ ☆ ☾

MOON

RULING PLANET OF CANCER

☽

MACRO (SOCIETAL)

The Moon shifts into a new zodiac sign approximately every two and a half days and orbits Earth in approximately 27.3 nights. Every month there are different phases of a Moon, starting with a New Moon and ending with a Full Moon. Since the Moon fluctuates the tides of our waters (water symbolizing life and emotions), it has a big impact on society's emotional energy.

Every New Moon brings in new emotional energy, whereas every Full Moon helps us release emotional energy. The type of emotional energy it brings is dependent on the zodiac sign it falls under. The phases of the Moon are often used for spiritual rituals, magical empowerment, and moonscopes (a type of horoscope based on the Moon's placements).

MICRO (PERSONAL)

The Moon is the second most important "planet" in your natal chart. It dictates your emotions, inner habits, instincts, desires, emotional intentions, and emotional reactions. It's how you see yourself in private, and it's the side people see when you're comfortable.

Depending on how compatible it is with the Sun or any other planet, it can show us if a person likes to internalize or vocalize their emotions, if a person likes to handle their emotions independently, or if they require assistance in processing and understanding their emotions. The Moon can also show us if we are insensitive or sensitive, logical, irrational, or if we are capable of higher emotional comprehension, vulnerability, or self-expression.

MERCURY

RULING PLANET OF GEMINI AND VIRGO

☿

MACRO (SOCIETAL)

Mercury, like Venus, is closer to the Sun than Earth. Mercury follows the path of the Sun, staying in its orbit in the same sign or one to two signs away. From an astronomical perspective, Mercury orbits the Sun approximately every 88 Earth days. From an astrological perspective, it stays in one zodiac sign for about 15–60 days, moving back and forth through one sign in a set of retrogrades, which can last 21 days or more each time.

Since Mercury influences the speed of communication as well as society's way of communicating and innovating, you will find that this planet deeply impacts our mental energy. It's how we perceive and communicate with one another in whatever form, whether it's online or offline. It also influences our way of thinking and how we create ideas, theories, and inventions.

MICRO (PERSONAL)

The energy of our Mercury sign works closely with our Moon and Sun sign, meaning Mercury is the third most important planet to know because it guides our logic and senses. Mercury influences and dictates how we communicate and engage with others, how we like to learn, our sense of organization or lack thereof, the speed of our thoughts and ideas, and our overall intellect and higher thought process.

Mercury can provide us with insights into our personal thoughts, beliefs, and values. It can tell us if a person is pessimistic, optimistic, witty, sarcastic, diplomatic, logical, or irrational. It helps guide our common sense, if a person has any to guide, and how and what we invest our mental energy into.

✷ ✫ ☾

MERCURY DIRECT

When Mercury is stationed direct, it means our thoughts and ideas are forward, progressive, rational, and productive. Depending on the sign and house it's in, it can also stimulate a more positive, productive, and intelligent mental energy.

Mercury stationed direct can boost our creativity, imagination, intuition, intelligence, and tact, and it can even heighten our engagement with others. It can be free-flowing or strict, open-minded or closed. It can spark innovation and invention when combined with a compatible planet or aspect, or it can create a mess of unpredictable and unorganized ideas if mixed with an incompatible planet or aspect.

MERCURY RETROGRADE (Rx)

When Mercury is retrograde (depending on which sign it's in), our thoughts and ideas are either backward, slow, reckless, or impulsive. It can mess with our forms of communication, providing a higher chance of technological failures, misdirection, indecisiveness, mental fogginess, or misunderstandings in even the simplest conversations. It can also mean that certain processes, meetings, or events are delayed or completely halted.

During this type of retrograde, our true voice and thoughts come out. We can and will learn a lot about human behavior and others' thought processes. This phase can show you the aggressive side of someone you thought was passive or shy, or it can show you how dark someone thinks. This can also show you how someone thrives under greater pressure.

Overall, a Mercury retrograde teaches us how to overcome the challenges of communication and how to resolve or correct the mental flaws we have in ourselves or with others.

☼ ☆ ☾

VENUS

RULING PLANET OF TAURUS AND LIBRA

♀

MACRO (SOCIETAL)

Like Mercury, Venus is closer to the Sun than Earth and stays either in the same sign or one to two signs away from it. From an astronomical perspective, it orbits the Sun in approximately 225 Earth days. From an astrological perspective, it stays in one zodiac sign for approximately 24–120 days, phasing in and out of retrogrades, which can last around 41 days each time.

Venus influences society's relationships, primarily feminine energy. It's how society views and values unity, partnerships, and community. It has a big impact on how we get along, how we nurture one another, and how we value and perceive beauty, whether it's a physical embodiment of beauty or material possessions, such as art.

MICRO (PERSONAL)

Venus is the fourth most important planet in astrology. It influences our internal feminine energy and how we utilize our feminine energy in our personal lives. It's how we define love, friendship, and family in present time. It can also give us insights into how we handle these relationships, what we want in a relationship, how we seduce and attract potential partners, and how we please our loved ones.

Our Venus placement can give us further information about which zodiac signs we are most compatible with. These relationships can be either platonic, professional, or romantic. It can also show us how a person defines and values beauty, how they choose to surround themselves with beauty, and how they practice self-love, self-care, and self-healing.

✸☆☽

Venus Direct

Venus is the feminine energy of society. Therefore, it symbolizes the heart of our society. When Venus is direct, it means there is positive growth or change in our relationships. Depending on the sign and house it falls in, we find that relationships undergo positive transitions, such as healthy unions, opportunistic partnerships, or more awareness in who we choose to love.

Venus direct focuses on the growth and balance of relatives, friendship, professional partnerships, romance, compatibility, self-development, and/or self-love. For society, it can predict positive changes for communities, group activities, social experiences, and higher advancement and reputation.

Venus Retrograde (Rx)

When Venus is retrograde, depending on the placement, relationships can undergo more negative transitions. Society can experience phases of isolation, privacy, adultery, manipulation, breakups, or the resurfacing of past wounds and trauma that need to be confronted.

There can be a rise of pettiness and shadiness among the community, an exposure of injustice and unfairness in a relationship, or a deep cleanse of someone's inner circle. We may learn there are many people who have poor judgment and rush into or stay in toxic relationships, or we learn that people can become wiser and get out of toxic relationships during this time.

Overall, people can get stuck in unloving and unhealthy relationships that have caused or are causing pain. It's up to the individual to heal from any hurtful relationships and move on without regret or guilt. This can be a release of our old self or a removal of relationships that are no longer beneficial. It's also a realization that we don't need to hold onto toxic relationships; instead, we can move on to more supportive and loving individuals, even if that means being our own partner.

☆☆☾

MARS

RULING PLANET OF ARIES AND CO-RULER OF SCORPIO

♂

MACRO (SOCIETAL)

Mars marks the end of the inner planets, which symbolizes our physical energy moving into the spiritual realm. From an astronomical perspective, it takes approximately 1.8 Earth years for Mars to orbit the Sun. From an astrological perspective, it can stay in one zodiac sign for 57–180 days, phasing in and out of retrogrades that can last about 72 days, more or less, each time.

Mars is an intense and powerful force that influences our physical energy, aggression, and strength in our society, primarily in a domineering and masculine way. It's the actions society takes when it comes to global or national situations, and it also reflects the speed and stamina of society in present or future time. It shows us how society will act when confronted with a situation that requires intense change.

MICRO (PERSONAL)

Opposite of Venus (which influences feminine energy), Mars influences our masculine energy, physical energy, aggression, and physical stamina. It can show us how we like to use our energy, how assertive or dominate our energy is, how we project our energy in the physical realm, and where we like to invest our energy.

Our Mars placement influences the actions we take in certain situations. Depending on which zodiac sign and house it falls in, it can provide insights into how we act during a physical confrontation, physical intimacy (sex), and affection. It can also point to a person's sexual preference.

✵✫☾

MARS DIRECT

Mars is the planet of war, which showcases our physical strengths in the physical realm. When Mars is stationed direct, it empowers our actions for better or worse, depending on the placement. What takes place is further progression and production in our physical environment, where individuals either come together or go solo in empowering themselves physically.

For societies to progress, governing countries, states, communities, and smaller organizations will perform with more tact and unity, such as with peace treaties, humanitarian acts, elections, change of law(s), change of industrial practices, change or evolution of businesses or types of industries, and beneficial partnerships.

MARS RETROGRADE (Rx)

When Mars is retrograde, we find society taking a few steps back in evolution. Depending on the placement, people can become power hungry, greedy, aggressive, abusive, or violent. Revolutions can take place through war, riots, protests, or any other act of extreme or irrational behavior.

During a Mars retrograde, a change of how people view intimacy can also take place, most times for the worst. People can become overly aggressive, argumentative, or violent/abusive with one another. Our true physical power and strengths come out without much self-control. It can take a lot of mental discipline to contain any anger or resentment we have been harboring before the retrograde took place.

Regardless of what happens, Mars retrograde usually creates an intense evolution into something more positive and impactful in society. Sometimes these evolutions can be quick and revolutionary, and other times they can be slow and counterintuitive. What we learn and see is the truth behind our actions and how past actions can affect present times.

✵ ☆ ☾

JUPITER

RULING PLANET OF SAGITTARIUS AND CO-RULER OF PISCES

♃

MACRO (SOCIETAL)

Jupiter marks the start of the outer/external planets, and since it's the biggest planet in our solar system, it has the biggest influence over society. From an astronomical perspective, it takes Jupiter 12 Earth years to orbit the Sun. From an astrological perspective, it shifts into a new zodiac sign every year, phasing in and out of retrogrades for about 121 days each time.

Jupiter influences how society receives and perceives luck, blessings, money, and fortune. It's how society philosophizes power and expansion. It's seeing everything from a higher and much more grand perspective, building tactics and perspectives that can expand or stunt our growth. It's also known as the Greater Fortune, with Venus being the Lesser Fortune.

MICRO (PERSONAL)

Jupiter is a big planet and impacts your chart in the same manner. This planet influences our luck, expansion, fortune, and blessings. When matched with certain aspects, this planet can provide us with further insights into our way of life, and it can also tell us how a person defines a meaningful, blessed, or lucky life. It can answer the following questions: Does a person like living grand and lavishly? Do they desire material wealth and traveling? If so, how?

Jupiter shows us how we justify our thoughts and how we philosophize money, power, prosperity, lifestyle, manifestation, and abundance. It's how a person explores and expands their way of life through mental and spiritual justification. It's good to note that some astrologers also consider Jupiter the planet of karmic values and beliefs.

✵☆☾

JUPITER DIRECT

Since Jupiter shifts into a new zodiac every year, it can predict the mental and spiritual changes society will undergo in relation to wealth, fortune, luck, and blessings. When Jupiter is stationed direct, we find society advancing outward through education, literature, philosophy, or a general way of life (evolution of society). It's more of a positive evolution of the mind.

Jupiter direct can show us what's past the horizon, as in what we can look forward to or what lessons we can learn throughout the year. Depending on the placement, it provides us with higher insights and spiritual perspectives in how we can resolve the bigger issues in our society, usually through more advanced ways of communication or technology that can help the masses move and think more efficiently.

JUPITER RETROGRADE (Rx)

When Jupiter is retrograde, depending on the placement, we can find society digressing rather than progressing. Keep in mind Jupiter is the ruling planet of both Sagittarius and Pisces (both mutable dual signs), which brings out the animalistic and unpredictable behaviors of both signs during this phase. Thus, restriction of spirit and mental stability are not prioritized, and freedom of spirit and mental spontaneity are.

Retrograde Jupiter can bring about sudden and urgent changes in society. It's a life-changing event that pushes society into a period of great spiritual and philosophical evolution. Even small innovations and creations should be considered, for these smaller changes are part of the greater vision and lead to the greater fortune of society.

What we inevitably learn as a society is how to think outside of ourselves, releasing old lingering traditions that have prevented us from attracting more positive opportunities for mental, spiritual, and environmental wealth.

✵ ☆ ☽

SATURN

RULING PLANET OF CAPRICORN AND CO-RULER OF AQUARIUS

♄

MACRO (SOCIETAL)

Saturn is the second biggest planet and influences how society governs itself, usually through a hierarchy such as a government. From an astronomical perspective, Saturn takes about 29–30 Earth years to orbit the Sun. From an astrological perspective, it takes approximately two and a half years to shift into a new zodiac sign, phasing in and out of retrogrades for up to 138 days each time.

Where Jupiter can be a bit unpredictable, abhorring routine, Saturn is the opposite, valuing structure, organization, justice, and respect. Saturn is very strict, disciplined, and responsible. This planet believes in management, rules, and guidelines for society to sustain itself. It shows where governing bodies need to restructure themselves. This is also a planet of greater environmental resources, and it shows us how we utilize our resources for the betterment of society.

MICRO (PERSONAL)

Saturn is a powerhouse in astrology, especially when it comes to the way we work and how we like to work. It is the governing body of self-direction. This planet influences our resourcefulness, discipline, personal boundaries, and limitations (what we're willing to use or sacrifice for personal success).

Saturn can show us how we define success and reputation and if we value or require approval from others. It can also provide insights into how we view justice, respect, politics, and the government. It can show if we are rebellious and willing to fight for what we believe in or if we are more likely to conform

✶☆☾

and abide by the rules of those in higher positions, such as the government.

SATURN DIRECT

When Saturn is stationed direct, depending on the placement, we can find society moving with the flow of governmental structure. It can show us if society is ready to make changes that either support or defy traditional laws, such as marriage, animal rights, civilian rights, climate change, etc.

Saturn direct can promote humanitarian efforts that help shape characters, cultures, or diversities within society. Saturn can also advance the need for greater architecture and inventions that support the well-being and structure of countries and their governing bodies. This also includes a country's people, plants, and animal ecosystem.

SATURN RETROGRADE (Rx)

Where a Jupiter retrograde affects the evolution of society's philosophical or spiritual perspectives on greater fortune, Saturn retrograde affects the evolution of humanity's connection with the well-being of all life-forms on Earth. When Saturn is retrograde, we find governing bodies restricting and may feel the need to restructure society to regain hierarchal power.

Depending on the placement, Saturn retrogrades can create rebellion and cause riots or protests against injustice. Saturn can also expose corruption in governments, overthrow hierarchies or monarchies, or push governments to restructure laws to appease the public. It can also predict a loss of resources, which impact our society for the worst.

Regardless of what happens, governing bodies (big or small) will learn to restructure themselves to achieve more success and a better reputation. This heavily includes financial obligations or laws that impact the welfare of people or animals.

✹ ☆ ☾

URANUS

RULING PLANET OF AQUARIUS

MACRO (SOCIETAL)

Uranus influences the way society evolves mentally and emotionally. From an astronomy perspective, it takes about 84 Earth years to orbit the Sun. From an astrology perspective, it takes about seven years to shift from one zodiac sign into another, phasing in and out of retrogrades that last approximately 151 days annually. Due to the length of time, Uranus is best interpreted in an aspect with other planets.

Uranus connects humanity with intuition. Keep in mind, this is not the same type of influence as Jupiter or Saturn. Uranus influences how society sees purpose within the community, utilizes intuition to create a change of purpose, and pushes for mental and emotional change that helps or reinvents how we engage with one another.

MICRO (PERSONAL)

Uranus influences change and originality in our lives. This planet can give us insights into how we like to change internally and externally, how well we follow the rules of society, and if a person is traditional, rebellious, gullible, intuitive, thoughtful, creative, or innovative.

Uranus can show us how we utilize our intuition and intellect, how we define and value independence, if we have co-dependent behaviors, how we like to evolve mentally and emotionally, and how we view humanity as a whole. When matched with a complimentary aspect, it can heighten our need to seek purpose in our community. When matched with uncomplimentary aspects, it can heighten the need to isolate ourselves from community.

URANUS DIRECT

When Uranus is stationed direct, depending on the placement, we find individuals using their purpose, skill, or expertise to connect with humanity. There can be a growth of humanitarian acts or a union of certain groups. These groups can be considered odd or non-traditional, wanting to connect mentally and intuitively with a common passion or just cause.

Regardless, there will be a lot of communication within these groups that expands in society. These groups prioritize freedom of choice and can stay in their bubble away from others who they consider judgmental, or they can become motivated to take their just cause publicly with the intent of educating and expressing their views on humanity.

URANUS RETROGRADE (Rx)

When Uranus is retrograde, depending on the placement, we can see a rise of dogmatism, anarchy, and rebellion within society. It represents the evolution of mental and emotional change (good or bad) where people start to shift away from the norm or distance themselves from humanity. Conspiracy theorists can come crawling out, wanting to provide perspectives that go against the system (usually the government).

Society can find itself becoming more passionate about its beliefs, wanting to enforce or force its beliefs onto others. It can be a separation of mind versus heart in society, where there is a clear segregation between two groups of people, though neither will have a clear understanding of where the other stands.

What we learn from this retrograde is how to accept the differences within diverse groups and cultures, where changing our perspectives for the better helps the overall mental and emotional balance of society.

✵ ✰ ☾

NEPTUNE

RULING PLANET OF PISCES

Ψ

MACRO (SOCIETAL)

Neptune influences society's imagination, intuition, spirituality, religion, divine gifts, and creative work, such as music, art, and writing. From an astronomical perspective, it takes Neptune approximately 165 Earth years to orbit the Sun. From an astrological perspective, Neptune shifts into a new zodiac sign every 13.5 years, phasing in and out of a retrograde approximately 158 days each time. Due to the length of time, Neptune is best interpreted in an aspect.

Since we are moving away from the Sun, everything society has learned through our major experiences from Jupiter through Uranus is turned inward for deeper reflection and projection. Neptune internalizes who we are in the world, our higher purpose in society, and how society internalizes the deeper issues of the world.

MICRO (PERSONAL)

Neptune primarily influences our intuition and imagination. It can show us whether we are intuitive, delusional, realistic, spiritual, imaginative, gifted, empathic, mysterious, or religious. It can show us how we internalize and reflect on life's deeper issues and how we project and express our beliefs and emotions through creative and spiritual endeavors.

Neptune helps us gain a deeper sense of purpose and opens up our third eye to the spiritual realm. In here, we can see ourselves more abstractly. After we fully embrace ourselves emotionally and spiritually, we can then start to heal through spiritual enlightenment and creative empowerment.

Neptune Direct

When Neptune is stationed direct, depending on the placement, we find society's creative and spiritual energy flowing steadily. Since its orbital path is much longer at 13.5 years, we find that this type of energy doesn't change very often. Therefore, it is more co-dependent on its planetary aspects.

Depending on its planetary placements, Neptune direct allows society to align itself with traditional or unconventional methods of self-reflection and creative outer expression. It can also help society elevate spiritually, where spiritual acceptance, spiritual enlightenment, emotional expression, and creativity take priority in the healing and understanding of our true selves.

Neptune Retrograde (Rx)

When Neptune is retrograde, depending on the placement, we can see a change in the way people perceive spirituality as well as creative endeavors like music and art. There can be a drastic change in these perceptions, which helps society or individuals cope with present circumstances.

During a retrograde phase, Neptune will disrupt our spiritual beliefs, which pushes society to rethink or reflect on its personal choices. It can be taxing on a person's soul knowing that their actions have affected their personal circle or even the wider community. However, this is a time where everyone must commit to deeper reflection and spiritual justification. It can also be a time where what we feel must be fully expressed into our environment.

What we learn from Neptune's retrograde is that we must break free from any emotional or spiritual restraints, unlearning what no longer benefits us in the present time. It's a long process to undo lifelong teachings, but it must be done so future generations can adapt and adopt new spiritual teachings. This inevitably helps us emotionally cope and express ourselves in new ways, especially through music, art, and writing.

☼ ☆ ☾

PLUTO

RULING PLANET OF SCORPIO

♇

MACRO (SOCIETAL)

Pluto influences great transformations and evolutions in society, usually in the form of greater spirituality and karmic values. From an astronomical perspective, it takes 248 Earth years to orbit the Sun. From an astrological perspective, it shifts into a new zodiac approximately every 20 years, shifting in and out of retrogrades for approximately 183 days at a time. Due to this length of time, Pluto is best interpreted with other planetary aspects.

Since this is the last and furthest planet away from the Sun, Pluto remains the black sheep of the planetary family, but this doesn't make it less important. Where the Sun is birth, Pluto is death. Pluto takes us deep into the void and teaches us how to interpret a soul. It also affects society's perspectives on the deeper meaning of what transformation and evolution is and how community and culture perceive death and the afterlife.

MICRO (PERSONAL)

Pluto influences our intensity levels of regeneration and transformation in our life. It tells us how we handle major life transitions, how we perceive life and death, and the energy we invest in creating a worthy and meaningful life. It can also give us insights into our life's journey and, for some, the true and deeper meaning of our true purpose in this lifetime.

Pluto is a mysterious planet that is full of karmic values when combined with other planetary aspects. It can show us how a person perceives karma, their spiritual principles, their beliefs of the afterlife, and how they perceive the meaning and value of their soul.

PLUTO DIRECT

When it comes to Pluto, it's not always as straightforward as other planets. Pluto is highly co-dependent on other aspects for interpretations to be more accurate. As a distant planet, one can interpret Pluto as a planet that sees life from an outsider's perspective but also one that can predict how certain events will play out since they're on the outside looking in. It's best to see this planet as a spiritual teacher who guides our higher intuition and soul transformation as a society.

Often overlooked, Pluto encourages society to create meaningful soul connections with one another and build awareness of how our actions can affect our soul in the afterlife. This, in turn, helps society make decisions that are based on its level of acceptance and understanding of its own soul's conscience. One must also be aware that those with incompatible Pluto aspects can manipulate others through their perceptions of the soul and abuse and impose a false meaning of it onto others for control.

PLUTO RETROGRADE (Rx)

When Pluto is retrograde, depending on the placement, we find that society's false, misunderstood, or manipulated perception of spirituality and afterlife starts to change. This is an intense transition into the meaning of life and what it means for humanity.

We can learn that a lot of spiritual beliefs, which are embedded in culture, can come back to its original state or be reinvented for modern times. We can see communities or individuals connect or reconnect with the spiritual realm through unconventional methods. This is also a time where people can release all superficiality and disconnect from their environment and community altogether, which motivates them to seek the meaning of their life through intense exposures in a new and enlightening environment.

✺ ☆ ☾

HEMISPHERES AND QUADRANTS

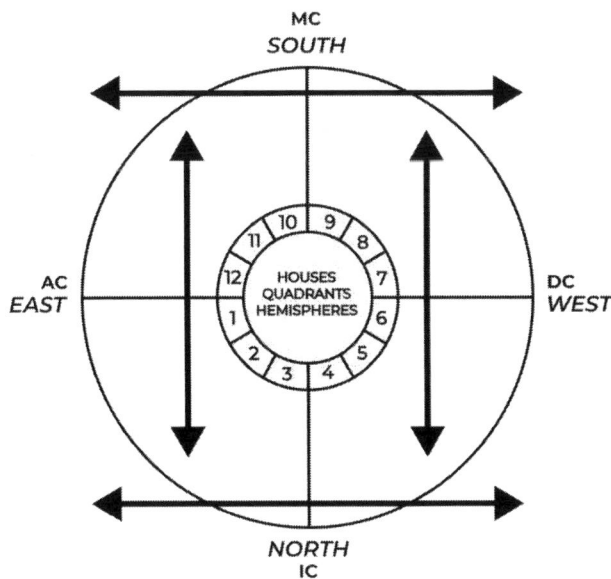

HEMISPHERES	QUADRANTS (CORNERS)	QUADRANT HOUSE
South: 7th – 12th Houses	**Midheaven (MC – Medium Coeli):** Starts at 90° but can change degrees and sway in different houses.	10th House – Capricorn (career)
North: 1st – 6th Houses	**Imum Coeli (IC):** Always opposite of MC at 270° or moves with the MC.	4th House – Cancer (home)
East: 10th – 3rd Houses	**Ascendant/Rising Sign (ASC or AC):** Starting at 0° for equal housing; can be dependent of the time of sunrise, which changes degrees within zodiac signs but remains fixed in the middle of the chart.	1st House – Aries (self)
West: 4th – 9th Houses	**Descendant (DC):** Always opposite of Ascendant, remains fixed at 180° or changes degrees with the zodiac sign following the AC.	7th House – Libra (partnerships)

✵☆☾

ASCENDANT & DESCENDANT

AC / DC

MACRO

Sunrise and East of the horoscope are represented by the **Ascendant (AC or ASC)**, always in the 1st house, which can start at 0° or the time of sunrise starting at a different degree in a zodiac sign. If a horoscope is interpreted through an equal housing system, such as Whole Sign, then the AC will start at 0°. If a horoscope is interpreted through an unequal housing system, like Equal House or Equal Midheaven, then the AC can instead point to the time and position of a sunrise.

Sunset and West of the horoscope are represented by the **Descendant (DC)**, which is always directly opposite of the AC and in the 7th House of Partnerships, starting at 180°. Like the AC, the DC can also point to the time and position of a sunset, but only if the AC points to the sunrise in the appropriate housing system. Regardless of the housing system, the AC and DC will remain a fixed longitudinal line that cuts the horoscope in half.

MICRO

The Ascendant, aka rising sign, governs the 1st House of Self (self-awareness). The rising sign influences our ascending outlook on life, how we like to present ourselves to the world (physical appearance), our direction of self, and our first impressions from others.

The AC focuses on external projection, so think of your rising as the shield you carry. It's what shields you from oncoming energy and the energy people sense before they get to your core. Simply put, it's the projection of what you want people to see. This sign is also used for personal horoscopes, as it dictates the starting degree/zodiac sign of every chart.

The Descendant, aka descending sign, governs the 7ᵗʰ House of Partnerships and influences our ties to love and relationships. Where the AC is more about what we want other people to see, the DC is more about the people we choose to see and surround ourselves with. It's also how we view ourselves in our community.

The DC focuses on the external projection of relationships, so think of it as the root of our love, where love stems from, and where love can be nurtured for ourselves and others. It's how you deal with your circle of relationships, which can be romantic, platonic, or professional. It can also point to who we are most compatible with.

The DC is not a common point that astrologers talk about, mostly because it isn't as influential as a Venus sign or other planetary aspects. However, you can include it in your readings if it resonates with your interpretations. Always follow what fits your type of reading.

✵☆☾

MIDHEAVEN & IMUM COELI

MC / IC

MACRO

Noon and South of a horoscope are represented by the **Midheaven (MC, aka Medium Coeli)** at 90°, which can reside in or around the 10th House of Career. Midnight and North of a horoscope are represented by the **Imum Coeli (IC)**, which is exactly opposite of the MC at 270°, residing in or around the 4th House of Home. Depending on the housing system, the MC and AC can change houses in a horoscope (unequal, Equal House, Equal Midheaven) or remain fixed to the cusp of the 9th and 10th houses (Equal House, Whole Sign).

The reason our MC and IC can change houses and degrees is because the MC can point to the time and position of when the Sun reached its highest point (noon), whereas the IC can point to the time and position of when the Sun reached its lowest point (midnight), all of which are dependent on certain time zones. This is an even bigger reason to have accurate information like date, time, and location.

MICRO

The Midheaven (MC or MSC) sign governs the 10th House of Career but can float in other houses nearby (dependent on the house system). Regardless, our MC influences the direction of our earthly purpose, such as career, finance, education, and investments of self. Simply put, it's our commitment and dedication to a higher purpose within our communities and families.

Since our MC lives in the upper/outer hemisphere of the horoscope, it is a projection of self-awareness in the physical realm. Think of this as the crown you wear. It holds major responsibilities and the burdens that come with them.

It can shine brightly when you've aligned yourself with your true purpose, but it can also dim and rust if you have not.

The MC should not be taken for granted, as it can show you how to use your energy to advance and succeed in your career, the work environment that best compliments your energy, and how you can excel when given the right tools and knowledge.

The Imum Coeli (IC) governs the 4th House of Home but can float in other houses nearby (dependent on the house system). Opposite of our MC, the IC influences a greater sense of self, how we feel about ourselves, where we come from, and how we perceive our childhood. Simply put, it's the traits we've adopted since birth.

Since our IC lives in the bottom hemisphere, it is a projection of our inner self-awareness in the spiritual realm. Think of this as your soul roots, which provide insights into how you view, value, utilize, and ground your personal experiences. Since the IC resides primarily in the 4th house, which encompasses the experiences that stem from our childhood home, our IC can point to how we have handled (or how we are handling) our childhood experiences (good or bad) in relation to our parental role models.

The IC can also be interpreted as the energy of home itself, where you can find comfort with the zodiac sign it resides in. For example, let's say the IC resides in the sign of Taurus in the 4th House of Home. This means the person finds comfort and security with family traditions they grew up with, food from their childhood, having material possessions that remind them of home, and the household routines they grew up with are inflexible and strict.

The IC, like the DC, is not a common point that astrologers talk about, mostly because it isn't as influential as other planetary aspects, though this doesn't make it less important. You can include it in your readings if it resonates with your interpretations. Always follow your intuition.

✵ ✰ ☽

Author Notes

One theory I have put together is that the sign your IC is in is the zodiac sign you gravitate toward the most, as in the one you find most attractive, because it reminds you of comfort and familiarity. This will be the sign you love or the one that loves you. However, this interpretation can be argued because of other planetary placements, such as the DC or Venus aspects.

☀ ☆ ☾

HOUSE SYSTEMS

Horoscopes are divided into four quadrants and four hemispheres, which are then subdivided into 12 houses and 12 zodiac signs.

Take note of the numbers 1–12 within the inner pie slices that run counterclockwise, the same direction as the zodiac. These are called houses. Houses provide further insight into our psyche (soul).

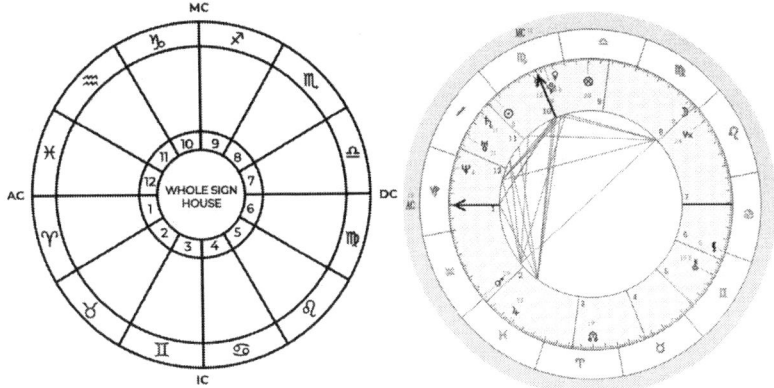

Equal Housing (Whole Sign) vs. Unequal Housing (Placidus)

There are two main house systems astrologers use: **equal and unequal housing systems.**

Unequal housing systems are dependent on the ecliptic (the apparent path of the Sun), as well as other celestial astrophysical factors, which calculate houses in unequal degrees instead of an even 30°.

Equal housing systems cast an equal number of 12 30° slices of either houses, zodiac signs, or both in fixed or unfixed quadrants, houses, and/or zodiac signs.

Regardless of which house system you're accustomed to or begin to use, houses can provide further insight into someone's personality or provide predictive insight into a future event.

✸☆☽

Think of the houses as seeing your energy from different perspectives, though your position in the stars will remain the same. Imagine standing up and looking at two cliffs, one side being unequal and the other equal. They're seeing you from the same position but will still offer similar, if not the same, insights from different houses. Most times, the degrees and positions of your planets and signs will remain the same. The major changes are the house positions and the size of houses, which can vary in degrees.

This book will not cover all house systems, but it will summarize the well-known ones. You can find more extensive information on any house system through online research. There are some astrologers who are loyal to one house system, while others use multiple house systems.

Author Notes

Personally, I prefer to use different types of housing systems for different horoscopes. I use Placidus when I'm writing a thorough natal chart because it offers more detailed information. I use Equal Housing for Energy Natal Charts (canvassed artwork) with quick summaries because the astrological information is easier to interpret into art form. I use Whole Signs for general zodiac horoscopes because it's broad and not dedicated to one person.

To me, and I know many will argue, all house systems can interpret a horoscope and come to the same or similar information about a person or event. My suggestion is to follow whatever house system resonates with you because we all learn and interpret astrology differently.

☼ ☆ ☾

EQUAL HOUSING SYSTEMS

Equal house systems are the simplest way of organizing horoscopes and the easiest way to digest, learn, and interpret astrological information. Equal housing systems are primarily based on an even 30° for houses and/or zodiac signs. The Ascendant (AC) and Midheaven (MC) can be fixed or adjusted based on the housing system used.

You may choose these types of housing systems if they prove to be easier to learn, more beneficial and accurate in your interpretations, or if you are more of an intuitive and free-flowing astrologer.

Well-Known Equal House Systems:

★ Whole Sign focuses on position
★ Equal House focuses on sunrise and noon
★ Equal Midheaven focuses on sunrise

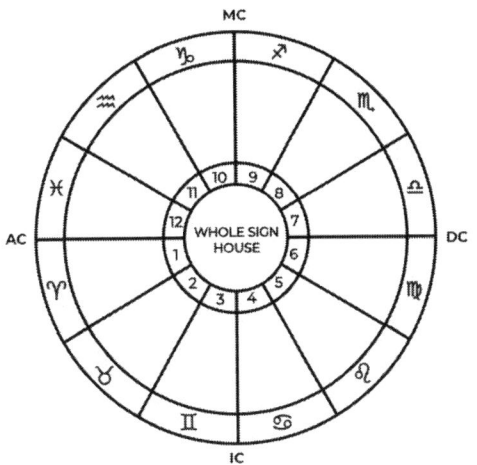

Whole Sign: The horoscope is cut into equal amounts of 30° for all 12 houses and 12 zodiac signs, starting at 0°. The Ascendant represents the rising sign on the cusp (the start) of the 1st house. The Midheaven is fixed at the cusp of the 9th and 10th houses at 90°.

✵✫☾

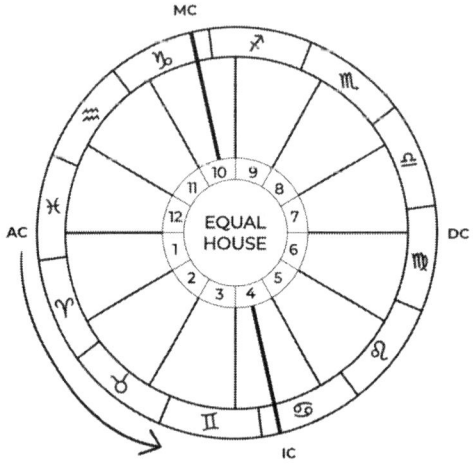

Equal House: The horoscope is cut into 12 equal houses, with 30° each. However, the start of the zodiac is dependent on the starting position of the AC, where the AC represents the time of sunrise. The MC moves houses and represents the highest point above the horizon (noon).

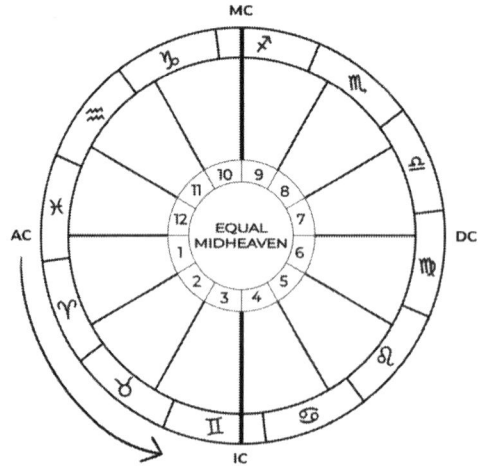

Equal Midheaven: The 12 houses are an equal 30°. The Midheaven is always fixed at 90° on the cusp of the 9th and 10th houses. However, the start of the zodiac is dependent on the starting position of the AC, where the AC represents the time of sunrise.

☀☆☾

UNEQUAL HOUSING SYSTEMS

Unequal housing systems are dependent on mathematical calculations based on specific time zones and locations, celestial movements within the house cusps, celestial equators, ecliptic arcs and horizons, and many other astrophysical factors. Thus, the 12 houses are constantly shifting in unequal degrees. The Ascendant (AC) and Midheaven (MC) are co-dependent on specific times, either sunrise or time of birth. The MC is not committed to the cusp of the 10th house, but rather may sway in and out of other houses nearby.

Many choose unequal house systems for overall accuracy of celestial time and space, so if you possess a more analytical mindset, then it's best to use an unequal house system for your horoscope interpretations.

Well-Known Unequal House Systems:

★ Placidus focuses on Earth's time
★ Koch focuses on birthdays
★ Regiomontanus focuses on the celestial time of our solar system

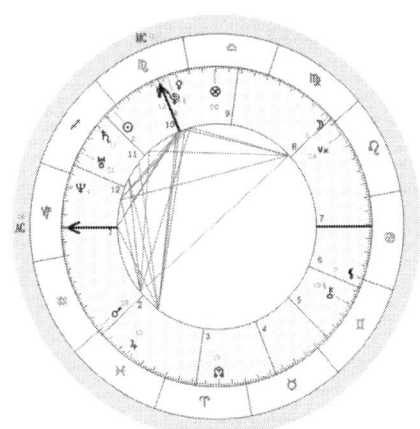

Placidus: This system is time-based, and it's one of the most popular modern house systems. This system calculates celestial movements above and below the horizon, where the AC represents the time of sunrise and the MC represents the highest point above the horizon (noon).

✵ ✰ ☽

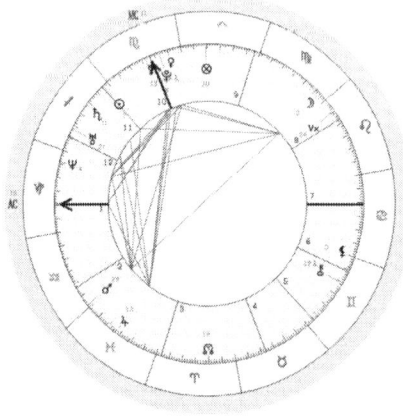

Koch: This system is time-based, and it's calculated by celestial movements on the horizon based on a person's date of birth. This house system is an extensive version of Placidus; however, it places significant importance on the MC/IC axis rather than the AC/DC axis, where the Midheaven refers to the time of birth.

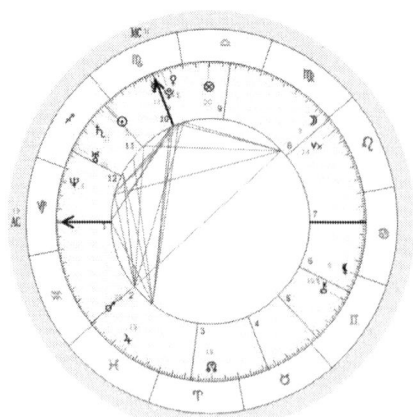

Regiomontanus: This system is derived from the Porphyry house system, and it's not commonly used in modern times, though it is still used by some. This system calculates horoscopes based on the celestial equator, which is divided into 12 then projected onto the ecliptic.

✲ ✦ ☽

HOUSES EXPLAINED

Just as there is an evolution with zodiac signs and planets, there is also an evolution between houses. As each house moves into the next, it takes with it the energy and lessons from the one before.

Houses are split between bottom (internal) hemisphere and top (external) hemisphere, and they are dependent on the planetary placements within them to make sense. Our **internal houses** focus on how we build ourselves in preparation for the outer world. It's the energy we use to build our internal character, beliefs, and values. Our **external houses** take what we've learned about ourselves and implements it into our direct environment (the outer world). **Opposite houses** work to balance one another's energies, thereby giving what the other cannot.

Houses without planetary placements often means there isn't enough energy to consider them. However, some astrologers interpret the house in connection with the zodiac sign it's aligned with. Example: 5th House of Creativity in Pisces with no planets within can still be interpreted.

HOUSES CHEAT SHEET

HOUSE	MOTTO	EVOLUTION	OPPOSITE HOUSE
1st	I am	Character Values	7th – Partnerships
2nd	I have	Material Values	8th – Regeneration
3rd	I think	Mental Values	9th – Mental Exploration
4th	I feel	Emotional Values	10th – Career
5th	I will	Skills and Talent	11th – Hopes & Friendships
6th	I analyze	Usefulness and Community	12th – Self-Undoing
7th	I balance	Value of Partnerships with Self	1st – Self
8th	I desire	Spiritual Wealth and Desires	2nd – Possessions
9th	I see	Perspectives and Experiences	3rd – Communication
10th	I use	Finances and Lifestyle	4th – Home
11th	I know	Value of Humanity	5th – Creativity
12th	I believe	Value of Higher Purpose	6th – Health and Service

✸✶☾

Bottom (Internal) Hemisphere

1ST – 6TH HOUSES

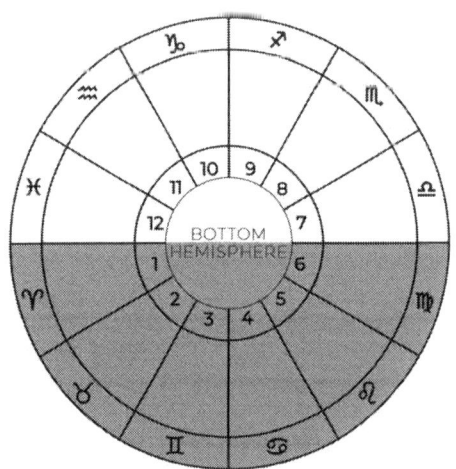

The bottom (internal) houses focus on the internal energies we face in our personal lives. It has more to do with our character's mental, emotional, and physical development (the self-development stages).

1ST HOUSE (SELF) "I AM"

Character Values

This house represents the development of self-awareness, our personal character, self-esteem, outward confidence, and sense of purpose and direction. Simply, it's how we view ourselves.

2ND HOUSE (POSSESSIONS) "I HAVE"

Material Values

This house represents the development of ourselves with things. It's how we value money, success, and possessions. It's our perspective of our physical environment, which influences our need to have or not have possessions.

3RD HOUSE (COMMUNICATION) "I THINK"

Mental Values

This house represents the development of our mentality as we maneuver through life. It's how we communicate with ourselves and others, as well as our perspectives, beliefs, and opinions of the world and everyone in it.

4TH HOUSE (HOME) "I FEEL"

Emotional Values

This house represents the development of our emotional attachments. It's how we value home, family, love, lifestyle, the comforts of the heart, our emotional expression, what makes us feel good, and what makes us feel at home.

5TH HOUSE (CREATIVITY) "I WILL"

Skills and Talent

This house represents the development of our greater ambitions. It's how we utilize our creativity, willpower, and drive. It's the pursuit of our deepest passions and strengths and the value of our skills and talents.

6TH HOUSE (HEALTH AND SERVICE) "I ANALYZE"

Usefulness and Community

This house represents the development of our physical well-being and our usefulness within communities. It's how we analyze our physical status in the community and how our analyzations and methods of self can be applied to better service our community.

✵ ☆ ☾

TOP (EXTERNAL) HEMISPHERE

7ᵀᴴ – 12ᵀᴴ HOUSES

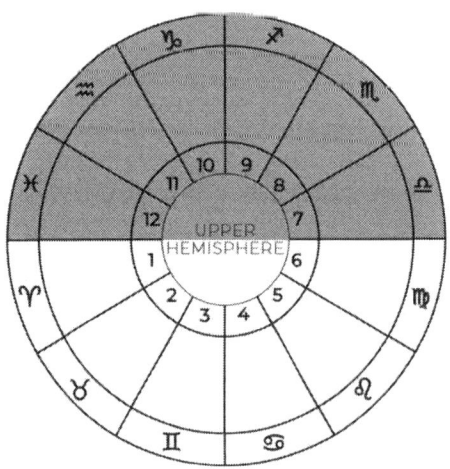

The upper (external) houses focus on the external energies we face in our environment. They have more to do with how our character maneuvers within the physical realm using what was learned from the self-development stages (the bottom hemisphere).

7TH HOUSE (PARTNERSHIPS) "I BALANCE"

Value of Partnerships with Self

Opposite of the 1ˢᵗ House of Self, this house represents how we view and balance ourselves with others, our compatibility with others, our partnerships and our purpose with others, and our values regarding who we are with our partners.

8TH HOUSE (REGENERATION) "I DESIRE"

Spiritual Wealth and Desires

Opposite of the 2ⁿᵈ House of Possessions, this house represents how we take our values from the 2ⁿᵈ house and apply them to worldly desires, how we regenerate our energy to possess and continue pursuing what we desire, and how our desires relate to a spiritual or divine meaning.

9TH HOUSE (MENTAL EXPLORATION) "I SEE"

Perspectives and Experiences

Opposite of the 3rd House of Communication, this house represents how we use our communicative skills to explore and expand our perspectives, ideologies, and theories through physical experiences and how we value what we see through multiple perspectives/experiences.

10TH HOUSE (CAREER) "I USE"

Finances and Lifestyle

Opposite of the 4th House of Home, this house represents how we move out of our home and create a financial means to support what and who we love the most, how we value finances, how we utilize career for status and wealth, and how we use our resources to succeed in life and build a home.

11TH HOUSE (HOPES AND FRIENDSHIPS) "I KNOW"

Value of Humanity

Opposite of the 5th House of Creativity, this house represents how we apply our creative senses, skills, and talents, which leads to us sharing our knowledge with others, building beneficial friendships, understanding how our strengths affect others, and our overall humanitarian values.

12TH HOUSE (SELF-UNDOING) "I BELIEVE"

Value of Higher Purpose

Opposite of the 6th House of Health & Service, this house represents how we apply our sense of self and purpose within our community and how we value our emotional and spiritual beliefs. It's about learning that we can sabotage all we've learned from prior houses, which then sends us back to the 1st house to rediscover who "I am."

✹☆☾

☼ ☆ ☾

HOUSE LANDLORDS

It's best to visualize the horoscope as a constantly moving community. Planets act as taxicabs, where their ruling sign(s) is/are the driver(s) who pick up other zodiac signs or ride solo and either drops them off at different houses for a vacation or parks in their ruling house for a staycation. Orbital paths are the GPS of the horoscope, aspects are freeways that connect our destinations, hemispheres (North, South, East, West) are the regions of the horoscope, and quadrants (AC, DC, MC, IC) are the governors of the hemispheres.

There are 12 houses within these hemispheres, with each house having a special landlord (zodiac sign) and representing a different meaning in a planet's orbital path. Landlords picked up by a traveling planet other than their ruler and dropped off into a house other than their own act as foreign visitors who borrow energy from a house's landlord and ruling planet.

HOUSE LANDLORDS CHEAT SHEET

HOUSE NO.	MOTTO	LANDLORD	HOUSE OF...
1st House (AC)	I am	Aries	Self (Self-Awareness)
2nd House	I have	Taurus	Possessions
3rd House	I think	Gemini	Communication
4th House (IC)	I feel	Cancer	Home & Family
5th House	I will	Leo	Creativity
6th House	I analyze	Virgo	Service and Health
7th House (DC)	I balance	Libra	Love and Partnerships
8th House	I desire	Scorpio	Regeneration and Transformation
9th House	I see	Sagittarius	Mental Exploration
10th House (MC)	I use	Capricorn	Career
11th House	I know	Aquarius	Hope and Friendships
12th House	I believe	Pisces	Self-Undoing

✵ ✫ ☾

Example 1: Let's say your Virgo Moon is in the 1ˢᵗ house (Aries landlord). Virgo is the foreigner because Virgo's ruling planet is Mercury and they own the 6ᵗʰ House. This means it's renting energy from Aries' 1ˢᵗ house and Cancer's Moon (the Moon rules Cancer).

We know the Moon influences our emotions and instincts, and we know the 1ˢᵗ house provides insight into our sense of self and direction. Because Virgo is the foreigner, we know it will be influenced by its new environment and adopt a few traits as a visitor. With that knowledge, we can interpret the energy as: This person possesses assertive and highly focused emotional energy. They like to organize and overanalyze their feelings. They can react emotionally cold and detached, especially if the situation or person is unreasonable. This person can be deeply critical of themselves or others and can even experience extreme anxiety when things aren't perfectly planned out. They are guided by logical, productive feelings and will remove themselves from situations they feel are unbeneficial to their emotional growth.

Example 2: Let's say your Scorpio Venus is in the 8ᵗʰ house. Scorpio has been picked up by Venus, so it's a foreign passenger because Scorpio's ruling planets are Mars and Pluto. However, it is not taking a vacation because it owns the 8ᵗʰ house. Therefore, it is having a staycation and taking a trip around its own house.

We know Venus influences love and relationships, and we know the 8ᵗʰ house provides insights into how a person regenerates their energy. It's also a house known for its intense spiritual/healing abilities, and it represents how a person perceives desire in relation to emotional fulfillment and spiritual justification.

With that knowledge, we can interpret the energy as: This person is both sensitive and self-controlled in love. They yearn to possess and be possessed. They find it hard to trust and be openly vulnerable, which is why they seek

☀ ☆ ☾

out soul connections where they feel an unbreakable and trustworthy bond. They can be jealous and spiteful when spurned but loyal and devoted when in love. This person is a strong believer of karma, though at a younger age they can be vengeful or use vengeance as a way to feel empowered. Their definition of love is gauged by the level of intensity in a relationship. They are challenged to learn that not all intense relationships arc hcalthy ones, nor do they define true love or romance. This can lead them down a cycle of abusive or traumatic relationships, by which they feel inspired to keep it going due to the extremes of it, as well as their undying loyalty to those they feel a strong connection with.

Important: These examples are just one part of a horoscope. Higher accuracy is based on aspects (relationships between planets). You also won't see your houses, your rising (Ascendant) sign, and sometimes even your Moon sign unless you know the time of your birth. To find your time of birth, check your birth certificate.

✸ ☆ ☾

HOUSE DOMINANCE

A person with dominant houses (multiple planets in the same house) in their horoscope means there is a heavier influence within those houses. Houses that do not have planets can be dismissed as a lesser influence or can be interpreted using the ruling planet of the zodiac sign in that house. This is ultimately your choice.

For Example: A natal chart has three planets in the 10th House of Career and three planets in the 7th House of Partnerships. Depending on the planets and the aspects of those planets, this person invests most of their energy into personal success and personal relationships.

DOMINANT HOUSE	DOMINANT MEANING...
1st House (AC)	Greater sense of self and direction, stronger zodiac traits
2nd House	Greater desire for material wealth and possessions
3rd House	Greater sense of communication and mental capacity
4th House (IC)	Greater desire for family, stronger definitions of family
5th House	Greater sense of creativity, imagination, and visualization
6th House	Greater sense of community, self-care, and overall health
7th House (DC)	Greater desire for meaningful and beneficial relationships
8th House	Greater sense of regenerative and transformative energy
9th House	Greater need for mental exploration and expansion
10th House (MC)	Greater ambition, motivation, and financial independence
11th House	Greater sense of humanity, friendships, culture, and diversity
12th House	Greater need for self-care due to self-sabotaging behavior

☼ ☆ ☾

1ˢᵀ HOUSE OF SELF (SELF-AWARENESS)

ARIES LANDLORD

♈

"I am self."

The 1ˢᵗ House of Self (aka House of Self-Awareness) is owned by Aries, a cardinal fire sign. This house has a major influence on how a person sees and values themselves and how a person develops their self-awareness. It is also the house that has the most authority over all the other houses because it is the start of every horoscope.

As we are birthed into the world, the 1ˢᵗ House of Self signals the start of our maturity levels, providing us with the energy needed to build our initial personality. It spreads our energy into other houses, helping us learn and develop parts of our personality in different areas of our lives.

Think of the 1ˢᵗ House as our primary household.

Think of the 1ˢᵗ house as our primary household. It houses and protects all of our personal values, and it influences our mental, emotional, and physical growth. It also impacts our natural instincts, habits, and traits. However, it is not more influential than your Sun sign unless your Sun is in the 1ˢᵗ house.

With Aries' influence, a planet in this house empowers our ambitions and gives us purpose to pursue our inner desires. It offers us courage to overcome certain challenges in our life and confront weaknesses that prevent us from being the person we envision.

When a planet is in the 1ˢᵗ house, it can emphasize a strong sense of self, confidence, and a desire to live life to its full potential.

2ND HOUSE OF POSSESSIONS

TAURUS LANDLORD

♉

"I have possessions."

The 2nd House of Possessions is owned by Taurus, a fixed earth sign. This house develops our perspectives on money, material wealth, and success. It's also our attachments or detachments to material or immaterial possessions.

From the 1st House of Self, we have learned to develop our character in the environment of our own homes. With the 2nd house, we learn that our character requires certain things that make us feel a sense of accomplishment or comfort and a physical environment that allows us to be ourselves.

Think of the 2nd house as our secret vault.

Think of the 2nd house as our secret vault. It houses and protects what we want to acquire, cherish, nurture, and possess in private. What we desire in ourselves must be projected into what we can see and feel, so this house can also show you the types of things that showcase how a person feels about themselves or show you role models this person strives to be.

With Taurus' influence, a planet in this house provides us with the energy needed to realistically achieve and obtain our desired possessions within the physical realm. It also offers strategy and focus to pursue whatever gives us a comfortable and pleasurable lifestyle.

When a planet is in the 2nd house, it can emphasize a strong desire to have material wealth and success and own/buy property and assets.

3RD HOUSE OF COMMUNICATION

GEMINI LANDLORD

♊

"I think communication."

The 3rd House of Communication is owned by Gemini, a mutable air sign. This house further develops our mental and social awareness (negatively or positively) and helps us engage with others through multiple forms, such as writing, music, art, technology, or anything else that helps us convey messages.

From the 2nd House of Possessions, we have learned that our possessions showcase our internal desires, but it has also trapped our private thoughts. With the 3rd House of Communication, we learn to go beyond our personal homes and communicate those thoughts with others.

Think of the 3rd house as our school.

Think of the 3rd house as our school. It houses the way we convey our thoughts and beliefs in ways that others can understand. It's also our social understanding and how we develop our character with others.

With Gemini's influence, a planet in this house provides us with the energy needed to interact, accept, and understand the needs of others through a series of communication. It also helps us bring awareness to how others perceive our thoughts and beliefs, which helps us create the intelligence and intuition needed to better engage, persuade, or argue.

When a planet is in the 3rd house, it can indicate a strong urge to express and understand multiple perspectives using several forms of communication.

✸ ☆ ☾

4ᵀᴴ House of Home

Cancer Landlord

♋

"I feel home."

The 4th house is owned by Cancer, a cardinal water sign. This house further develops our emotional awareness and emotional needs. It helps us gain more self-awareness through emotional processing and projection.

From the 3rd House of Communication, we have learned how to engage with others and convey our thoughts and ideas. With the 4th House of Home, we learn to express and understand the feelings behind our thoughts and ideas. It is the deeper meaning of what makes us think the way we do.

Think of the 4th house as our parents' house.

Think of the 4th house as our parents' house. It represents the comforts of the heart and our emotional attachments to home, family, and love. It is also how we define the meaning of our attachments and the impact it has on us as we move further away from the 1st House of Self. Simply put, it's how we feel when we move out of our home and live by ourselves.

With Cancer's influence, a planet in this house provides us with the energy to develop our emotional senses and reactions to people and things. It brings us a sense of what love is or could be. It also influences our emotional control when it comes to the things or people that mean the most to us.

When a planet is in the 4th house, it can emphasize a strong desire to have emotional attachments, feel at home, and feel loved by family.

5ᵀᴴ HOUSE OF CREATIVITY

LEO LANDLORD

♌

"I will create."

The 5th house is owned by Leo, a fixed fire sign. This is also known as the House of Pleasure and Sex, but it's more about our creative ambitions and our drive in developing our special skills and talents for the world to see. It also helps us further develop and assess our self-worth.

From the 4th House of Home, we have learned to develop our emotional senses and define our emotional attachments in the world. With the 5th House of Creativity, we learn to pour our emotions into projects that help us see our self-worth and build our talents to exceed our personal value.

Think of the 5ᵗʰ house as our work studio.

Think of the 5th house as our work studio. This house represents how we utilize our creativity and willpower to pursue our deepest passions. It's how we improve on our greatest strengths and develop our skills in preparation for the physical realm.

With Leo's influence, a planet in this house provides us with a stronger sense of creation and innovation, as well as purpose and direction. It helps us focus our energy into dreaming bigger and better without limitations.

When a planet is in the 5th house, it can point to a strong imagination and creative vision and a strong urge to dream and create a new reality.

✹☆☾

6ᵀᴴ HOUSE OF SERVICE & HEALTH

VIRGO LANDLORD

♍

"I analyze service & health."

The 6ᵗʰ house is owned by Virgo, a mutable earth sign. This house marks the end of the bottom (internal) hemisphere, getting us ready for the upper (external) hemisphere. It's the preparation of everything we've learned about ourselves in prior houses and how we include it in our communities.

From the 5ᵗʰ House of Creativity, we have learned to build our skills and pursue the things that give us value, purpose, and self-worth. With the 6ᵗʰ House of Service and Health, we learn to utilize and share our professional expertise, greater strengths, and talents and skills with our communities.

Think of the 6ᵗʰ house as our hospital.

Think of the 6ᵗʰ house as our hospital. It represents how we analyze our physical well-being, our physical status in the community, our physical values, and how it all can be applied to better service our community. It's also how we like to help and serve others and how we want to be useful in the world.

With Virgo's influence, a planet in this house provides us with the energy to utilize and refine our skills and talents to benefit others or create the changes needed to obtain a healthier lifestyle.

When a planet is in the 6ᵗʰ house, it can indicate a strong sense of duty to service others and a need to help the community and master human well-being.

7ᵀᴴ HOUSE OF LOVE & PARTNERSHIP

LIBRA LANDLORD

♎

"I balance love & partnerships."

The 7th house is owned by Libra, a cardinal air sign. This house marks the beginning of the upper (external) hemisphere, which focuses more on how our character develops in society (physical realm). It is the house that defines and further develops the meaning of unity and partnerships with others.

The 7th House of Love and Partnerships is opposite of the 1st House of Self. With the 1st house, we learned to value ourselves and develop our initial characteristics. With the 7th house, we learn to balance love of self with love of others. This house gives insights into our compatibility with others, no matter the type of relationship, and how we value ourselves with others.

Think of the 7th house as the court room.

Think of the 7th house as the court room. It houses equality and justice, as well as marriage and divorce, although at times, it can have a negative effect, tilting toward injustice and inequality in relationships. Therefore, this house allows us to play the judge and can show us people's true intentions when it comes to any relationship or partnership we pursue.

With Libra's influence, a planet in this house provides us with the energy to differentiate realness and superficiality when it comes to compatibility. It also shows us how a person utilizes their relationships to benefit themselves.

When a planet is in the 7th house, it can indicate a strong desire to build, balance, and maintain relationships.

☼☆☽

8ᵀᴴ HOUSE OF REGENERATION & TRANSFORMATION

SCORPIO LANDLORD

♏

"I desire regeneration & transformation."

The 8ᵗʰ house is owned by Scorpio, a fixed water sign. This house helps us further develop our connections with material and immaterial possessions. It's how we define our attachments through spiritual justification.

The 8ᵗʰ House of Regeneration and Transformation is opposite of the 2ⁿᵈ House of Possessions. With the 2ⁿᵈ house, we learned to possess the things that make us feel comfortable. With the 8ᵗʰ house, we learn that certain things do not provide us with the happiness we need to live an emotionally fulfilling life. We then take a more spiritual or abstract approach to search for a meaningful link into what makes us truly happy.

Think of the 8ᵗʰ house as an Egyptian tomb.

Think of the 8ᵗʰ house as an Egyptian tomb. It's the house of the occult and spiritual senses; it's the one that relates to death and afterlife. Within that tomb, we find many possessions we believe will help us in the afterlife. We then search for the things we can take with us in death, even if that means taking immaterial wealth.

With Scorpio's influence, a planet in this house provides us with energy to take a more spiritual, intense, and in-depth approach to life. It helps us continue pursuing our desires with deeper meaning and soul purpose.

When a planet is in the 8ᵗʰ house, it can indicate a strong sense of intuition, spiritual growth, and mastering one's internal evolution.

9TH HOUSE OF MENTAL EXPLORATION

SAGITTARIUS LANDLORD

"I see mental exploration."

The 9th house is owned by Sagittarius, a mutable fire sign. It is a house that further develops our mentality, instilling in us more faith and wisdom to view life more philosophically.

The 9th House of Mental Exploration is opposite of the 3rd House of Communication. With the 3rd house, we learned to communicate our inner thoughts and ideas. With the 9th house, we learn to strategize and refine our ideas and theories, as well as utilize our communicative skills to expand our perspectives through physical experiences, such as travel.

Think of the 9th house as a yacht.

Think of the 9th house as a yacht, one that is always moving and built to travel. It houses where our mind wants to travel, how we value education and personal experiences, and our understanding of culture and diversity. We see that life is filled with opportunities to evolve our mentality, especially as we move around and adopt other customs and cultures.

With Sagittarius' influence, a planet in this house provides us with the energy needed to view life from an optimistic and open-minded perspective. It encourages us to pursue the truth behind everything and everyone.

When a planet is in the 9th house, it can point to a strong sense of justice, research, and philosophy and the urge to seek the truth in all situations.

10ᵀᴴ HOUSE OF CAREER

CAPRICORN LANDLORD

♑

"I use career."

The 10ᵗʰ house is owned by Capricorn, a cardinal earth sign. It further develops our need to provide for ourselves and our family. It shows us how we value and utilize our finances to better our environment or status.

The 10ᵗʰ House of Career is opposite of the 4ᵗʰ House of Home. With the 4ᵗʰ house, we learned the meaning of family, love, and emotional attachment. With the 10ᵗʰ house, we learn that love is not enough to feed us. We then go out into the world, with family in mind, and take our skills to obtain financial support, which provides the necessary resources to survive or gain reputation.

Think of the 10ᵗʰ house as the White House.

Think of the 10ᵗʰ house as the White House. It represents power, status, ambitions, profession, order, and hierarchy. It's our most successful and most resourceful house that provides us with the knowledge to take our dreams and ground them in reality. However, it can also stomp on youthful dreams and pressure you to conform to societal norms.

With Capricorn's influence, a planet in this house provides us with energy to take responsibility and accountability and be disciplined in using our skills to create a stable environment for ourselves and our families.

When a planet is in the 10ᵗʰ house, it can emphasize a strong desire to build, achieve, and master success through experience and education.

11ᵀᴴ HOUSE OF HOPE AND FRIENDSHIPS

AQUARIUS LANDLORD

♒

"I know hope and friendships."

The 11ᵗʰ house is owned by Aquarius, a fixed air sign. This house further develops our humanitarian needs and encourages causes that educate people to be friendlier, kinder, and more humane.

The 11ᵗʰ House of Hope and Friendships is opposite of the 5ᵗʰ House of Creativity. With the 5ᵗʰ house, we learned to define what our greater strengths are and how to utilize them to express ourselves. With the 11ᵗʰ house, we learn to take these skills and educate others, relieving ignorance and ego.

Think of the 11ᵗʰ house as a spaceship.

Think of the 11ᵗʰ house as a spaceship that launches you into a new world where you can connect with alien life-forms. It houses your hopes and dreams in building peace and harmony by sharing knowledge and sustaining beneficial partnerships through deeper understanding and acceptance. You may even have to take a more creative and eccentric approach to form bonds.

With Aquarius' influence, a planet in this house provides us with energy to see life from multiple unbiased perspectives, which helps us gain clarity and focus to create the change necessary to evolve humanity as a whole.

When a planet is in the 11ᵗʰ house, it can point to a strong sense of faith and an urge to do good in the community and be a friend or role model of the world.

12TH HOUSE OF SELF-UNDOING

PISCES LANDLORD

♓

"I believe in self-undoing."

The 12th house is owned by Pisces, a mutable water sign. This house marks the end of the horoscope's life cycle, therefore ending our personal journey. It helps further our spiritual and emotional values, as well as our greater sense of purpose in the world. It can also be a house of self-sabotage.

The 12th House of Self-Undoing is opposite of the 6th House of Service and Health. With the 6th house, we learned to be of service to our community by sharing our skills and wisdom. With the 12th house, we learn that there is a deeper meaning to community, as well as a deeper meaning to our life choices, where we can feel rejected or accepted by them.

Think of the 12th house as the church.

Think of the 12th house as the church or the place we visit to repent. It's the house of greater reflection, housing our karma and providing us with our life's greatest punishments or rewards. It heavily influences our emotional, mental, and spiritual perspectives. We overcome these challenges by uplifting our spirit and receiving professional help, self-medicating, or participating in self-love and care.

Since this is the last house, it will always transition back into the 1st House of Self, where we experience our next evolution and further develop our character. One would call this a birthday, where we continue to revisit all we have learned internally and externally over the years.

With Pisces' influence, a planet in this house provides us with the energy to see life more vividly, spiritually, and sensitively. We learn to be kind and caring to ourselves by reflecting on our lives and seeking the help we need through our respective communities. We must also learn that we are only human and that our human nature is to sabotage or destroy parts of ourselves to evolve into a stronger being.

When a planet is in the 12th house, it can indicate strong rebellious desires that sometimes lead to self-sabotaging behavior, yet there is a strong sense of self and authenticity no matter what.

✷☆☾

☼ ☆ ☾

ASPECTS

Aspects are the relationships between planets. Planetary aspects are the traditional way to read energies and one of the more accepted ways by professionals. Depending on what aspect your planets have with one another, it can create harmony or disharmony between your energies.

Note: Aspects are divided between major aspects and minor aspects. Some astrologers include minor aspects and others dismiss them altogether. The choice is up to you; however, this book will not cover minor aspects.

Orbs & Degrees

MAJOR ASPECTS	DEGREES	MAXIMUM ORB DEGREES
Conjunction	0°	0°–10° (8° without the Sun or Moon)
Sextile	60°	3°–6°
Square	90°	5°–10°
Trine	120°	5°–10°
Opposition	180°	5°–10°
MINOR ASPECTS	**DEGREES**	**ORB DEGREES**
Semisextile	30°	1°–1.5°
Semisquare (octile)	45°	1°–2.5°
Sesquisquare (tri-octile)	135°	2°–2.5°
Quincunx	150°	2°–3°

Unaspected Planets: These types of planets still have some energetic influence in a horoscope. You can read them independently or gain even further insight with their compatibility to other planets using elements and zodiac signs.

✺ ☆ ☾

ASPECT CHEAT SHEET

MAJOR ASPECTS	DEGREES	RELATIONSHIP	ASPECT MEANING
Conjunction	0°	MARRIED	Powerful and intense connection between planets
Sextile	60°	DATING	Opportunity and harmony between two planets
Square	90°	DIVORCED	Challenge and tension between two planets
Trine	120°	PROFESSIONAL	Favorable and beneficial energy between two planets
Opposition	180°	COMPLICATED	Opposing energy that creates challenges between two planets

Degrees between aspects is an important factor, as well as the orb it creates from its angle. The reason why astrologers use orbs instead of angles is because the degree of angles (depending on the house system) is sometimes not the exact degree it should be. To be clear, the orb degree is the number of degrees outside of the stated aspect degree.

For Example: A square aspect is noted as 90°, but it can still be considered a square aspect if two planets are 95° apart. Therefore, the orb degree is 5°.

Keep in mind that some astrologers use **different amounts of orb degrees**, but it's widely accepted that Sun and Moon aspects can have a wider orb of up to 10°. Regardless, one thing is certain: the closer the orb, the stronger the relationship between planets and the more impact and significance it has.

For Example: If an orb degree for a square aspect is less than 3°, then it has more impact than one that has an 8° orb. If a square aspect is exactly at 90° (0° orb), then it will have more impact than an aspect with an orb of 3°.

☀☆☾

ASPECT MEANINGS

CONJUNCTION (MARRIED)

TWO PLANETS AT 0° DEGREES

A conjunction occurs when two planets are 0° apart and usually reside in the same zodiac sign. Conjunction aspects provide insight into how a person utilizes their energy for the betterment of themselves (good or bad). They will have heightened energy in all traits, sharing both negative and positive energies. Think of this aspect as a married couple that fully accepts and understands one another's strengths and weaknesses. However, there will still be arguments between them, whether it's petty or not (depends on the aspect).

If we take a look at numerology, the number zero represents completion, full circle, and infinity. Therefore, this aspect tells us about the completion between two planets and the energy that makes a person complete or whole.

SEXTILE (DATING)

TWO PLANETS 60° DEGREES APART

✳

A sextile occurs when two planets are 60° apart and can reside in zodiac signs that are elementally compatible. Sextile aspects provide insight into how a person develops and progresses when given certain opportunities. They work together harmoniously, each taking its turn to balance and learn from one another. Think of this aspect as two people dating, where they appreciate one another's positive traits but can be dismissive of their negative traits.

If we take a look at numerology, this aspect creates the number six, which represents harmony, compassion, and love. This tells us that these planets have more positive influences over one another, and it can also tell us that a person will choose positive growing opportunities.

Square (Divorced)

Two planets 90° degrees apart

□

A square occurs when two planets are 90° apart and share the same modality (cardinal, mutable, or fixed) but are elementally incompatible. This aspect provides insight into a person's negative traits and behaviors and the challenges they face when trying to conquer them. Think of this aspect as a divorced couple whose incompatible traits create intense friction. There will be a strong learning curve between them, but overcoming these curves will bring forth stronger traits of perseverance over self.

If we take a look at numerology, this aspect creates the number nine. The number nine represents greater inner wisdom, problem-solving, discipline, and tolerance. This aspect tells us that these planets will work harder to resolve the issues between them, but there are no guarantees.

Trine (Professional)

Two planets 120° degrees apart

△

A trine occurs when two planets are 120° apart and share the same element. Trine aspects provide insight into how a person utilizes their strengths and skills and how they share their talents with others. They understand how to work with one another for the betterment of themselves with consideration of the effects it will have on others. Think of this aspect as a beneficial professional relationship, where planets share the same goal.

If we take a look at numerology, this aspect creates the number three, which represents creativity, divinity, generosity, communication, and sociability. This tell us that there are powerful influences between these two planets, and the person will be influenced to create more magical or beneficial relationships.

OPPOSITION (COMPLICATED)

TWO PLANETS 180° DEGREES APART

☍

An opposition occurs when two planets are 180° apart and can share the same modality and are elementally compatible. Opposition aspects provide insight into how a person balances their negative traits with their positive traits. These planets create a yin/yang type of energy, of which they can balance or unbalance one another. Think of this aspect as a complicated union, where they are either the best of friends or the worst of enemies.

If we take a look at numerology, this aspect creates the number nine. Similar to the square aspect, the number nine represents greater inner wisdom, problem-solving, discipline, and tolerance. Where it differs is that an opposition aspect will resort to balance instead of resentment. What this tells us is that these two planets must endure a constant battle for dominance, which can tilt from positive to negative.

☀☆☾

AUTHOR NOTES

Reading an aspect accurately depends on the information of both planets. Aspects not only define the relationship between planets, but they also define the relationship of the zodiac signs and the houses within them.

For example: Sun in conjunction with the Moon is expanded into Sun in Scorpio in the 10th house in conjunction with the Moon in Taurus in the 5th house.

Every planet can have a relationship with another planet, even without an aspect present. A planet's elemental energy and zodiac sign can still be interpreted to be compatible or incompatible with another planet. At the end of the day, it's up to you to decipher every planetary relationship.

✴ ☆ ☽

ELEMENTS

Elements add specific traits that affect zodiac signs' personality and aura. There are **four types of elements** and **three zodiac signs per element:** fire (spirit), earth (body), air (mind), and water (heart). There are compatible, incompatible, and neutral compatible elements.

Envision elements as groups of families. In a family, there are two boys (masculine elements) and two girls (feminine elements). As you learned earlier, there is an evolution between zodiac signs; therefore, there is also an evolution between elemental siblings.

★ **Fire (spirit):** our spirit, passions, and desires
★ **Earth (body):** our physical body and material wealth
★ **Air (mind):** our mentality, ideas, and thought process
★ **Water (heart):** our emotions, sensitivity, and love

GLYPHS	SIGN	ELEMENT	ENERGY
♈	Aries	Fire	Masculine
♌	Leo	Fire	Masculine
♐	Sagittarius	Fire	Masculine
♉	Taurus	Earth	Feminine
♍	Virgo	Earth	Feminine
♑	Capricorn	Earth	Feminine
♊	Gemini	Air	Masculine
♎	Libra	Air	Masculine
♒	Aquarius	Air	Masculine
♋	Cancer	Water	Feminine
♏	Scorpio	Water	Feminine
♓	Pisces	Water	Feminine

✹☆☾

COMPATIBLE ELEMENTS

COMPATIBLE	INCOMPATIBLE	NEUTRAL
Fire and Air	Fire and Water	Fire and Earth
Earth and Water	Earth and Air	Water and Air

COMPATIBLE ELEMENTS

Compatible elements create positive energy and work together to uplift and encourage one another. They have a natural flow to sustain one another and get along effortlessly.

Fire (spirit) and air (mind) move upward into the heavens, which spreads enlightenment and empowerment. Earth (body) and water (heart) cover the lands with nourishment and maturity.

INCOMPATIBLE ELEMENTS

Incompatible elements create negative energy, which brings tension and turmoil to both the heavens and earth. Fire (spirit) and water (heart) can create aggression and overreaction. Earth (body) and air (mind) can create confusion and irresponsibility.

NEUTRAL ELEMENTS

Neutral elements can create negative or positive energy. Fire and earth can either create wealth and power or poverty and defeat. Water and air can create intelligence and intuition or senselessness and delusions.

☀☆☽

FIRE SIGNS (SPIRIT)

ARIES, LEO, AND SAGITTARIUS

△

Fire signs light the way for others, and like fire, they leave behind the smoke and ashes of everything and everyone they've consumed. They are ambitious, impulsive, aggressive, passionate, and fiery. Their strength lies within their desire to be the best and live out their wildest dreams. They can be selfish and self-centered, yet that's what makes them focused and fearless leaders.

Fire signs require a lot of **physical stimulation**. They yearn to take control of destiny in a physical sense, and they find it hard to sit still, always needing to stay active in mind, heart, and spirit. They are affectionate lovers, as well as short-tempered, even violent, fighters. They often have difficulty with authority, as they want their flames of glory and success to light up their lives without feeling restricted or limited by others.

Fire signs help ignite physical action in others. They represent the torches for dreams and ambitions. Without them, humanity would lack passion, drive, and influence.

FIRE SIGN EVOLUTION

Aries, a cardinal fire sign, is the eldest of the three and the first zodiac sign (oldest zodiac sign). They have discovered fire and have begun to utilize it out of necessity for survival and innovation. Leo, a fixed fire sign, is the middle child. They have learned to master the fire's potential for control and power. Sagittarius, a mutable fire sign, is the youngest. They have learned the true essence of fire, using it for spiritual and mental purposes and allowing it to burn freely without restraint.

EARTH SIGNS (BODY)

TAURUS, VIRGO, AND CAPRICORN

Earth signs build structured foundations for others, moving away from emotion and finding strength in logic and resourcefulness. They are reliable, patient, tolerant, stable, disciplined, and reserved individuals. These signs are built on stamina, hard work, longevity, and commitment.

Earth signs require **financial security and stability.** Money and career are big motivators for earth signs, so it's natural for them to create long-term goals, financial independence, and savings accounts at an early age. They can get anxious and depressed when they're not progressing. They are instinctual signs and like to stick to strict routines but are also very cautious when making major decisions. They strive to have and build perfection and organization in everything they do.

Earth signs ground the energy of others. Their discipline and strictness are the soil and fertilizer to our dreams. Without them, humanity wouldn't have a structure or a foundation to stand on.

EARTH SIGN EVOLUTION

Taurus, a fixed earth sign, is the firstborn. They have discovered earth and have learned to nurture it out of necessity for long-term survival and growth while also creating structure and seasonal routines. Virgo, a mutable earth sign, is the middle child. They have learned to analyze the earth, creating ways to repurpose and restructure natural resources for maximum efficiency. Capricorn, a cardinal earth sign, is the youngest. They have learned to utilize the earth to build homes and architecture, which then creates the need for power and status.

Air Signs (Mind)

Gemini, Libra, and Aquarius

Air signs create balance in thoughts, ideas, and communication for others. They are persuasive, flighty, talkative, creative, thoughtful, whimsical, and eccentric individuals. They have a lifelong journey for knowledge, as they strive for total mental awareness and mental freedom.

Air signs require **a lot of mental stimulation**. Their minds never stop moving. They see life from multiple perspectives and believe there are multiple ways to accomplish one thing. Just like air, they can be unpredictable and uncontrolled. Communication and socialization will be important to them, as they find it challenging to keep their thoughts to themselves and find it hard to be alone. The freedom to convey their ideas and challenge the norm will also be prioritized, as they feel suffocated by the things they cannot vocalize and are naturally rebellious.

Air signs release the mental energy of others. They represent our most bizarre and creative ideas and deeper imagination. Without them, humanity would be bland, routine, and robotic.

Air Sign Evolution

Gemini, a mutable air sign, is the firstborn. They have discovered a wind of ideas and have learned to utilize the air of communication out of necessity to debate, convey, and socialize with others (good and bad). Libra, a cardinal air sign, is the middle child. They have learned to utilize the persuasion of ideas to gain power, status, and material possession. Aquarius, a fixed air sign, is the youngest. They have learned to master research, knowledge, perspective, and speech to better educate humanity.

✺☆☾

WATER SIGNS (HEART)

CANCER, SCORPIO, AND PISCES

Water signs bring life into our emotions and dive deep into the meaning of a soul. They are intuitive, compassionate, receptive, emotional, moody, and sensitive individuals. They believe in having total emotional awareness and sustaining and managing our emotional wellness.

Water signs require **emotional stimulation, reassurance, and security.** And yes, they need all three to balance their complex emotional sensors. Like water, their spirits and emotions must flow freely, otherwise they create an overwhelming tsunami for others to drown in. They find it difficult to control the tidal waves of their emotions because they easily soak in the energies of other life-forms. They feel and sense things most people can't, which provides them with more sensitivity, depth, soulfulness, intuition, and receptivity than other zodiac signs.

Water signs, when they've mastered their emotions, become a peaceful rain that brings life and meaning to others. Without them, other signs would lack the emotions needed to feel love, hate, life, and death.

WATER SIGN EVOLUTION

Cancer, a cardinal water sign, is the firstborn. They have discovered water, bringing emotions into humanity and utilizing them to sustain life and cleanse our thoughts and actions. Scorpio, a fixed water sign, is the middle child. They have learned to internalize and control emotions through deep reflection and psychic intuition. Pisces, a mutable water sign, is the youngest. They have learned how to master intuition and emotion through spiritual connection and creative expression.

MODALITIES

You learned that zodiac signs with the same element are like siblings, and now you will learn that zodiac signs who share the same modality are like cousins. Modalities, sometimes known as qualities, for zodiac signs dictate specific traits in positive or negative energy (drive, motivation, passivity).

There are **three types of modalities**—cardinal, fixed, and mutable—and there are four zodiac signs assigned to each modality. Two signs are positive, and two signs are negative, which creates energetic balance between them.

★ **Cardinal:** self-awareness, ambition, and resourcefulness
★ **Fixed:** desire, willpower, focus, and material success
★ **Mutable:** freedom, intellect, communication, and beliefs

GLYPHS	SIGN	MOTTO	MODALITY	ENERGY
♈	Aries	I am	Cardinal	Positive
♋	Cancer	I feel	Cardinal	Negative
♎	Libra	I balance	Cardinal	Positive
♑	Capricorn	I use	Cardinal	Negative
♉	Taurus	I have	Fixed	Negative
♌	Leo	I will	Fixed	Positive
♏	Scorpio	I desire	Fixed	Negative
♒	Aquarius	I know	Fixed	Positive
♊	Gemini	I think	Mutable	Positive
♍	Virgo	I analyze	Mutable	Negative
♐	Sagittarius	I see	Mutable	Positive
♓	Pisces	I believe	Mutable	Negative

☀☆☾

Cardinal Signs

Aries, Cancer, Libra, and Capricorn

Cardinal signs embody our self-awareness, ambition, and resourcefulness. They are the projection of self into the outer world. As natural-born leaders, they strive to do their best in everything they do. They can be aggressive, stern, and direct, wanting to empower people with their actions and motivate them with their words. However, none of their amazing leadership skills would manifest if they didn't first invest all of their energy into building themselves up and launching themselves forward.

Cardinal signs possess more energy than other zodiac signs, which is needed for their larger-than-life goals. They tend to prefer quick progression and maximum production, otherwise they become frustrated and challenging to deal with. They are the type to commit to the challenges ahead and invest time in educating themselves, unwilling to quit until they've overcome their personal or societal obstacles.

Cardinal signs can manage multiple projects but have difficulty trusting others who don't follow their lead, so they struggle with delegation. They believe and expect others to keep up without questioning their methods or authority. Positively, cardinal signs are one of the most trusted signs when it comes to management and career, mostly because they've built up a resumé of skills and talents that others can't deny.

Cardinal Sign Evolution

Aries (I am) embodies physical self-awareness, Cancer (I feel) embodies emotional self-awareness, Libra (I balance) embodies mental self-awareness, and Capricorn (I use) embodies societal and environmental self-awareness.

FIXED SIGNS

TAURUS, LEO, SCORPIO, AND AQUARIUS

Fixed signs embody our desires, willpower, focus, and material success. They are the projection of self-worth and possession. As the focused signs of the zodiac, they filter out the noise of others and are possessive and protective over their beliefs. They find it difficult to consider other perspectives without good reason or personal experience.

Fixed signs do not trust easily because they are fully aware that others can manipulate situations, which is why they prefer to experience things for themselves. Once convinced, they will not budge from their judgment (good or bad). Needless to say, they are loyal to the choices they make and rarely regret them. This type of energy bleeds into their relationships, finances, and careers, all of which they can become overly possessive or protective over, so long as their attachments remain loyal and trustful.

Fixed signs value and uphold their self-worth. They strongly believe there is a right and wrong way to do things and anything in between serves as nothing more than a distraction of realistic expectations. Positively, they weed out irresponsibility from their lives and focus on the underlining meaning of everything and everyone. This helps them stay on their desired journey of self-fulfillment, self-respect, and self-worth.

FIXED SIGN EVOLUTION

Taurus (I have) embodies material desires, Leo (I will) embodies physical desires, Scorpio (I desire) embodies emotional desires, and Aquarius (I know) embodies mental desires.

☼ ☆ ☾

MUTABLE SIGNS

GEMINI, VIRGO, SAGITTARIUS, AND PISCES

Mutable signs embody our freedom to think, our intellect, communication, and beliefs. They are the projection of mentality within society. As the most adaptable signs of the zodiac, they strongly believe in the freedom of choice and embrace consequences both optimistically and pessimistically. They often see and experience life from both sides of the coin, choosing to toss it up on the chance for a better life. "Whatever happens, happens" should be their motto.

Mutable signs are free-flowing individuals who find it difficult to ground their dreams realistically. They can commit to journeys but abandon them halfway through out of fear of restriction and conformity. To see a project to completion, they need to feel strongly passionate about the subject. These signs require a lot of mental and creative freedom, otherwise they will feel stifled by their thoughts and ideas.

Mutable signs are expressive mentally and emotionally, finding it easier to communicate verbally or creatively than other zodiac signs. Their perceptions in life tend to be different than others', as they find solace in justifying their actions or consequences through spiritual, scientific, or philosophical means. Positively, these signs are often lighthearted and playful, choosing to live life day by day instead of obsessing over what they cannot control.

MUTABLE SIGN EVOLUTION

Gemini (I think) embodies perception and creativity, Virgo (I analyze) embodies logic and reconstruction, Sagittarius (I see) embodies faith and philosophy, and Pisces (I believe) embodies intuition and spirituality.

✹ ☆ ☽

ZODIAC SIGNS IN DETAIL

As there is an evolution with planets, there is also an evolution for zodiac signs. All signs learn from the last sign in hierarchy, modality, and element.

SUN SIGN

These sections will detail the energy of each Sun sign and how they've evolved before the sign before them. Our Sun sign carries the bulk of our energy. It is the core of our personality; therefore, it will have the most information. **You can also read this section** for your Rising sign and Moon sign. If you are a cusp baby, then read both of your Sun signs.

UNEVOLVED SUN SIGN

The negative, highly toxic, and dark energy of a Sun sign, this is meant for people to see themselves from a highly immature, toxic state.

EVOLVED SUN SIGN

The positive, enlightened, and fully awakened energy of a Sun sign, this is meant for people to see themselves from a highly mature, enlightened state.

MOON SIGN

The Moon influences our emotional energy, so these sections will detail how we perceive, react, and handle our emotions based on our Moon sign. Keep in mind these are general interpretations. Accurate interpretations are dependent on a mixture of celestial factors, such as aspects and houses.

SIGNS IN OTHER PLACEMENTS

Zodiac signs in Ascendant/Rising (AC), Midheaven (MC), and all other planetary placements describe how they influence our personalities. These sections are general interpretations. Accurate interpretations are dependent on a mixture of celestial factors, such as aspects and houses.

☼ ☆ ☾

ZODIAC CHEAT SHEET

GLYPHS	SIGN	MOTTO	TRAITS	TRADITIONAL DATES	RULING PLANET(S)
♈	**Aries**	I am	Fire, Cardinal, Positive, Masculine	March 21 – April 19	Mars
♉	**Taurus**	I have	Earth, Fixed, Negative, Feminine	April 20 – May 20	Venus
♊	**Gemini**	I think	Air, Mutable, Positive, Masculine	May 21 – June 20	Mercury
♋	**Cancer**	I feel	Water, Cardinal, Negative, Feminine	June 21 – July 22	Moon
♌	**Leo**	I will	Fire, Fixed, Positive, Masculine	July 23 – August 22	Sun
♍	**Virgo**	I analyze	Earth, Mutable, Negative, Feminine	Aug. 23 – Sept. 22	Mercury
♎	**Libra**	I balance	Air, Cardinal, Positive, Masculine	Sept. 23 – Oct. 22	Venus
♏	**Scorpio**	I desire	Water, Fixed, Negative, Feminine	Oct. 23 – Nov. 21	Pluto and Mars
♐	**Sagittarius**	I see	Fire, Mutable, Positive, Masculine	Nov. 22 – Dec. 21	Jupiter
♑	**Capricorn**	I use	Earth, Cardinal, Negative, Feminine	Dec. 22 – Jan. 19	Saturn
♒	**Aquarius**	I know	Air, Fixed, Positive, Masculine	Jan. 20 – Feb. 18	Uranus and Saturn
♓	**Pisces**	I believe	Water, Mutable, Negative, Feminine	Feb. 19 – March 20	Neptune and Jupiter

☼ ☆ ☾

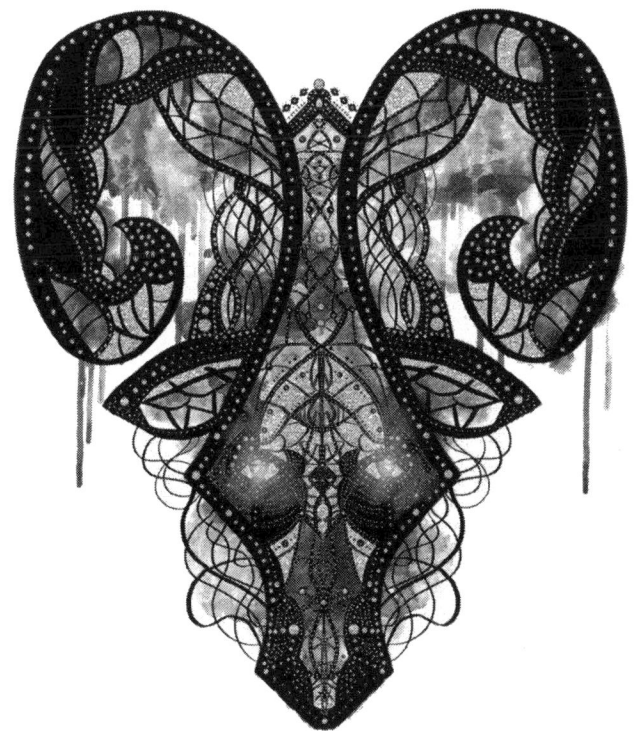

ARIES

Martian Ram

♈

March 21 – April 19
Element: Fire
Modality: Cardinal
Ruling Planet: Mars
Symbol: The Ram
Motto: I Am

ARIES SUN

♈ ☉

"I am."

Aries is a cardinal fire sign, guided by the Ram and ruled by the planet Mars. It shares this planet with Scorpio. As the firstborn star child, first fire sign, and first cardinal sign, Arians feel destined to capture and engulf the world with their vibrant wildfire. In the dark void of the galaxy, they become the light that ventures out into unexplored worlds, viewing them as an open sandbox where everything they touch burns with the brightness of their youthful imagination. Because of their need to continuously explore, the universe has blessed them with brave hearts and more energy to keep their spirits marching forward into the great unknown.

Arians are naïve, even gullible, to the world and its surroundings because they are the firstborn, but they also hold more experience because of it. As the true leaders of the zodiac, their mighty horns ram through and pave the way for the rest of the signs to follow. Rarely do they look back to see what others will do with their paved pathways after they've departed from it. With that said, they do not feed off the energy of other signs; they lead without it.

As the Martian Ram, they are guided by the planet Mars, which is befitting for this zodiac sign. Mars embodies physical energy and aggression, which is everything Aries personifies. Mars is the red sandbox, brewing with Aries' powerful wildfire and providing Arians with ferocious drive and purpose. This planet constantly spits out fiery warriors, releasing them into the universe to discover new and exciting worlds to play in. This can be a good or bad thing, depending on the maturity levels of a born Aries.

With torches in their hand, Arians are entrusted by the universe to spread

their light of innovation and creation. However, unevolved Arians can take advantage of this trust, turning into spiritual arsonists and burning bridges along the way. Evolved Arians, on the other hand, will inspire others with the creation of fire. Regardless of their intentions, Arians were meant to light up and go, leaving the cleanup for the next zodiac sign (Taurus).

Arians' strengths are more physical than mental or emotional. As a Mars sign, they experiment with all physical sensations, even sexually. Touch and affection will be extremely important to them when making connections with others. Sitting still can also be hard for them. A body part is always moving anxiously about, ready to start the next journey. This type of impulsivity and impatience is what drives them to always push ahead no matter what.

If an Aries finds themselves in a situation they can't physically get out of, their minds will race to explore an imaginative world or fantasy, one where they see themselves physically getting away. Their visions and dreams are usually packed with exciting, intense action or laughable, comedic moments. They are known to be thrill seekers and thrill givers, and they love seeing the physical reactions of others (mostly laughter or fear). They also have a great sense of humor and always see the funny or sunny side of life's situations. You will find many famous Aries entertainers, professional fighters, police officers, firefighters, military personnel, comedians, directors, screenwriters, or any other profession that allows them more physical action or reaction.

The Aries symbol is the ram, and like a ram, Arians charge in headfirst, demanding everyone to step aside and make way for their greatness. Their mighty horns symbolize their physical power and inner strengths. However, like a fiery ram, they come in hot and ready for anything. Yet, with all that fire inside, their ego can be overly sensitive, and it doesn't take much to get them riled up and ready to buck.

Arians have been known to resort to aggression or violence to protect those they love, stand up for themselves, show dominance, and get their point

✷✧☾

across—whichever comes first or whomever challenges their authority. Naturally dominant and competitive, they love a good challenge, which allows them to show off and use their horns. When their eye is on the prize, they'll utilize their physical prowess to win it or take it by force

With all that fiery energy, Arians are not always heated or aggressive; they are usually happy-go-lucky individuals who are always optimistic about their future. They love to be wild and playful, and you can find many who are always smiling and seeing the humor in their traumatic situations. They have a strong belief that it's better to laugh than cry in any given situation, and it's this type of behavior that makes them so robust.

Arians love to have a good time. It's the thrill of life that brings them zeal, so they want to experience everything life has to offer. Arians are powerful manifestors and tend to go after everything they desire. To them, everything and everyone can be obtainable so long as there is a passion and drive for it. As impatient as they can be when it comes to meaningless paths, they can be extremely patient when it comes to long windy roads. Regardless of where they go, they will always enjoy the journey for what it is because they see every experience as a great adventure in which they can become stronger than they were before.

Arians are naturally curious and eager to experiment. They are fiercely independent at an early age. In their younger years, their little hands can be seen tinkering with their toys, even destroying and testing their breaking limits. After they've learned the ins and outs of their toy, they can get bored with it in a day, wanting something new the next. It can be incredibly challenging to hold their attention or affection after the honeymoon phase has passed. This can be alarming for others who want to possess them, but that's the thing: you cannot possess them. Like fire, they need oxygen to grow and consume. It's also not in their spirit to be submissive to anybody or anything.

Arians can't wait to take the world by storm, but if for some reason they

☀ ☆ ☾

are limited by adults, they can build resentment and live by the code, "I'll show you who's boss one day." This warrior-like mentality creates a strong sense of urgency and ambition most zodiac signs do not have. They also have an undefeatable mindset that helps drive their ambitions. As they get older, they tend to adapt the idea that things and people can be consumed and tossed away without much thought. It's not to say that they cannot love or cherish things or people. It's just that empathy, attentiveness, patience, and nurturing are not their strongest traits. Assertiveness, courage, power, and projection of inner and outer strength are.

Since Arians burn through things and people so quickly, long, boring, or slow situations can create frustration and restlessness in their energy. They like to jump straight to the point of any given situation. The more challenging and complex a person or object is, the longer attention span they'll have toward it. However, if they discover that this new world is a façade that lacks an epic adventure, they'll abandon it for someone or something that does.

The Aries motto is "I am." Their life challenge is overcoming themselves since their entire life is based on self-discovery. To overcome this, they must always remind themselves that to be true to self is to find one solid destination that defines who they really are. As they maneuver through life's obstacles, they begin to build extreme confidence in who they are and what their limitations are as a person.

Arians experience a lot of pressure to "be somebody," especially because they are the first zodiac sign. This can create a lot of identity issues. They are also prone to being impressionable, especially in their younger years. They can trust easily without question, believing that they cannot be harmed or giving a person too much credibility without any real proof. They eventually learn through experience that not everyone is as genuine or honest as they are but can be jaded by it. They must learn to use discernment where needed.

Arians absolutely hate when people tell them who they are. With their

☀ ☆ ☾

motto being "I am," they want to be able to tell others who they are and who they are not, even if the other person is speaking the truth. Arians are constantly trying to change narratives, especially when it comes to themselves. Their trigger word is "control." They don't like when people tell them they are controlling, even though this is a trait that everyone else acknowledges. It's hard for them to see the negative sides of themselves because they prefer to see only the positive. However, control is not a bad trait at all. Like a general in war, they see all positions on the field and master the tactics to take down any invasions or conquer when they're expanding.

As a cardinal fire sign, they instinctively take initiative and/or control of every situation. Their energy requires them to constantly consume and expand, otherwise they will burn out and become frustratingly stagnant and uninspired. With their strong sense of purpose, they genuinely believe that life is an obstacle course asking to be defeated. They are their own superheroes in life, and submitting to a tedious and domesticated lifestyle is rarely a life goal for them.

Although Arians have a great sense of purpose and drive, they tend to constantly experiment and dabble in numerous projects, careers, or quick changes in lifestyle. It will take a lot of trial and error, failures, and successes before they learn where they truly belong. If they are the extremely restless type, then their path can lead to an endless cycle of different adventures in one lifetime (good or bad). Settling down and becoming complacent can be hard for these adrenaline junkies, but with full commitment, there's nothing they cannot achieve.

Overall, Aries Suns embody physical mastery. Always true to themselves, they are living and breathing warriors who teach other zodiac signs how to overcome their environment mentally and emotionally. They teach all zodiac signs to pursue their dreams fearlessly with all their physical might. No matter the cost, it will all be worth it if you push your limitations to succeed.

✹ ☆ ☾

UNEVOLVED ARIES – WILD BARBARIAN

Unevolved Arians lack respect for those who come after them. They believe that everything they do and say is law and that all should follow it. Reasoning with them can be a challenge or a full-on fight, which they embrace and pursue without fear of consequences.

Unevolved Arians can become easily angered, taking everything as a personal attack. They can find it difficult to overcome their insecurities, making it a point to defend themselves whenever they feel triggered. Because of this, they can be highly volatile, even violent, especially when it comes to their ego or if someone challenges them vocally or physically. If they do not prioritize physical wellness, they can also be severely lazy and lack ambition.

Since the Aries motto is "I am," unevolved Arians have a challenging time fully understanding who they are and what their purpose is. They become wild barbarians who are unable to control their wildfire, mostly using it for selfish, egotistical reasons. Rather than using their willpower to defend or uplift others, they get into the habit of overpowering others to boost their self-esteem. Their sense of determination is only used to fulfill their desires, pushing people out of the way or forcing others to bend to their will.

As a cardinal fire sign, unevolved Arians can be extremely immature, never wanting to take responsibility for their actions or acknowledge any wrongdoing. They either play around too much, never taking life seriously, or they take life too seriously, never wanting to play. It's black and white to them, where the ultimate outcome is whatever serves their best interest. They do whatever they feel, whenever they feel, dismissing all consideration on how it will affect loved ones around them.

☀ ★ ☾

EVOLVED ARIES – WISE GENERAL

Evolved Arians are the true masters of physical sense and evolution. Their horns of brilliance light the way for others, providing hope for better and stronger days. Evolved Arians are not selfish; they are extremely generous and eager to help others who are vulnerable or physically weaker than them.

When they meet new people, they bring them in with warm hugs and a smile. They are always thoughtful and considerate of others, being one of the best gift givers because they love to see people's positive reactions. Their youthful and jovial spirit is never extinguished. The older they get, the more playful, inspiring, humorous, and lighthearted they become.

Since their motto is "I am," evolved Arians have the strongest sense of purpose and determination to overcome themselves and any obstacle they come across. They fight what is right in the world, using their bravery and fearlessness to become a solid and successful role model for others. They utilize their physical and mental strengths to pave pathways for others to cross. They do not discriminate or use their power or status to belittle others. Their only intent is to create a legacy that is innovative and life changing for those who come after them.

As a cardinal fire sign, evolved Arians are wise generals who guide and inspire others to find their true purpose in life. They are passionately creative and project optimism and perseverance in everything they do. As a natural leader, they will pick you up when you're down and become a true and loyal ally who reminds you of your self-worth. They remind people to explore their greatest passions and embrace every challenge confidently.

☀ ☆ ☾

ARIES MOON

♈ ☽

"I feel what I am."

An individual with an Aries Moon will handle their emotions with more passion and aggression, but it depends on other celestial factors. Mixed with fire, they can be emotionally explosive but also more fearless and active. Mixed with earth, they are determined and focused but emotionally selfish and unapologetic. Mixed with air, they are more thoughtful and outspoken with their emotions but can be disrespectful and impolite. Mixed with water, they can overreact and become volatile but are more sensitive, loving, and compassionate.

Emotionally, Aries Moons draw on their strengths when they're down and out. What you see and hear is usually what you get. They hold nothing back. They are progressive with their emotions, finding relief when they can resolve emotional issues quickly. It is too burdensome for them to harbor any negative emotions; therefore, they tend to release and forget them. However, they are still very sensitive to the world around them, finding it difficult not to take things too personally. They can become violent or aggressive if they feel the need to defend themselves or someone they love.

Aries Moons are emotional firecrackers with a higher probability of being explosive and destructive. However, most of them tend to be jovial and optimistic. They love to laugh, play, and find humor in every situation. They are often emotionally optimistic and an open book who welcomes others with warm hugs and open arms. Everyone is an ally until proven otherwise. Aries Moons can be emotionally impulsive and impatient, wanting to reveal their intentions and leave a lasting mark in people's lives (good or bad).

☀ ★ ☾

ARIES ENERGY IN OTHER PLACEMENTS

ARIES ASCENDANT (RISING)

♈ AC

"I am myself."

Aries Risings project a sense of realness, strength, purpose, and power in everything they do. Upon first impression, they come off as extremely friendly and fun-loving. They like to make everyone feel welcomed, but they also make it known that they don't play any games. They are highly self-assured, believing that inner strength and power should never be too obvious.

When it comes to their physical appearance, they like to project a sense of dominance, flashiness, or masculinity in their style. They prefer to not follow popular trends, choosing to set trends that express how they feel internally.

ARIES MIDHEAVEN (MC)

♈ MC

"I am my career."

Aries Midheavens like to have control and purpose in their career. They prefer to have powerful positions that allow for quick growth and room to do as they please. As avid problem-solvers, they thrive in intense situations. They enjoy projects that challenge their mental and physical abilities because they are very confident that they can overcome any obstacle.

If a career is stagnant or less than exciting, they become restless and easily frustrated with everything and everyone. They are prone to job-hopping until they find a thrilling career that offers status, self-growth, and power.

ARIES MERCURY

♈ ☿

"I am what I think."

Aries Mercurians are progressive in their thought process. The majority are social, solitary, and physical learners who are talented when picking up any skill and experimenting with different methods. They like to resolve issues quickly and are not the type to dwell on or entertain pessimism. They are also innovative and quick to act on their ideas, not wanting to let opportunities pass them by.

When they express themselves, they stand with conviction, have a deep sense of self-worth, and possess strong likes and dislikes. They embrace challenges and risks because they have high confidence in their skills and abilities, plus they are strong believers of mind over matter.

ARIES VENUS

♈ ♀

"I am love."

Aries Venusians are very selective types who come off shy and nervous when they meet someone they like. The more captivating someone is, the more they are attracted to them. Once they fall in love, they revolve their world around their partner; all they want is to feel their presence, even if they're not doing anything. However, if they become bored or restless, they will lose their passionate steam and find more exciting love elsewhere.

Aries Venusians are at their best with those who have strong self-awareness and are committed to inspiring life goals. They vibe with people who aren't afraid to be powerful, optimistic, strong, and successful.

☼ ☆ ☾

ARIES MARS

$$\Upsilon \ \sigma$$

"I am physical power."

Aries Martians embody physical power and intensity, and most are daredevils looking for the next adrenaline rush. Needless to say, they require a lot of physical stimulation and find value in anything that offers physical strength and energy. With their high stamina, they are more than capable of pushing their bodies past their physical limits.

Aries Martians are very dominant, and they like to feel stronger or more powerful than other people. Status in the physical realm will be very important to them, as this allows them to utilize their strengths. They are also the type to act on how they feel and aren't afraid to get physical to defend themselves or get their point across.

ARIES JUPITER

$$\Upsilon \ \jupiter$$

"I am expansion."

Aries Jupiterians are expansive in both the spiritual and physical realms. They are explorers of worlds, searching for something mentally and spiritually exciting. They require constant growth to feel fulfilled in life and can grow impatient with tedious learning phases. They prefer to have hands-on experiences that allow them to learn and grow at a faster pace.

Aries Jupiterians create their own luck in life and are motivated to be pioneers in whatever industry they take on. They yearn to expand their knowledge for others to learn from or refine. They ultimately dream of leaving behind a legacy that creates new pathways for others to travel on.

ARIES SATURN

♈ ♄

"I am restriction."

Aries Saturnians take life very seriously. They believe that having a strong discipline of good habits and a restriction on bad habits create inner power and worldly success. They possess strict boundaries and will enforce them if need be. They are not afraid to use force to get ahead in life and aren't against restricting others they feel are competition. They also make sure that people know their place and respect their authority and status.

Aries Saturnians are a force to behold in the physical realm, ramming their way through any obstacle that gets in the way of their life goals. They have a strong sense of direction and believe in being decisive and strategic, while ensuring that they have an intelligent and strong-willed team who is willing to help them reach their worldly dreams as one unit.

ARIES URANUS

♈ ♅

"I am change."

Aries Uranians create change in people's lives. They believe in being a leader of the people who provides direction and purpose. They fight for causes that help communities become stronger, more vocal, and physically dominate, some even being pro-war and avid supporters of military power.

Aries Uranians are not against force, especially when it serves the greater good. However, they are not without a heart. They will fearlessly stand up for the weak and the poor and become the voice for those who are unheard. They use their strengths to inspire people to be the change they preach.

✵ ☆ ☾

ARIES NEPTUNE

♈ ♆

"I am spiritual."

Aries Neptunians require physical experiences to really connect with their spirituality. They embrace and embody masculine divinity, so they are not afraid to undergo rigorous rituals that will make them feel physically stronger and more confident about their path in life. Many explore different countries to gain a deeper sense of spirituality through native cultural beliefs.

Aries Neptunians' physical well-being usually aligns with their spirituality, where they feel more connected with others using their outer senses, such as touch, smell, and sight. This often bleeds into their imagination and creativity, where their personal experiences allow them to create more powerful work for others to physically experience.

ARIES PLUTO

♈ ♇

"I am evolution."

Aries Plutonians prefer to evolve and transform independently. They focus more on physical evolution and worldly success. What they can feel, touch, and experience provides them with true emotional fulfillment. In a lifetime, they will try to prove their worth and value in their respected community, showing others that evolution starts with good judgment, brave decisions, constant challenges, and self-improvement.

Aries Plutonians' life goals usually have to do with leaving their mark on the world and discovering or inventing something that will have a deep impact in society long after they depart into the afterlife.

✷ ☆ ☾

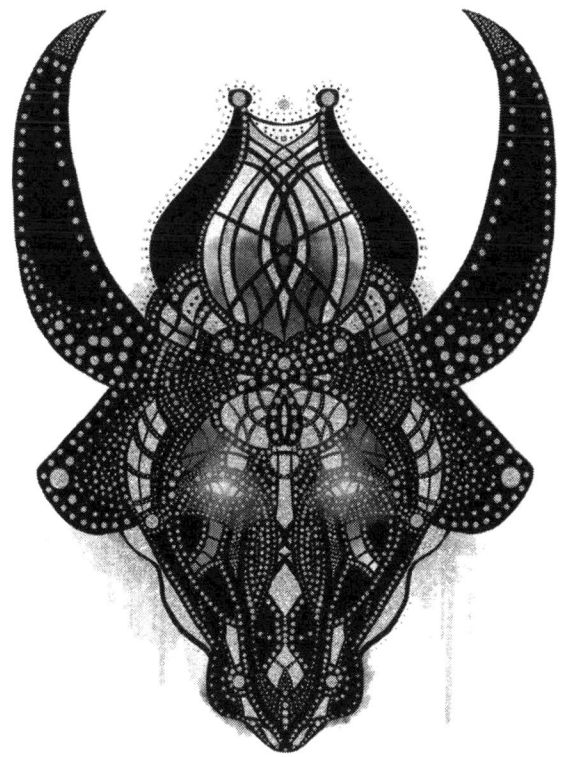

TAURUS

Venusian Bull

April 20 – May 20
Element: Earth
Modality: Fixed
Ruling Planet: Venus
Symbol: The Bull
Motto: I Have

TAURUS SUN

♉ ☉

"I have."

Taurus is a fixed earth sign, guided by the Bull and ruled by the planet Venus. It shares this planet with Libra. As the second star child, first earth sign, and first fixed sign, Taureans feel a sense of duty and burden to replant and nurture parts of the world that Aries left in ashes. Taureans value and honor patience, time, material wealth, and worldly possessions. Due to this, the universe has blessed them with eyes to observe and focus on the natural, even superficial, beauty of the physical realm and all who dwell in it.

Taureans understand the true meaning of investment and are deeply aware that hard work and patience pays them a more comfortable and higher quality lifestyle. Because of this, Taureans are possessive of everything they create and build. Once they stake their claim on a piece of land or person, nothing in this world can tear it away from them. Thus, change and adaptability can be extremely difficult for them to accept and adopt, as they require the stability of routine and familiarity to feel fully secure.

As the Venusian Bull, Taureans are guided by Venus, which heightens their love of things they can touch, feel, use, wear, and possess, such as money, fine art, quality food, good music, literature, and anything or anyone beautiful. They also love to smell things and people; anything sweet-smelling is intoxicating to them. You will know if they are in love with something or someone through their gaze. Some may think it's rude of them to stare so long and silently, but they take their time observing all the little details and soaking in the sight of whatever or whomever they find beautiful.

With Venus guiding their vision and standards, they are the selective and

expensive type, only wanting quality objects and valuable people around them. Because of this, Taureans can be extremely judgmental, criticizing those who do not fit in their field of beauty. If they are disgusted by someone, they will not hesitate to express their disdain.

Taureans love owning masterpieces, so they take extra precaution when dealing with their possessions. If you truly want to know how a Taurus feels about themselves, look at their home and inner circle of people. Every possession is a projection of how they see themselves. They strongly believe in investing in people or things that last long term rather than investing in anything cheap and useless. They highly cherish and value their possessions with utmost care and devotion. It's also good to note that when Taureans are in love with something or someone, they have already accepted it as is. This type of love is only given when they feel that the other party has accepted all of them as well.

Taureans are known to be enablers who allow and tolerate good and bad behavior from loved ones because they believe in unconditional love and full acceptance of people as they are. They are true believers that someone's natural character (flaws and all) is what defines natural and real beauty. However, their Venusian sight can cloud their better judgment when it comes to physical appearance. They can fall hard for beauty and can get into very unhealthy relationships because of Venus' influence. However, once they see that someone or something is ugly or worthless, they will not hesitate to throw it out like yesterday's trash.

The Taurus symbol is the Bull. Like a bull, they are very stubborn and unwilling to budge when it comes to their beliefs. Even though they are patient and tolerant, they can be quite bullish when provoked, aiming their horns at those who intrude on their personal space (traits learned from Arians). However, they usually have extraordinarily strong boundaries when it comes to strangers outside of their herd, whereas everyone within the fence gets a

☼☆☾

few passes so long as they remain loyal and appreciative.

Speaking of the herd, Taureans are extremely family-oriented. Even if they go rogue and travel solo, they will remain connected and loyal to their family. Their family doesn't always have to be blood-related either. Possessive as usual, they will hold onto people they allow into their space, which can take a bit of time because they don't trust easily, but once you're in, you're in for the long haul. However, if you take advantage of their space or betray their trust, they will kick you out and hold an unshakeable grudge for life. The more dominant and stubborn ones will keep reminders to bulldoze you out of their way if they are forced to be around you.

The Taurus motto is "I have," and their favorite word is "mine." They use it often. Many Taureans are possessive of their material wealth, often finding it hard to part with anything they buy or earn. Their life's challenge is the need to accumulate and possess material wealth, which can cause Taureans to feel like nothing in life is ever enough. To overcome this, they must learn to find true happiness and success in making peace with what they earn and receive and be content and appreciative of the present time. If Taureans are not careful, they can become obsessed with possessing things that aren't meant for them.

Regardless of their situation, money and rewards will continue to be an important asset in their lives because it buys them the comfort and beauty they so often desire. Money will be a constant topic that they love to talk about because it's something they know how to control and manage. It offers them stability and security, and they are fully aware that it's a reward for all of their hard work, so they take it seriously. Since they're the ultimate masters of coinage, quality, routine, and cleanup, they do well in the military, stock market, managerial positions, or as business owners in retail or food.

As a fixed earth sign, these bulls were created to endure a lot of weight on their shoulders. It can take a lot to break them mentally and emotionally, but

✵ ☆ ☾

when they do, they tend to dwell on and internalize the pain. As said before, it can be hard for them to accept change—any change. It makes them feel uneasy when things are out of place. You will probably find them placing objects around the house, never to touch them again. Once it's there, it's there for good, just like everything and everyone else in their life.

As a fixed sign, privacy and intimacy are important to them, and although, Taureans appear hard on the outside, they are extremely sensual and soulful on the inside. They are irrevocably sweet, tender, and good-natured yet stern, hardcore, and logical. Their calm and subtle energy masks their intense emotions, all of which creates more depth in their silent yet highly observant characters. Though most say they are dull or too routine, they only show that side to people they will never trust.

It can take years for Taureans to open up emotionally, and if they don't trust you, they'll never even give you a sneak peek. Needless to say, Taureans find it challenging to trust others. They will run a series of secret tests when getting to know someone. If you pass them, they will mentally agree to possess you. However, let's be clear. Their type of possession is different than any other sign. They still believe in letting people live their lives, but they want to be the only person you run to at the end of the day. They love the idea of being relied on and being someone's protective shelter, but only when they have made the decision to be a part of your life. Otherwise, if they don't care for you, they won't answer the phone.

Like their fellow earth siblings, Virgo and Capricorn, vulnerability is considered a weakness that must be kept in the comfort of their home and with people who already accept them as is, flaws and all. You have a better chance getting them to open up in their safe spaces. Don't forget the food and wine because eating and drinking are their greatest comforts.

Taureans ground themselves in all earthly things, all man-made things, and all that is natural and real; and although they present themselves as grounded,

✲☆☾

they can be narrow-minded and judgmental. They prefer to see the negative before the positive, which serves more as a defense mechanism. As a fixed sign, they are overly attached to their beliefs, unwilling to budge, even with reason. They possess very realistic and pessimistic views in life and view life as black and white, yes or no, with nothing in between.

Some Taureans believe in herd mentality, where everyone must follow their lead because they know what's best for them. Some are also known to bully their beliefs onto others if they feel strongly about them. Fortunately, most go by the "live and let live" mentality, choosing to ignore everyone else's beliefs other than their own and allowing people to live blissfully ignorant lives so long as they aren't bothered by it.

As a fixed sign, Taureans are labor-intensive signs who possess strict routines, especially when it comes to work and financial responsibilities. They put their duties above everything and everyone else, believing that their purpose in life is to nurture their environments through hard labor. If left unproductive, they will become emotionally unfulfilled. They need to keep their physical demands in tune with their spirits and their pockets, otherwise they will feel useless and helpless, and they are far from that. Even if they need help, they will refuse it, as they strongly believe in maintaining their dignity; and when left between a rock and a hard place, they will dig their way out without a helping hand. This is what makes this sign so magnificent.

Overall, Taurus Suns embody material possession, labor, and sensuality. They master all senses of quality and natural beauty, teaching others how to build when starting with nothing and inspiring those who need to rebuild when they've lost everything.

☼ ☆ ☾

UNEVOLVED TAURUS – STUBBORN DICTATOR

Unevolved Taureans are stubborn dictators who don't know when to stop bullying others into their radical beliefs or traditions. They take structure and regiment to the extreme and cannot handle innovation unless it is created by them. Unevolved Taureans are pessimistic and judgmental of the world and everyone in it. They feel that everyone, except for them, is a burden to the world, which is the result of sentiments of the unevolved sign before them, Aries. They are so burdened with the cleanup duty of others that they fail to see anything good come out of it.

Since their motto is "I have," they can find themselves becoming bitter or jealous of those who have what isn't meant for them or what they choose not to work for. They are possessive in an unhealthy manner, where changes in life are seen as a huge threat to their livelihood. They hoard their money selfishly and possess people like they're objects. Needless to say, they have serious abandonment issues. Unevolved Taureans need to be in control of every outcome. When they are not in control, they will complain for hours and dwell in the bottomless pit of their negativity.

As a fixed earth sign, unevolved Taureans are unable to see other people's perspectives in life. They believe there is only one way to live and only one way to resolve issues: their way. If you are unable to see their perspective, you are useless and a waste of space to them. They can also have a hard time with authority, always wanting to prove that the only authority in existence is themselves. All of this leaves them with more disappointment and frustration in humanity due to their own actions and thought processes.

✹ ☆ ☾

EVOLVED TAURUS – LIFE MENTOR

Evolved Taureans are patient and nurturing life mentors who live to build and create stable and solid families. They welcome everyone into their herd and appreciate others with unwavering loyalty and devotion. What they've learned from Aries, the evolved sign before them, is to inspire others with actions. Due to this, evolved Taureans act with a higher sense of responsibility and dedication to work and family. They are also good listeners who offer logical and sensible guidance to everyone they come across.

Since their motto is "I have," evolved Taureans are possessive creatures who love and nurture things and people. However, they do not hold anybody hostage. They allow people to live and love freely without judgment. They are willing to break their backs for people they love and care for and will give whatever they have to make others happy and comfortable. They have a great sense of duty to the world and nature, choosing to involve themselves in causes that create sustainability and efficiency for everyone. They practice gratitude for everything they have and will always make sure loved ones feel special, appreciated, and adored every day.

As a fixed earth sign, evolved Taureans are fixated on providing quality, comfort, and beauty in the world. Although they are naturally materialistic, evolved Taureans know how to balance material wealth with internal wealth, understanding and accepting a more spiritual and holistic approach to life. They observe the world and eat life lessons for breakfast, lunch, and dinner. They share their wisdom with those they eat with, always leaving an empty seat for wandering souls who need stability and life guidance.

✵ ☆ ☾

TAURUS MOON

♉ ☽

"I have what I feel."

An individual with a Taurus Moon will handle their emotions privately and cautiously, but it depends on other celestial factors. Mixed with fire, they can be highly stubborn and power hungry but more affectionate and passionate. Mixed with earth, they are emotionally reserved, patient, and nurturing but come off as cold and emotionally detached. Mixed with air, they can be outspoken and lively, but they can be more judgmental and obnoxious. Mixed with water, they can be sensual, sensitive, and loving but dwell longer in their negative emotions.

Emotionally, Taurus Moons often internalize their feelings and find it difficult to express how they feel when things are not guaranteed. They are cautious when making emotional decisions. What you see is definitely not what you get, as they often hide behind their cool and grounded exteriors. They are highly loyal, observant, and especially private, wanting to keep extra sensitive issues within the household. They tend to have a higher tolerance when it comes to others, preferring to always remain calm in tense situations. However, they can lose their patience if they feel they are being constantly harassed or when they are betrayed.

Taurus Moons find trust and vulnerability difficult to uncover in others, yet they're not against giving it to the ones they love. As a possessive sign, change is very difficult, and they will hold onto people out of fear of being uncomfortable. Taurus Moons yearn for comfort and material wealth, finding financial stability and possessions to be more valuable. They also prefer to go at a very slow pace, being unbothered by the busy highways of others.

✵☆☾

TAURUS ENERGY IN OTHER PLACEMENTS

TAURUS ASCENDANT (RISING)

♉ AC

"I have myself."

Taurus Risings project stillness, tolerance, and self-control in everything they do. Upon first impression, they can come off as quiet and unbothered, which they usually are. However, they tend to be more observant and focused on whatever's in front of them, usually taking a more serious approach to life.

When it comes to their physical appearance, they are reserved and dress for comfort in public spaces but love to be nude in the privacy of their homes. They tend to invest their money in items that will last long term, usually preferring high-end designer brands and precious gems, like diamonds.

TAURUS MIDHEAVEN (MC)

♉ MC

"I have my career."

Taurus Midheavens prefer steadily growing careers that offer longevity and wages that match their strong work ethic. They have herd mentality and are capable of carrying large workloads, but only if everyone follows their lead and doesn't stray from their process. If someone strays, they'll bully them back in line without hesitation.

Taurus Midheavens love the accumulation of money and tend to be good at anything that has to do with financial decisions, savings, or investments. They can also be trusted with vital information, as they value confidentiality.

TAURUS MERCURY

ŏ ☿

"I have what I think."

Taurus Mercurians have very stern thoughts and ideas. It can be difficult to change their views because they aren't easily persuaded with pretty words. They are logical thinkers who are focused on their responsibilities and providing for their family. Most are visual or mathematical learners who need time to process all the facts before making a rational decision.

Privacy and trust will be very important for them, otherwise they will keep their thoughts to themselves. If they're silent, they're either observing your actions or quietly judging you. When they do express themselves, they are surprisingly very sweet, loving, and understanding, unless you've made them mad. If you did, you're in for the hard truth.

TAURUS VENUS

ŏ ♀

"I have love."

Taurus Venusians are gentle and nurturing individuals who take love very seriously. They are cautious when choosing a partner, mostly because they don't trust easily, and they want someone ready for a long-term commitment. They take their time in love and like to live in the moment with someone new, finding beauty in the natural process of love.

Taurus Venusians are at their best with those who are patient, affectionate, and responsible. They vibe with responsible and secure people who prioritize their family. They tend to join a herd of mature and extremely loyal people who are committed to having long-term friendships grow into a family.

TAURUS MARS

ஃ ♂

"I have physical power."

Taurus Martians are very dominant and determined signs, but they aren't the type to boast about it. They are strong believers that actions speak louder than words, and they prefer to project their dominance through self-control. For the most part, they are passive and keep to themselves. They try not to intrude on other people's business and expect the same in return.

Taurus Martians are patient and tolerant of other people's actions, and they are not easily provoked. However, they will see red and bulldoze you into the ground if you go too far. Fortunately, these signs are too focused on building themselves up to worry about others.

TAURUS JUPITER

ஃ ♃

"I have expansion."

Taurus Jupiterians have highly realistic and pessimistic views. They are highly tactical individuals who harbor brutally honest opinions and stand by facts. They don't entertain people's opinions or conspiracies, finding more value in scientific methods. They are more environmentally expansive and believe that everything can be proven, disproven, or improved upon over time through human invention, historical discoveries, or natural evolution.

Taurus Jupiterians don't believe in luck because they feel that success and fortune are earned through hard work. They build the lifestyle they want and believe that as long as they don't give up, their hard work will not be in vain and their life goals will eventually be fulfilled through steady growth.

TAURUS SATURN

ʘ ♄

"I have restriction."

Taurus Saturnians possess strong discipline and stubborn boundaries that are hard to break. They are highly responsible signs that seem to have their priorities all figured out. They are punctual, respectful, and honorable signs who expect the same from others. They also believe that everyone has a role to fulfill, whether at home or at work, and that they should play their role correctly or dismiss themselves for someone else to do it.

Taurus Saturnians have very strict rules in and out of their home. They strongly believe that people should be responsible and accountable for their actions, where punishment and rewards are based on said actions. If you don't like their rules, they won't stop you from leaving or kicking you out.

TAURUS URANUS

ʘ ♅

"I have change."

Taurus Uranians have a difficult time with change and are uncomfortable when things move too quickly. It's not to say that they cannot change; they can and do, but they don't believe in changing for others' sake. They prefer to move at their own pace, which can be slow and tedious for those who are more impulsive and reactive.

When it comes to community, they don't really bother to lead emotionally charged mobs, and most prefer to get involved in causes that have to do with animals and nature. They find it easier to leave people to their own thoughts and emotions, believing that sensitive topics will get figured out on their own.

☀☆☾

TAURUS NEPTUNE

ᛦ ♆

"I have spirituality."

Taurus Neptunians believe in spirituality but not organized religion. They don't like the feeling of being controlled or manipulated. Most have a strong spiritual connection with nature and animals and will utilize Earth's natural resources to their full extent. They are lovers of stars, water, crystals, herbs, or anything tangible that fills their sacred spaces with beauty and comfort.

Being connected with the earth and partaking in daily rituals helps them stay grounded and peaceful. It also helps them nurture others with more love and attention, all of which they master the more they become enlightened.

TAURUS PLUTO

ᛦ ♇

"I have evolution."

Taurus Plutonians embrace natural evolution and accept the aging process, even death. Material possessions, comfort, financial security, and a loving family bring them true emotional fulfillment. In a lifetime, they will embark on a journey of pleasure, food, and history. They want to have many youthful stories to tell their children and grandchildren. If they don't have families, they will live a life of serenity and peace with books of their work.

With full acceptance of both life and death, Taurus Plutonians spend their lifetime constantly building and providing for their families. It's extremely important for them to leave behind structure, life lessons, and material wealth after they depart into the afterlife. This ensures that their family continues to grow and evolve with them in mind.

GEMINI

Mercurian Twins

♊

May 21 – June 20
Element: Air
Modality: Mutable
Ruling Planet: Mercury
Symbol: The Twins
Motto: I Think

GEMINI SUN

♊ ☉

"I think."

Gemini is a mutable air dual sign guided by the Twins and ruled by the planet Mercury. It shares this planet with Virgo. As the third star child, first air sign, and first mutable sign, Geminis are the thinkers of the zodiac who yearn to expand mentally and creatively. With Arians busy burning through new worlds and Taureans nurturing worlds with their noses in the ground, Geminis look upward and outward, springing with ideas on how to make life more pleasurable and entertaining and less tedious and dutiful. Because of this, the universe has blessed the Mercurian Twins with free-spirited hearts and eccentric and flexible mindsets to wander the world with a higher intellect and imagination than Aries and less restriction and discipline than Taurus.

Geminis take life's evolution a step further and redefine reason and logic from Taurus and refine creativity and talent from Aries. Geminis explore the true meaning of what mental restlessness and empowerment really is. They make it a point to be different and rebel against the norm, which allows them the opportunity to explore any and all curiosities. Their mentality also provides them with sets of diverse and cultured life perspectives.

As the Mercurian Twins, Geminis possess a very versatile thought process, along with a clever wittiness that can outthink and outsmart any sign. Naturally intelligent, they constantly seek mental stimulation, are quick learners, and are known to be linguistic experts. They utilize their communicative talents and otherworldly thinking skills to gain a unique understanding of the world and its people. This can lead to them being misunderstood, as they tend to think and say things that seem unrealistic or

☼ ☆ ☾

inconceivable to others with much blander imaginations.

Because of Mercury's restless energy, Geminis find it difficult to stay still and silent. Always needing to keep their minds or mouths busy, they find it mentally fulfilling to find answers and resolutions for every situation. Many like the challenge of DIY, scientific, or mathematical projects, where their minds can explore complex situations and come up with unique ways to problem-solve. This also helps them build higher ingenuity and intelligence, which is something they embrace proudly. Since they are heavily influenced by Mercury, Geminis excel in any career that involves complexity and creativity. They can work alone or in a group; it doesn't matter to them so long as they are in control of creative processing instead of organization.

As the first air sign, they connect with others on a mental level. It's not to say that they can't feel what others feel; they do, but it's not prioritized when they're engaging with others. Guided by Mercury, Geminis are always expanding their perspectives, often swaying back and forth between multiple personas to discover how far they can push their mental state. Mercury heavily influences the speed of the mind, allowing Geminis to come up with fresh, eccentric ideas and opinions within seconds. Great examples of Mercury's influence are Gemini actors and actresses who play various roles and characters, never allowing themselves to be defined by one face or archetype.

Mercury gifts Geminis with the ability to negotiate and communicate. They can talk their way in or out of anything or anyone. They can mentally break someone with words alone. Depending on which twin wants to act, they can be either thought-provoking or blatantly ignorant. They can spew a mix of random or unpredictable ideas at people just for the sake of filling the silence in the room or to play on people's reactions. They prefer to shake people out of their conformed behaviors, as this allows them to see people's true selves. This in turn helps them learn people's mental limitations, which also shows them what they can or can't get away with when toying with

☼☆☾

people's greater imagination.

Since Mercury prioritizes speed over tact, Gemini's mind will also race faster than their mouth, and most are unable to catch the impact of their words until after they're said. They are also not fully aware of people's sensitivity to certain topics, nor do they believe that people should be sensitive to any topic. When someone corrects them, they can be genuinely confused on why they are so upset. To them, they were only saying the truth or trying to entertain others, even if it was said in ill humor. You won't find many who apologize for what they said because they said what they said, and it's final.

Freedom of expression and uncontrolled mental thoughts are especially important to Geminis. They express themselves without fear of consequences, and they love to write and journal their thoughts and feelings. Family and friends may find letters written to them out of nowhere. On top of that, they are highly interactive, talkative, and playful. They love to surprise others by playing pranks or vocalizing what everyone is or is not thinking. They really enjoy the shocked reactions they receive when they say or do something spontaneous. Whether they pursue a good or bad reaction really depends on which twin wants to play that day: the good one or the bad one.

The symbol of Gemini is the Twins, making it the first dual sign in astrology, which means Geminis possess both negative and positive energies: yin and yang. One twin is the voice in the shadows, and the other twin is the voice in the light. The shadow twin possesses realistic and destructive perspectives, whereas the light twin possesses whimsical and optimistic perspectives. The light twin always thinks of pushing equality and freedom of choice into the world and beyond, whereas the shadow twin always thinks of pushing rebellion and mental games into people's heads. Both are masters of communication, controversy, imagination, and wit.

The twins live life like a theater, always in character and ready for the stage. As a very social sign, they can adjust their mental energy to whomever

✵ ☆ ☾

they speak to, and if they feel like it, they can mentally manipulate someone to extract information from them. Their remarkable psychological skills also help them learn characters quickly and adopt traits they like in others. It doesn't mean they'll pretend to be someone else, unless it's for professional means; it means they take pieces from people and tweak it into themselves so they can continue to understand, convey, and accept multiple perspectives.

The Gemini motto is "I think." This goes hand in hand with their ruling planet, which further guides them away from their emotions and into their higher thinking. Their life's challenge is based on their own mental well-being. Their thoughts can be their worst enemy or their best friend, which can confuse their direction in life or remove opportunities. The power to think is what makes them stand out from the rest, but their dark thoughts can turn against them, causing them to spiral out of control and hide behind pleasure and temptation to cover their insecurities. To overcome their life's challenge and maintain their mental well-being, they must commit to higher knowledge, self-awareness, and enlightenment.

As a mutable air sign, Geminis are highly adaptable in their thoughts and ideas. There is never a dull day with these twins, as they cannot be still or controlled like earth signs. The twins must soar high like Dorothy from *The Wizard of Oz* in a hot air balloon or ravage the skies on a broom like the Wicked Witch of the East. Regardless of which twin wants to play pilot, they know how to maneuver through turbulence and can make quick, calculated changes when the need arises. This type of mentality helps them achieve much success in their later years, as they are able to adapt without complaint.

As a zodiac sign that hates being controlled, it's not a surprise that Geminis find it even harder to control themselves. They feel suffocated by the rules and restrictions of society. They yearn for ultimate freedom in everything they do, which can ultimately lead them toward their greatest success, as it helps them come up with innovative ideas that change the world. To them, anything

✸☆☾

is negotiable and anything is possible if you're smart enough to overcome it. However, when it comes to emotional control, they can become overwhelmed by it and sink into long-term depression or mental anxiety.

It can take the twins a while to process their emotions since emotions are more complex and confusing than logic or reason. They strongly believe that emotions are limiting and restricting toward their sense of freedom. It's usually a battle between the mind and the heart because it's hard for them to trust how they feel when their brain tells them that anything can be resolved. This can cause relationship issues, where they are unsure of how to think or feel, often dragging things out longer than they should. They must prioritize mental organization, mental wellness, and further emotional intelligence before they can commit themselves to anything or anyone long term.

Geminis' unpredictable behavior and curious eccentricities are what makes them so special. It's because of their unique mindset that they are notorious in provoking others; but if you look at it from a higher perspective, the world wouldn't be as colorful or inventive without their presence. Yes, it's with their need to explore the unexplored that pushes society to think outside its comfort zone. Depending on the twin, it can be a much-needed breath of fresh air or a suffocating gas chamber.

Overall, Geminis master mentality in all aspects of life. They teach other zodiac signs to vocalize and express themselves unapologetically. They give life and set the stage for all the open-minded, odd, outrageous, rebellious, and spontaneous characters of the world. They understand what it means to think outside of the box, and they are true advocates of diversity and eccentricity.

✼ ☆ ☾

UNEVOLVED GEMINI – CHAOTIC GOSSIPER

Unevolved Geminis are chaotic gossipers who revolt all authority, responsibilities, and restrictions that have been pushed onto them from the sign before them, unevolved Taurus. With the need to escape, they disrupt traditions and organization, becoming chaos itself. With their mouths moving 10 times faster than their minds, they lack the self-control needed to create long-lasting relationships with others. Vocal expression is used more for personal attacks on people's characters.

Since their motto is "I think," unevolved Geminis can go into a mental spiral of all the things that can go wrong in their make-believe world. They jump to assumptions rather than collecting the evidence needed to make sound and reasonable judgments. When they're confronted, they can manipulate thoughts to benefit the outcome they want. Their energy can go from zero to 100, switching back and forth after a few seconds. They like being unpredictable and random, messing with people mentally for their own personal amusement. Everything is a sick joke to them.

As a mutable air sign, unevolved Geminis can be extremely flighty and unorganized. They can become a flight risk for anybody who wants to get involved with them professionally or romantically. Unevolved Geminis are commitment-phobic and find it too hard to stay with one person for too long. They believe that freedom is doing whatever you please whenever you want and valid requests of commitment from others are taken as a serious threat to their so-called "freedom."

✵☆☾

EVOLVED GEMINI – CREATIVE COMPOSER

Evolved Geminis are highly creative composers who utilize their mental strengths to invite imagination into reality. What they've learned from Taurus, the evolved sign before them, is to devote their time in observing and welcoming others. Evolved Geminis use these traits and apply them in all their creative endeavors and social interactions. They are friendly, non-judgmental, and expressive individuals who accept all types of people. They help others unleash their full creative powers and be themselves no matter what people may think.

Since their motto is "I think," evolved Geminis have an optimistic point of view unlike any other zodiac sign. They are freethinkers who stay away from those who try to suffocate their ideas. This type of mental freedom allows them to dream and imagine a world full of creative possibilities. Their keen observation skills and quick thought process is an advantage, which helps them resolve situations through multiple perspectives with consideration of everyone involved. They lend their expressive voice to help those who don't have a voice, oftentimes joining causes for poverty-stricken communities. They fight for the underdogs in the world and push for full inclusivity.

As a mutable air sign, evolved Geminis are a dual sign that see both the positive and negative in life. They accept and embrace both sides, being fully aware that both are needed for mental balance and genuine self-expression. They are not superficial and will oftentimes choose to live a non-traditional and non-conforming lifestyle. They believe that self-expression and mental freedom is not just for them but for everyone.

☼☆☽

GEMINI MOON

♊ ☽

"I think what I feel."

Individuals with a Gemini Moon are open-minded and vocal about their emotions, but it depends on other celestial factors. Mixed with fire, they can be playful and honest but lack tact in their expression. Mixed with earth, they are grounded and strategic but more insensitive and aloof. Mixed with air, they are communicative and witty but more argumentative and unaware of personal boundaries. Mixed with water, they are imaginative and creatively expressive but lack mental and emotional self-control.

Emotionally, Gemini Moons think of their emotions constantly. It may even feel alien-like because they like to view their emotions through multiple perspectives, which can often confuse their judgment. They are very friendly and outspoken, and they openly accept diversity in all types of people. They also prefer people to show their true faces, as they are fully aware that traditions and laws can restrict people's natural behaviors. They, in turn, do not believe in holding back their truth or their true selves from the world. They do not judge others and are not ones to prevent others from expressing their true and honest feelings.

Gemini Moons are expressive types who feel suffocated by their thoughts and emotions, so they naturally throw it up, with most of it being positive because they tend to see the good in people first. But if you show your evil side, they are not the type to stand aside and remain silent. Gemini Moons may not have the emotional self-control of other signs, but that doesn't make their emotions less valid. They have what others do not dare to have: emotional freedom, which is a trait that is rare and unique only to them.

☀☆☽

GEMINI ENERGY IN OTHER PLACEMENTS

GEMINI ASCENDANT (RISING)

♊ AC

"I think for myself."

Gemini Risings project eccentricity, sociability, and open-mindedness in everything they do. Upon first impression, they are chatty and a little awkward but humorous and accepting. They tend to not take life too seriously, finding it easier to take a more carefree approach to things and people.

When it comes to their physical appearance, they dress however they want to. The more it doesn't fit the norm, the better. They prefer to dress colorfully, quirky, and flashy, not because they want attention but because they believe their style should express how they think and feel about themselves.

GEMINI MIDHEAVEN (MC)

♊ MC

"I think career."

Gemini Midheavens prefer to have creative freedom and expression in any career they pursue. If they feel their creative or intellectual minds will be stifled or controlled, they will quit their jobs unexpectedly to find a job that is less suffocating.

Communication is their forte. They like to be in positions where they can socialize and interact with different types of people. Learning something new helps them stay motivated and focused. They are quick learners who get restless easily and perform best when they have multiple pots on the stove.

GEMINI MERCURY

♊ ☿

"I think to communicate."

Gemini Mercurians are in their true element. They value and utilize the freedom of expression and thought (good or bad). Most are mathematical, verbal, or social learners who find it easy to pick up multiple languages, solve complex problems, and multitask. They are also accepting of different cultural behaviors and beliefs, can adapt quickly to new environments, and will adopt what they've learned into their personal lives.

As highly intelligent signs, they are naturally witty, inquisitive signs with a busy mind that is hard to silence. They require a lot of mental stimulation, and many love researching conspiracy theories or anything that is intricate, technical, odd, or abnormal.

GEMINI VENUS

♊ ♀

"I think love."

Gemini Venusians are very open about love and can love more than one person at a time, but that doesn't mean that they can't be monogamous. They think of love constantly but find long-term commitments challenging, as they hate being controlled or feeling mentally suffocated. When in love, they offer absolute freedom to their partners and find open communication, honesty, trust, and friendship easy to give.

Gemini Venusians are always looking for their twin and are at their best with those who allow them the freedom to express how they feel, be themselves, and fully accept their unpredictable thoughts and actions.

✵ ✯ ☾

GEMINI MARS

♊ ♂

"I think physical power."

Gemini Martians have powerful mental abilities that allow them to get out of sticky situations through quick mediation and clever problem-solving. However, they can be very reactive to certain situations and aren't afraid of a fight or argument. They can even instigate fights if they feel like it. Luckily, most of them will try to mediate a situation with humor before it escalates.

Gemini Martians tend to think out loud because they believe in speaking their thoughts into existence, and although they talk openly about their ideas, they can find it hard to ground them with action. Their restless energy can get bored with tedious work, so to be productive, they require small, quick goals without long-term commitments.

GEMINI JUPITER

♊ ♃

"I think expansion."

Gemini Jupiterians are mentally expansive, finding education, technology, science, and creative work valuable. They strongly believe that not everything is what it seems and not every solution is the right solution. They tend to have and pursue groundbreaking ideas that evolve humanity in ways people didn't think was possible.

Gemini Jupiterians are out-of-the-box thinkers who believe in luck, fate, and initiative. They focus on building their intelligence and skills more than accumulating material wealth or status. To them, the human mind and how it expands is much more fascinating and less boring than money.

GEMINI SATURN

♊ ♄

"I think restriction."

Gemini Saturnians are the opposite of restriction; they are unrestricted and undisciplined but not for the reasons you think. They rebel against authority because they hate to be controlled or manipulated into conforming. They are fully aware of what conforming does to the human mind (loss of true self), so naturally they will move against it.

Gemini Saturnians are more disciplined when it comes to their mentality. Their intelligence is what makes them so successful. They strongly believe that minds should think freely without limitations or restrictions. This allows them to flourish creatively and resourcefully in any work they pursue.

GEMINI URANUS

♊ ♅

"I think change."

Gemini Uranians view life from multiple perspectives (good or bad). Since they are so adaptable, they are constantly adjusting their habits and mentality as the world changes around them. As a rebellious sign, they love to interact with underground societies. The stranger, the more technologically advanced, or the more non-conforming the society, the more engaged they are.

Gemini Uranians mostly fight for causes of the unheard voices or those who are being silenced. These causes may not have a lot of backing, but that's what makes them more inspired to advocate for them. They are also known to join causes for literature, art, and any other form of communication or media.

✹ ☆ ☽

GEMINI NEPTUNE

♊ ♆

"I think spiritual."

Gemini Neptunians are the light and dark twins of spirituality and use it as another way of connecting with others and maintaining their free spirit. They often practice or develop their spirituality or spiritual gifts through the use of black and white magic, astral projection, energy work (reiki), or any other divine or supernatural practice (good or bad).

Gemini Neptunians tend to stay away from organized religion, as they feel it suffocates their natural beliefs. If they grow up in a religious household, they tend to stray away from it once they're older, as they hate to conform and be controlled. They prefer to fill their spirit with information they can collect through their own research and practices.

GEMINI PLUTO

♊ ♇

"I think evolution."

Gemini Plutonians evolve and transform mentally, where true emotional fulfillment is based on how much knowledge and experience they've gained in one lifetime. They are not the types to stay at home and wait for death to come knocking. They like to live life to the fullest, ensuring that they do not miss anything exciting or worthwhile.

Gemini Plutonians tend to experience the good, the bad, the ugly, and the beautiful in life, whether they choose to or not. This ultimately helps their creative efforts, where they can express their life's story in a creative format for others to enjoy long after they've departed into the afterlife.

CANCER

Moon Guardian

June 21 – July 22
Element: Water
Modality: Cardinal
Ruling Planet: Moon
Symbol: The Crab
Motto: I Feel

☀✫☾

CANCER SUN

♋ ☉

"I feel."

Cancer is a cardinal water sign, guided by the Crab and ruled by the Moon. As the fourth star child, first water sign, and second cardinal sign, Cancerians bring forth the emotional tides of sensitivity, receptivity, and intuition. Like the rushing waves of the ocean, their emotions are productive and aggressive. Their rivers of emotional healing flow through Taureans' soil, bringing life to their fields while also helping to extinguish the wildfires of Arians, who come and go as they please. Unlike Geminis who soar the skies with their expansive thoughts and ideas, Cancerians dive deep into the abyss of all emotions and reflect on the deeper meaning of self-reflection, self-awareness, self-expression, and self-love. Because of this, the universe has blessed them with heightened intuition and the sensitivity to feel everything and everyone, helping them to connect with all life-forms on a soul level.

Cancerians have a deep connection with and an appreciation of all the work from the zodiac signs before them. Cancerians take the passion of Aries, the hard labor of Taurus, and creative thoughts from Gemini and merge them together to create more insightful and intuitive life perspectives. They add sensitivity and emotional depth to all their skills and traits, bringing forth their soul's purpose and drowning out any superficial attachments. Naturally, they talk openly about their emotions, finding it emotionally fulfilling to express their deepest feelings. This behavior allows them to connect with others on a much deeper level than any other zodiac sign.

Cancerians are ruled by the Moon, thus becoming the Moon Guardians of Earth since they revolve around it. From this cosmic perspective, Cancers are

highly in tune with every life-form and are deeply aware of the importance and effect water has in sustaining life. They are the true masters of emotions and are capable of controlling it in themselves and others when they reach their evolved states. However, since they feel everything and everyone, it can be very difficult for them to control the number of emotions and energy they absorb.

Just as our Moon brings the tides of the ocean in and out, it does the same with the everchanging moods of Cancers, where their sensitivity levels can easily shift their emotions from negative to positive. They are destined to feel all emotions in one lifetime, even undergoing traumatic events to experience them. However, since they are natural-born empaths, they do not always have to endure the trauma themselves to fully comprehend it; instead, they can easily learn these emotional experiences from others they engage with. With this gift, they must be cautious not to carry the burden of others.

Just as our Moon is left in the darkness of space, Cancerians are often left in the dark void of their emotions. It can be difficult for this sign to hold back their feelings, as it is always important for them to express them. Yet, they will withdraw behind their infamous crab shell and process their feelings independently if they feel they will not be understood or accepted. This type of regenerative isolation gives Cancerians a chance to fully comprehend their emotions from a much deeper level than any other zodiac sign. Therefore, it is strongly encouraged for them to release their emotions as they feel them, otherwise they can accidentally drown people with their pressurized feelings.

The Cancerian symbol is the Crab. Like crabs, they can move in and out of water effortlessly, which symbolizes the movement of emotions onto Earth. Cancerians, like the crab, can live a lonely existence or swim with large groups. It depends on the rest of their placements, though the majority of the time they prefer less people intruding in their private lives. Instinctually, they are highly alert and guard themselves well behind their strong shell and

✵☆☽

pincers, yet underneath they are soft and affectionate.

With their thick shell, they can be slow to open up to others, yet they yearn to be loved and give love openly without having to hide. Love is something they give without limitations, especially if they vibe with you. However, if they've been jaded by the world, you will find them emotionally distant, distrustful, or shy. Because of their empathic nature, if they feel someone is energetically off, they do their best to stay away or express their revulsion to keep someone away permanently. If provoked, they will use their iron pincers to defend themselves or overwhelm their opponent with a surge of aggressive emotions. The same energy is used when protecting loved ones.

Cancerians guard themselves well against others. Their strong intuition can feel if someone is genuine or not. If they have a strong emotional attachment to someone and that person hurts them, they will take it very personally and will go out of their way to make them feel the way they feel. It can also jade them from loving others wholeheartedly, especially if the person that hurt them was a relative. This can create very tumultuous emotions that they constantly battle with in their later years, especially if they are not able to confront them.

If Cancerians are able to confront what hurts the most, they can become one of the most emotionally intelligent signs. They use their emotions to motivate themselves into elevated emotional states, meaning they no longer see their emotions as weak and they no longer reciprocate pain with pain; instead they show love and compassion where needed. They enjoy and praise people's personal success of overcoming their darkest emotions. They will also no longer hide behind a wall of insecurities and will use their shell to protect others who need it the most.

The Cancerian motto is "I feel." Their life's challenge is controlling their emotions, which can ultimately be their downfall. Their emotional habits can create toxic relationships or battles with self-worth and self-love. They require

☀ ☆ ☾

plenty of emotional reassurance, which can prevent them from relying on their intuition. To remove any doubts of how they feel, they must learn to embrace and work with their emotions rather than fear or neglect them. They must also learn to manage their expectations of others, realizing that not everyone holds the same emotional values.

Unlike Geminis, who use their mind more than their heart, Cancerians lead with their heart on their sleeve unapologetically. They can have a hard time accepting that others are incapable of doing the same. This can lead them down a road of emotional isolation, where they feel that nobody truly understands them on an emotional or soul level. Many Cancerians become severely depressed because of it; however, this is not the majority. Most Cancerians continue to push forward regardless of if their feelings are reciprocated, showering their intuition and good vibrations on those they love.

As a cardinal water sign, Cancers continue to promote love and healing above all else and always push for emotional change in themselves and others. Yet they are also productive, goal-oriented, and love hoarding money. They tend to take on careers that promote overall self-care, self-love, or an expression of their true self while still managing to consistently expand the flow of their money. You will find many who believe in money manifestation rituals or any other sacred ritual that helps them obtain emotional release and empowerment. Once they cling onto a dream, they never let it go. Their perseverance makes them one of the most successful signs of the zodiac.

Cancerians have an amazing gift of rinsing their emotions through creative projects. They are soulful creators devoted to the power of positive emotions, and most will talk openly about their emotional disorders to help spread awareness. When they've mastered their emotional responses and emotional control, they will use it to provoke or inspire others (depending on their mood and the person(s) involved). The majority of them record their healing journey either for themselves to reflect on or to enlighten others. This helps them teach

✴☆☾

others how to overcome their circumstances by understanding and accepting the root of their deepest issues.

Fortunately, the majority of Cancerians love to see positive reactions, such as laughter, tears of joy, smiles, etc., a trait learned from their cardinal cousin, Aries. You will find many Cancerian actors, comedians, artists, musicians, etc. who express their negative emotions and recycle them into positive and productive emotions. This helps them heal through their own pain. You will also find a lot of Cancerian healers, whether they are doctors, psychiatrists, or spiritual healers. They have the amazing ability to feel and fix the pain in others, and although they are natural shamans, Cancerians strongly believe that you are responsible for taking care of your own emotional well-being.

Indeed, Cancerians are one of the most emotional signs of the zodiac. They cry to release pain and trauma, and although it can be overwhelming to others, it is the only way they can get through to others. Yet, they are one of the most caring and authentic signs. They put their heart in everything they do, and they are always considerate of others, which is hard to find in a sea full of superficial people.

Overall, Cancerians embody emotional mastery and true unconditional love of self and others. They teach other signs how to express their emotions without judgment, stay true to how they feel, value and prioritize their emotional well-being, and follow their purpose with full acceptance of both heart and soul.

☀ ☆ ☾

UNEVOLVED CANCER – EMOTIONAL WRECK

Unevolved Cancerians are permanent victims in all aspects of their lives, and when they victimize others, they feel it was deserved because they were somehow hurt first. They will then drown you in their endless tales of victimhood, becoming what they're best known for: emotional wrecks. They manipulate emotions the same way unevolved Geminis (the sign before them) manipulate thoughts. If confronted, they will be extremely defensive and can stoop so low as to use your trauma against you to make you feel pain.

Since their motto is "I feel," unevolved Cancerians can be cruel and unforgiving when it comes to their emotional fulfillment. They also have no emotional self-control. They can overwhelm others with their issues or selfish desires because they only care about their feelings. When it's your turn to vent, they do well to dismiss your situation and always find a story to outdo yours. They trauma-bond with others only to feel better about their own situation. They seek out people who live at the bottom of the abyss, anchoring them in their negativity and never allowing them to seek the air of freedom.

As a cardinal water sign, unevolved Cancerians are co-dependent to the extreme. They find it difficult to make their own decisions without someone else involved. If they have an emotional attachment to you, they will find it difficult to let you go. They will guilt-trip and gaslight you to get you to stay. Their aggression can hit people unexpectedly like a tsunami, washing away any loving or healthy opportunity. If left alone, or if someone finally escapes, they are left with the guilt and disappointment of their uncontrolled emotions, which will be deflected and projected onto someone else.

☼ ☆ ☾

Evolved Cancer – Emotional Master

Evolved Cancerians are true emotional masters of reciprocation, self-care, and self-love. From Gemini, the evolved sign before them, they have adopted the art of self-expression, but they use this trait more for emotional mastery than mental mastery. They've also learned from their cardinal cousin, evolved Aries, to pursue the deeper meaning of self. Due to this, evolved Cancerians are the healers of the zodiac who teach others how to overcome their darkest nights. They take their traumas and achievements in life as examples to inspire and motivate others into understanding and accepting any emotional situation.

Since their motto is "I feel," evolved Cancerians feel and embrace every emotion. They befriend their feelings and project them in the right spaces. If they feel any pain or hurt, they internalize these feelings and produce works of art or music to release them. If they do not gravitate toward art, they will find another healthier alternative to release any negative vibrations. They reciprocate any emotion given to them and are highly compassionate souls who genuinely care for the internal well-being and emotional health of others.

As a cardinal water sign, evolved Cancerians are productive souls who strive to be successful providers for their families and friends. They often put loved ones before themselves, becoming self-sacrificing for the betterment of those around them. They also possess strong boundaries and know when to say no or distance themselves to regenerate energy. Though they can hibernate in their infamous shell for long periods of time, they always come out to remind people of the importance of self-care and self-love.

☼ ☆ ☽

CANCER MOON

♋ ☽

"I feel what I feel."

Individuals with a Cancer Moon handle their sensitive emotions through deep reflection and isolation, but it depends on other celestial factors. Mixed with fire, they can be highly romantic and optimistic but can overreact and play victim. Mixed with earth, they are emotionally balanced and grounded but can be guarded and pessimistic. Mixed with air, they are expressive and talkative but can lack true understanding of personal emotions. Mixed with water, they are highly intuitive and receptive but are prone to having severe mood swings and a lack of emotional control.

Emotionally, Cancer Moons are sensitive signs who wear their hearts on their sleeves. Depending on their mood, they either internalize how they feel or they express their feelings as they feel them. They are often self-sacrificing and find it hard to enforce their personal boundaries because they prefer to love freely, faithfully, and deeply with all their heart and soul. However, they will be truly heartbroken if their feelings are not reciprocated and will recede in their shell. In hiding, it can take them a long time to process their emotions.

Cancer Moons tend to romanticize and feel every situation. With such high intuition, they become natural empaths who feel more connected with people on a heart and soul level. They have strong emotional attachments and find it hard to detach once they've committed. Since they have strong emotional awareness, they are comfortable talking about their feelings. They also love to heal and guide others through them. Cancer Moons are genuinely kind souls who choose to recycle their emotions through productivity, believing it takes love to heal trauma.

✸☆☾

CANCER ENERGY IN OTHER PLACEMENTS

CANCER ASCENDANT (RISING)

♋ AC

"I feel myself."

Cancer Risings project emotion, passion, romanticism, and intuition in everything they do. Upon first impression, they come off as either warm and affectionate or shy and standoffish; it depends on their mood. They can get irritated by other people's attitudes very quickly, so however you present yourself is how they will reciprocate.

When it comes to their physical appearance, they're like a human mood ring and will often dress in styles that express their mood for the day. They can be casual one day, sexy the next, or dark and gothic another.

CANCER MIDHEAVEN (MC)

♋ MC

"I feel my career."

Cancer Midheavens pursue careers that involve a lot of money. Like water, they want their money flowing into a waterfall of abundance. They are very passionate and sensitive leaders who aren't afraid to get to the heart of any situation, even if it means getting their hands dirty.

Cancer Midheavens are highly intuitive and creative signs that need a way to release and express their emotions frequently, especially in their careers. They find emotional expression as a way to heal themselves and others, so if they can find a career that pays to heal, they will flourish.

CANCER MERCURY

♋ ☿

"I feel my thoughts."

Cancer Mercurians are very intuitive and perceptive when it comes to their thoughts and ideas. They are masters in listening to others, but they also want to be heard by others equally, especially when it comes to sensitive topics. Although they are highly compassionate beings, they can retreat into their dark shells when they're feeling vulnerable or misunderstood. It can be hard to break their guard once it goes up.

Cancer Mercurians are very intelligent, and the majority of them are social and auditory learners. You will find many of them pursuing music, art, or dance because it allows them to express their ideas more freely. They can also be expert teachers who find it easy to connect with others emotionally, persuading others to follow their hearts through emotional appeal.

CANCER VENUS

♋ ♀

"I feel love."

Cancer Venusians love to love and find it hard not to share their love with others. They are true romantics who fall in love with someone who isn't afraid to be vulnerable and someone who can be the strength to their weakness. They reciprocate this with all their mind, heart, and soul and are always willing to do the most for their partners in and out of the home.

Cancer Venusians take love and marriage very seriously. They yearn to have an ideal partnership with an unbreakable bond, a loving home, and a family with someone who's committed to all the trials and rewards of love.

✵☆☾

CANCER MARS

♋ ♂

"I feel physical power."

Cancer Martians are highly aggressive and emotional signs who believe that emotions guide true power. They unleash emotions in opportune times to overcome anything or anyone that stands in their way. However, this proves to be the biggest challenge for them because they can be consumed by their emotions and not always in a good way.

Cancer Martians can create tsunamis when provoked or challenged, yet they are just as passionate with those they love, submerging them in waters of affection and protection. They often use their crab-like shell as a shield to defend themselves and others. They can also be very sensitive and are prone to overreacting, but once calm, they will always choose love over hate.

CANCER JUPITER

♋ ♃

"I feel expansion."

Cancer Jupiterians feel that true expansion is more about emotional growth than mental, physical, or spiritual growth. They are strong believers that luck, faith, and abundance are based on how you feel about yourself and what you project into the physical realm. They are also protectors of fortune and will hoard away their savings for stormy weather.

As emotional manifestors of positive opportunities, Cancer Jupiterians are always working toward a better tomorrow and want others to feel the same. They look to expand and heal others by teaching them self-love and emotional self-control, which leads them down the path of success and prosperity.

CANCER SATURN

♋ ♄

"I feel restriction."

Cancer Saturnians are emotionally strict and find it challenging to break their routines for anybody. Discipline and emotional control allow them to pursue their career or goals relentlessly, all of which they are willing to sacrifice anything or anyone for to be successful and live a meaningful life.

Leadership for Cancer Saturnians will be very important, as they yearn to control their environment with their iron pincers. They have high standards and even higher expectations from those around them. To them, emotions can be a sign of weakness or great strength that they can utilize for the betterment of themselves, even if that means restricting or taking advantage of someone else's emotions to serve the greater good.

CANCER URANUS

♋ ♅

"I feel change."

Cancer Uranians feel that emotional change is necessary when saving and healing the world, which plays a huge part in their journey. Their compassion for others can lead them down many roads of advocacy, as they feel every pain and trauma of every life-form. Many will have a strong connection with water and will try to save ocean wildlife from being hunted and killed.

As natural empaths, it's challenging for Cancer Uranians to turn a blind eye to any type of emotional abuse or suffering. Undeniably, they fight for life and love. They strongly believe that change is loving the unloved and having compassion to save those who come from neglected or abused homes.

✴ ☆ ☾

CANCER NEPTUNE

♋ ♆

"I feel spiritual."

Cancer Neptunians are intuitively powerful and utilize their spiritual gifts to feel the souls of others. They often commit to long spiritual journeys of the heart and soul, usually travelling to any place with bigger bodies of water. Their journeys are almost always triggered from a near-death experience or traumatic childhood event.

Cancer Neptunians can welcome organized religion, as it is a way for them to connect spiritually with others; however, they may not always welcome the strict rules that come with it. They prefer to abide by their own spiritual beliefs, and most will believe in the supernatural and the occult.

CANCER PLUTO

♋ ♇

"I feel evolution."

Cancer Plutonians evolve emotionally, undertaking a lifetime of constant shifts. During their lifetime, they will undergo an intense spiritually cleansing journey full of emotional, even traumatic, challenges, which only proves to strengthen their resolve. This inevitably helps them accept every situation from a higher spiritual perspective.

Before Cancer Plutonians depart from this world, they'll experience every emotion life has to offer. Ultimately, they'll learn that the pursuit of love and companionship in all aspects of their life and sharing a loving home with true family and friends is more enriching than any material wealth. This, in turn, helps them become true masters of emotions in the next lifetime.

✵ ✩ ☾

LEO

Sun Queen/King

♌

July 23 – August 22
Element: Fire
Modality: Fixed
Ruling Planet: Sun
Symbol: The Lion/Lioness
Motto: I Will

LEO SUN

♌ ☉

"I will."

Leo is a fixed fire sign, guided by the Lion/Lioness and ruled by the Sun. As the fifth star child, we discover that Leo separates itself by shining brighter than any other zodiac sign. Because they are the second fire sign and second fixed sign, Leos have become competitive and are at constant war with themselves and the other signs before them to be first place in everything they do. Unlike their fixed cousin Taurus, who is focused on steady growth, Leos are focused on aggressive growth. Unlike their fire sibling Aries, who paves pathways for others, Leos focus more on paving pathways for themselves. Unlike Cancer, the sign before them, whose sole intent is to build emotional awareness, Leo's sole intent is to build stronger self-awareness.

Leos are birthed into the world with the burden of royal greatness on their shoulders, and they feel the heightened pressure to succeed. They also possess a stronger sense of entitlement and stricter beliefs and faith in their destiny and purpose. Due to this, the universe has blessed them with heightened vigor, willpower, focus, and physical stamina.

With the Sun guiding them, these Sun Queens/Kings are deeply aware that to become a strong ruler, they must rid themselves of any physical, mental, and emotional weaknesses. With the weight of the crown on their head, they feel the need to control others, which can be seen at an early age. During their younger years, you will see them develop their roar, mark their territory, and assert their dominance, using their voice to command and demand those around them, especially any siblings. Without the security of status, territory, or power, they feel helpless, weak, or vulnerable.

Like the Sun, Leos do not allow anyone or anything to shade their sense of self and purpose. They often rise above their circumstances, hungry to hunt, survive, and consume. They invest most of their energy in developing their talents and skills, all while strategizing how to conquer the world. This type of mentality is what sets them apart and is one of the main reasons why they often reach greater heights of success than other signs.

Leo's energy goes hand in hand with the Sun's movements. You will find many Leos becoming moody when they're not basking in the Sun, when the seasons grow cold or dreary, or when the Sun is blocked by the clouds. They often like their rooms as hot as the safari or dream about vacationing in some very hot and tropical destinations. Needless to say, Leos personify the Sun's radiance and temperature and have a much shorter temper and tolerance than Aries. They can be warm and sunny one day but can burn and scorch you the next, especially if you provoke their ego.

In reality, all Leos want to do is shine without any limitations. They hate when people tell them no. They are at their best when they're allowed to burn brightly and are the center of attention, and they abhor anything or anyone who tries to rain on their parade. If their circumstances prevent them from shining, they can become resentful and bitter of those who do shine. The rage in them can become an uncontrollable force of jealousy and cattiness, but it depends on their other placements. Fortunately, the majority of them will just eat the loss then train harder to overcome their competition.

Leos have extremely strong boundaries, a trait learned from their fixed cousin Taurus, and will enforce them at will. They do not care to listen or take advice from those who they feel lack credibility or authoritative power. Even so, they do not want to be a "puppet king." They prefer to rule alongside trusted advisors and those who will respect their gifted talents. This isn't to say that Leos cannot work well with others or respect what others who don't have authority have to say. That is far from the truth. They are not the type to

☀☆☾

shade others from sharing their expertise. So long as they can be the only Sun in the room, working with them won't be difficult. They are known to be highly generous individuals who reward loyalty, affection, and appreciation.

Many Leos seek guidance in their greater purpose. They seem to have control over everything else, but they are constantly worried if they are on the path toward greatness or not. If they are not, they will immediately correct themselves. Their commitment to self is what makes them so successful. Every Leo wants to be greater than they were last year, and even though they can be stubborn and inflexible, they will listen to sound advice after they've reflected on its importance.

The symbol for Leo is the Lion/Lioness. Leos are just as regal, noble, and grand as these mighty cats, and they are just as hungry to survive. They use tact and instinct to hunt down their bigger-than-life dreams. Like the great lion, they are naturally territorial, and many strive to be at the top of the food chain, wanting to rule over everything and everyone. They also want to be recognized for their successful hunts and educated on any failed hunts. They do not like being belittled for any choices they make, even if they're wrong. To them, anything they do deserves credit.

Like all cats, Leos love to be petted and adored. They yearn to be praised, complimented, and recognized for all of their greater efforts because they do the most for others and push themselves past their limitations to fulfill their great destiny, which oftentimes falls on the deaf ears and blind eyes of those who refuse to see their true potential. Yet, even with all the naysayers, Leos take this type of negative energy and use it as motivation. It's also good to note that they never forget their haters. They can hold a grudge for as long as they breathe. Most Leos also do not believe in apologies or forgiveness. It's beneath them to show any loyalty or kindness to cruel people.

Contrary to popular belief, Leos do not live in a delusion of grandeur. They dream big with the intent to make their dreams a reality. They also feel that

☀ ☆ ☾

anything can be conquered so long as you have the willpower to succeed. This makes them a good fit as CEOs, entrepreneurs, or business owners. Since they also love an audience, they can be amazing entertainers as well. You will find many Leos who fall in love with the stage because they were born with stage presence. They understand how to wow a crowd, and like the lion, they are unafraid of challenges and will devour them as they come.

As all cats are known for their grooming rituals, so are Leos. Though they can rough it in the wilderness, they still believe in maintaining their physical selves with utmost care and affection. A majority of them like to have a thick mane of some sort, and those who do will take great care in combing and styling it to perfection. If they have fair or thin hair, they will find ways in making it thicker. It will be hard to find a Leo that doesn't care about hygiene or having a clean castle. They can be extreme neat freaks and can change their surroundings constantly if they feel trapped by them.

Unbeknownst to many, most Leos love puzzles and mystery games, and they are really good at virtually any game that involves some kind of hunt. If you've ever been to an escape room or if you ever want to go, you should bring a Leo with you. If it has anything to do with life or death, bring a Leo. They don't mind getting their hands dirty, which is a trait passed down by their fixed cousin, Taurus. Although they prefer hard work instead of sitting by idly, any tedious work will be delegated, as they want to be part of the main stage, not hidden behind a curtain. The applause of others is important in building their confidence.

The Leo's motto is "I will." Their life's challenge is their own sense of entitlement. They must learn to define what great destiny truly is. Since they are born with the burden to succeed, they tend to receive heavier judgment from others. To overcome this, they must learn the grace of handling criticism, not overreacting under pressure, and utilizing their intellect and charm to persuade others into adopting their greater vision.

✵ ☆ ☾

Leos possess fierce willpower and are determined to exceed society's expectations. They have a heart as big as the Sun and are extremely generous individuals who value companionship, friendship, family, and partnership. Loyalty and love are qualities they live by, and they expect the same in others. When let down, they can take it as an insult to their greatness. This can lead them down a path of endless failures because, like Cancer, they can play the blame game and overdramatize situations.

As a fixed fire sign, Leos are focused on physical power. Instinctually, they take on more than they can chew. Like their fixed cousin Taurus, they can be stubborn and unwilling to bend for anybody. Like their fire sibling Aries, they are consumed with passion and aggression. With that said, Leos roar as loud as lions and are prone to throwing raging temper tantrums, especially unevolved types. However, they possess unbelievable stamina, direction, and focus, which helps them curb their appetite for blood.

Fortunately, Leos work toward becoming a good ruler and protector of their environment. They will defend all that they love to the death using their sharp claws and teeth. They shine their rays of optimism and hope of a better life to warm the world, giving people the strength and energy needed to be their own ruler and make their wild dreams a reality.

Overall, Leo Suns embody greater physical strength, force, willpower, and a higher purpose/destiny. The path of the unknown invigorates their spirit, giving them the courage it takes to explore what they feel in their spirit. They teach other zodiac signs to be the greatest version of themselves, helping them find the strength to overcome any physical or environmental challenges that may arise.

☀ ☆ ☾

UNEVOLVED LEO – DRAMATIC DIVA/DIVO

Unevolved Leos are entitled to the extreme. They believe that everything and everyone should bow down to their needs and desires, which is a trait they learned from their fire sibling, unevolved Aries, as well as the sign before them, unevolved Cancer. Like their fixed cousin, unevolved Taurus, they have been taught to hold onto their radical beliefs. However, unevolved Leos take everything a step further and sum up their unreasonable and unrealistic expectations as "deserving" of only the best, even if they have not earned it.

Since their motto is "I will," unevolved Leos can willfully punish anybody who threatens their spotlight. They will utilize their power or status (if any) to prevent further opportunities for any of their competitors. They don't believe in sharing, but if they do give willingly, you are obligated to pay them back in some way. Unevolved Leos turn on the drama and turn up the heat in any given situation to get what they want in life, becoming best known as dramatic divas/divos. If they don't get what they want, they will throw a temper tantrum and their roaring voice will make your ears bleed. The only way to turn it off is by giving them what they want.

As a fixed fire sign, they are fixated only on their greedy life goals. They can be petty to the extreme, focusing on how to beat everybody else. If their enemy fails in life, they'll sit back and laugh at their fall from grace. To them, the strong eat the weak; it's a part of the natural life cycle, and those who are strong shouldn't feel sympathy for it. Needless to say, they possess unrealistic demands and believe that superficial fame, money, and power can provide and sustain their noble status. In their head, the world revolves around them, and they'll behead you if you don't bow down.

☀☆☾

EVOLVED LEO – PASSIONATE VISIONARY

Evolved Leos are passionate visionaries who are constantly working on self-empowerment and conquering their worldly dreams. They've learned from the sign before them, evolved Cancer, to love freely and generously. They've learned from their fire sibling, evolved Aries, to follow their greatest passions and lead with confidence, and they've learned from their fixed cousin, evolved Taurus, to be loyal and nurturing to those around them. Due to this, evolved Leos are one of the top passionate and loyal leaders who encourage others to dream big without limitations.

Since their motto is "I will," evolved Leos have undeniable willpower and are motivated to rule with people in mind. They inspire others through their words and actions, always seeing the grand picture in every situation. They have extreme faith and confidence in their abilities and skills. They never second-guess themselves when they come across a challenge; instead, they fight fiercely to overcome it. They work hard for their dreams and possess extreme focus and determination to do whatever it takes to reach their full potential. Even when faced with failure, they will get up and keep trying.

As a fixed fire sign, evolved Leos are strong believers of fate and destiny, which pushes them to pursue their true purpose in life. They strive to be role models for their audience, so fulfilling their destiny is not just for them; it's for everyone who has a dream. Regardless of their upbringing, evolved Leos remain optimistic about their futures because whatever they manifest often comes true. They add flash and color to people's lives, showing them that life can be grand at any phase and on any stage in your life.

✹ ☆ ☾

LEO MOON

♌ ☽

"I will feel."

Individuals who have a Leo Moon process their emotions passionately and with a little bit of drama, but it depends on other celestial factors. Mixed with fire, they are intensely affectionate and fiercely protective, yet they are more aggressive and impatient. Mixed with earth, they are determined and focused but can be stubborn and egotistical. Mixed with air, they are highly optimistic, creative, and bubbly, yet they are boisterously loud and have a hatred of authority. Mixed with water, they are sensitive and inviting but are easily angered and can hold much longer grudges.

Emotionally, Leo Moons like to exaggerate how they feel because they like to put on a show, but it usually comes from a good space. They like to feel like they're starring in their own soap opera, which makes it more entertaining for them and everyone else who has to listen. They may not have the greatest storytelling abilities, but they have stage presence and they like to be the center of attention. Whatever they feel is what they want others to feel, whether it's good or bad. They embrace and accept their emotions, and they expect others to do the same.

Leo Moons do not believe in limitations of the heart. They believe that if you feel love, hate, or anything in between, you should always express it without fear. They really don't care if you like them or not; they will shine bright no matter what. However, if they love and care for you, they will be the umbrella that guards you from those who try to rain on your parade. Their optimistic views on life uplift the spirits of everyone around them. After all, Leo Moons are the stars in the night, distant Suns that light up any void.

✺ ☆ ☾

LEO ENERGY IN OTHER PLACEMENTS

LEO ASCENDANT (RISING)

♌ AC

"I will be myself."

Leo Risings project a sense of regal authority. Their confident, vivacious energy electrifies the room with warmth, superiority, and inspiration. They know how to wow their audience with their flashiness. Upon first impression, they come in hot and passionate when they are being assertive, when they're attracted to someone, or when they're talking about a sensitive subject.

When it comes to their physical appearance, Leo Risings love to stand out from the crowd with anything that makes them look more graceful or expensive. They also love jewelry because they love to shine.

LEO MIDHEAVEN (MC)

♌ MC

"I will be my career."

Leo Midheavens pursue creative careers that focus more on art, entertainment, or any career that gives them a higher status, a bigger audience, and recognition for their efforts. They shine the brightest when in command and in demand. As natural leaders, they pursue challenging projects, and their confidence to succeed inspires their team to follow and push through.

Since they take pride in themselves and their work and will invest time in building themselves up, they require salaries and bonuses that match their confidence, talent, and skill set. Any less and they'll throw a raging fit.

LEO MERCURY

♌ ☿

"I will think."

Leo Mercurians are driven to pursue and become the greatest versions of themselves. The majority of them are visual and physical learners who need to see and act out a skill to fully adopt and master it. They take pride in their natural skills and talents and are highly disciplined learners who are always focused on the end goal.

Leo Mercurians are extremely private about their personal lives, though it may not seem like it at first since they are quick to vocalize their thoughts and opinions. They are fearless thinkers who do not believe in limitations, and they are big dreamers who work toward a luxurious lifestyle.

LEO VENUS

♌ ♀

"I will love."

Leo Venusians love with all their being. They are extremely affectionate and like to be catered to, or even spoiled, by their partners. However, they're not completely selfish when it comes to love. In fact, they are highly generous and will treat their partner like royalty so long as it is reciprocated. They are the most loving with those who constantly recognize and appreciate their love.

Leo Venusians take love very seriously and are not the type to settle. This can lead them into multiple relationships until they find a strong mate who is more ambitious than they are. They are also highly territorial and do not like to feel second best to anybody. If they feel like they have to compete for love or attention, they will leave without notice.

☀ ☆ ☾

LEO MARS

♌ ♂

"I will be physical power."

Leo Martians aggressively work toward having and sustaining power in all aspects of their life. They need to take the lead role in everything they do, and if they have to, they will claw people out of their way to get where they need to go. They are the stubborn, hot-headed types who can get into a screaming match if they're being challenged, so bring earmuffs.

Leo Martians prioritize their physical well-being and find physical strength empowering. It becomes their type of meditation, which ignites their need for more power and stamina to take on the world. If they are not exercising their bodies, they will exercise their minds and strategize and hunt down multiple opportunities of growth and prosperity.

LEO JUPITER

♌ ♃

"I will be expansive."

Leo Jupiterians possess wildly enormous and expansive goals. As talented visionaries, they dream of winning the world over with their creations. They are often motivated by luxury, fortune, and travel and see material expansion as proof of their royal greatness.

Leo Jupiterians live for the stage, so showcasing their talents and skills is a requirement. They want an audience to hear their life stories, praise their efforts, and expand their journey by buying and consuming whatever they preach or sell. With an audience, they become an unstoppable force that is relentless in pursuing true wealth and fame.

LEO SATURN

♌ ♄

"I will be restriction."

Leo Saturnians are physically strict with themselves and others. They live to dominate and delegate. They like to keep others in line and can be very forceful when getting their way. However, it proves that they are highly organized and focused and are aware that people need leadership and guidance to be successful. As strict as they are with others, they go even harder on themselves, maintaining strict physical discipline to achieve their much sought-after goals.

Leo Saturnians are fiercely protective and loyal, and they will fight to the death defending the things and people they care about the most. They have difficulty trusting, so they will be cautious and selective when dealing with others. Nobody is considered an ally until they have proven their loyalty.

LEO URANUS

♌ ♅

"I will be change."

Leo Uranians make the most of their life by weeding out their weaknesses and developing their core strengths. They seek to be idolized and rewarded for the changes they make in their communities. Therefore, they invest a lot of their energy in becoming the change people want in themselves.

Leo Uranians strongly believe that change starts with great leadership. With their charm, they inspire others to find and join like-minded prides who hunt and eat together. Though there will still be a strong chain of command in which they are the leader, they will allow others to shine without envy.

✺ ✯ ☾

LEO NEPTUNE

♌ ♆

"I will be spiritual."

Leo Neptunians place high value on spirituality, seeing it as a source of great power and divine empowerment for themselves and others. Being a fiery lion/lioness, they are naturally connected with wild animals (mostly predators), fire, heat, and the Sun. They love to feel warm, radiant energy and travel to places that allow them the comfort of the Sun's exuberant vibration.

Leo Neptunians often take on lead spiritual positions, such as preachers or shamans. Like all other Leo placements, they require a following. They are adept at teaching others how to develop their senses and can apply fear or a chance of reward to inspire others in taking their spirituality more seriously.

LEO PLUTO

♌ ♇

"I will evolve."

Leo Plutonians evolve with the intent to overcome themselves and pursue all that is pleasurable and invigorating to their spirit. They feel the weight of the crown on their head, creating the pressure needed to push them forward; and once they have a taste of success, they clamp down and never let go.

Before Leo Plutonians depart from this world, they want to leave behind a legacy full of triumph and tributes to society. During their lifetime, they will undergo many challenges that test their willpower and devotion to self. Though their bodies age, their spirit is forever youthful, and they will continue to dream as big as their spirit until the day they evolve into the spirit realm.

☼ ☆ ☽

VIRGO

Mercurian Saint

August 23 – September 22
Element: Earth
Modality: Mutable
Ruling Planet: Mercury
Symbol: The Virgin
Motto: I Analyze

☀ ☆ ☾

Virgo Sun

♍ ☉

"I analyze."

Virgo is a mutable earth sign, guided by the Virgin and ruled by the planet Mercury. They share this planet with their mutable cousin, Gemini. As the sixth star child, second earth sign, and second mutable sign, Virgos are the diplomats and architects of the world. They use the skill of language, thought, and perspective to shape our mentality. Unlike their mutable cousin Gemini, who utilizes creative eccentricities that enlighten the world, Virgos use their mental abilities to refine ideas and create efficiency, organization, respect, manners, and perfection for humanity.

Like their earth sibling Taurus, Virgos are focused on the work ahead and devote their time to crafting skills to obtain financial security and stability. Unlike Taureans, Virgos are not as strict when it comes to physical labor and do not push or bully their beliefs onto others. They instead use their powers of intelligence and persuasion to inspire others on why they should work and perfect themselves to gain the lifestyle they desire. Due to this, the universe blesses them with keen analytical eyesight and cunning intelligence.

As Mercurian Saints, Virgos are guided by Mercury's quick insight and believe in doing what's best, not just for themselves but for humanity as a whole. They strongly believe there is a reason and purpose for everything and everyone. To fulfill this, Mercury instills them with the ability to focus on the smaller details in every situation, ensuring that nothing and nobody is left out. With these smaller details, they are then able to establish a technical and logical solution for any imperfections they come across.

With such a sharp mind, Virgos enjoy assessing, observing, and judging

the world around them, including people. They are extremely quick learners, with the ability to learn through other people's experiences (good or bad). Through observations, they collect the information needed to make better life choices. They strongly believe that a person is capable of reaching absolute human perfection and that it is a disciplined and responsible choice to work on yourself internally as well as externally. To them, there is no other way of obtaining the ideal lifestyle.

Virgos keep a mental databank of observations, experiences, and theories of life and people. They apply this databank to create standards for humanity as a whole. In utilizing these standards, they commit themselves to sustaining a more peaceful, good, and balanced lifestyle. They pride themselves in being diplomatic mediators, choosing peace over violence most times. However, this doesn't make them physically weak. Just like the sign before them, Leo, they can use violence or aggression to get people in order. Luckily, the majority of Virgos prefer to use their brain over their brawn. They are deeply aware that people are more willing to cooperate through intelligent communication rather than by force.

Virgos are progressive architects who see an opportunity to build, rebuild, and expand everything and everyone. Unlike their earth sibling Taurus, who doesn't mind long hard labor, Virgos prefer to work smarter not harder. They are masters in creating more efficient ways to work longer, with less backbreaking routines. However, once they've developed an effective system, they can fall victim to their own process and become extreme workaholics. If they are not working or being progressive, their talkative Mercury energy will be used in unproductive ways, such as petty gossip, harsh criticisms, hypocritical judgments, or overthinking negative insecurities.

Virgos usually pursue and obsess over projects that are very complex and involve the full use of mind and body or the evolution of humanly needs. They value intelligence and higher learning. Therefore, it is an important goal for

✸✰☾

them to pursue quality education, whether it's through an accredited school, work experience, mentorship, or self-education. Needless to say, they are both students and teachers of life experiences and life lessons. To them, every situation is a teachable moment for them or others they involve. This brilliant and highly productive mindset is what makes them stand out from the rest of the zodiac signs.

Since Virgos can learn just about anything, you will find many who make a career in technology, teaching, health care, nutrition, cosmetology, fitness, sports, music, art, writing, counseling, or science—any career that combines the mental with the physical. And with Mercury's influence, they are at their best when their career involves a community of people they can educate in some way. They are really adept in articulating their words and having very practical techniques that anybody can follow.

The Virgo symbol is the Virgin, but this doesn't mean they are prudes. It means they keep their personal lives private and are aware that people are judgmental and hypocritical of physical appearance and demeanor. They also value purity and cleanliness of the mind, body, and soul. This is a key reason why they strive for flawlessness. You will find many who devote themselves to body purification and are obsessed with researching how the body works with the mind. To them, mastering purity and perfection is what makes a person complete, and if a person chooses not to strive for it, they should be judged by a jury of their peers.

With the saintly Virgin guiding their instincts, Virgos prioritize disciplined behavior and routines, especially personal hygiene, fitness, and nutrition. They also value integrity, respect, and good manners. They are disgusted by rude, lazy, smelly, or dirty people. You can see it in their faces, even if they're trying hard not to vocalize it. The majority of them are also very conservative and selective in what they wear, believing that how you appear influences how people respect you. This goes to say that Virgos have very responsible

✸ ☆ ☾

and realistic perspectives when it comes to societal norms and traditions.

The Virgo motto is "I analyze." Their life challenge is their own criticism and judgments of what perfectionism means for themselves as well as others. They can also overanalyze their skills and decisions while harshly critiquing themselves for their flaws, which leads to stagnation, pessimism, or procrastination. They can also neglect their emotional needs, believing that emotions only deter them from making logical decisions. To overcome this, they must learn to be kind to themselves, trust their instincts and intelligence, and learn that perfection itself is not a realistic achievement, that there is perfection in imperfection.

Virgos notice all the smaller details of everything. At times it doesn't matter if everything else was positive; if something negative is said, they will investigate the thought process behind it or they will focus on it with such pessimism that they cannot look into the deeper meaning of it. However, when they are open to constructive criticism or realistic perspectives, they will adapt and adopt to change, especially when it helps them reach perfection. That's the wonderful thing about Virgos: they are always willing to fix themselves.

Virgos are not without emotions. Like Gemini, they are challenged by their complexity. They are unsure of how to balance what they feel with what they think is right. This type of confusion can create a lot of anxiety, but they won't let the world know. They can have a still face even though they are freaking out on the inside. They prefer to work on their emotions independently and will organize how they feel about a situation before they act on it. This can lead them to jump to assumptions or coldly dismiss the other party's feelings if they do not feel they are wrong.

As a mutable earth sign, Virgos are adaptable in their thinking and actions. They mutate and soak in their environment with the intent to learn and refine it. They believe that in order to service others, one must service themselves first. By mastering their analytical skills, as well as their reasoning talents,

☀ ☆ ☾

they are able to embrace their incredible attention to detail and forethought without adding negative judgments or unnecessary criticisms. This helps them reach their version of higher intelligence, which leads to their success.

When Virgos know something or someone is unreasonable, illogical, or no longer serves their overall well-being, they will weed it out of their system permanently. They strongly believe that evolution of the mind and body is what makes humans human. Thus, many travel to experience an evolution in others or within themselves, which helps them accumulate new ideas and perspectives. You will find many who keep a detailed log of their traveling observations, ready to share them with anyone who will listen.

With earth grounding their sensibilities, Virgos are known to be shrewd and frugal with their money. Unlike Taurus, who places a higher value on expensive products, Virgos are the opposite, considering expensive items an unnecessary expense. The majority are low maintenance and only purchase things out of necessity. Practicality is important to their lifestyle, so if it doesn't add up financially or have long-term benefits, they will dismiss it. This isn't to say that they won't go on spurts of shopping sprees and spend all their money in one day. They can, and they surely have. However, they will oftentimes have buyers' remorse afterward or extreme anxiety about how they spent their money so frivolously. Fortunately, starting over, saving up, or reinventing themselves is never an issue.

Overall, Virgos embody mastery over self and community. They do not believe in hoarding knowledge. They prefer to educate and enlighten those around them with realistic perspectives and well-researched studies. Through this, they motivate others to achieve purity and perfection in all aspects of their lives by embracing who they are and who they can learn to be.

☼ ☆ ☾

UNEVOLVED VIRGO – ANXIOUS CRITICIZER

Unevolved Virgos are anxious criticizers who overanalyze and overthink their environment and everyone in it. From their earth sibling, unevolved Taurus, they've learned that everyone must follow strict rules. From their mutable cousin, unevolved Gemini, they've learned that unorganized ideas and thoughts bring only demise and instability. From the sign before them, unevolved Leo, they've learned that personal power is more important than relationships. Because of all the signs before them, unevolved Virgos have been given the painstaking duty of reorganizing everything and everyone.

Since their motto is "I analyze," unevolved Virgos tend to criticize every scenario, usually harboring pessimistic views. Their minds are on a never-ending playlist of everything that's wrong with humanity. They see only what they feel needs fixing. Even if it's trivial and meaningless, they're not afraid to nag about it. They disguise their disgusts as constructive criticism, when deep down they believe you're incompetent. They can be extremely hypocritical and are prone to deflecting or projecting their insecurities onto others.

As a mutable earth sign, unevolved Virgos believe that perfectionism is the only thing that matters in life. Due to this, they can be severely fearful, cautious, and anxious when making decisions, believing that all failures can be prevented, though most of those fears are based in paranoia. If they mistakenly choose wrong, they are harsh and cruel to themselves and will mentally punish themselves for their imperfections. They can try so hard to be socially acceptable that they end up excluding themselves from anything or anybody good.

☼ ☆ ☾

EVOLVED VIRGO – TACTFUL ARCHITECT

Evolved Virgos are tactful architects who strategize and organize self improvement. They've learned from the sign before them, evolved Leo, to dream big without limitations. They've learned from their earth sibling, evolved Taurus, to guide others unbiasedly. And they've learned from their mutable cousin, evolved Gemini, to think creatively and freely. Due to this, evolved Virgos utilize their strengths to provide rational thoughts and concise mental processing to create a higher standard of living for all.

Since their motto is "I think," evolved Virgos are highly detailed signs who think with the intent to improve. They are strong listeners who offer logical solutions based on a person's individual needs. They do not criticize or judge others; instead, they appreciate everyone's ability to think and judge for themselves. The health of self and community will be a priority for them, as they often join causes that promote it. They utilize their mental strengths to perfect efficiency in every task and routine, which ultimately leads to a more peaceful and healthier lifestyle.

As a mutable earth sign, evolved Virgos are flexible yet regimental types with pure intentions, which allows them to stick to their strong moral beliefs. They collect and analyze every fact and piece of evidence to make sensible decisions and form unbiased opinions. They are natural teachers who teach others to adopt practicality and maintain integrity. They also aren't afraid to voice their thought and ideas, yet they are fully aware of the weight and responsibilities of having one. As such, they become the voice of every person who seeks self-awareness and self-improvement.

☼☆☾

VIRGO MOON

♍ ☽

"I analyze what I feel."

Individuals with a Virgo Moon analyze their feelings rationally with tact and sensibility, but it depends on other celestial factors. Mixed with fire, they are straightforward and optimistic yet are easily irritated by those they feel are incompetent. Mixed with earth, they are committed and tactical but find it difficult to see things from an emotional perspective. Mixed with air, they are intelligent and soak in information effortlessly, yet they find it challenging to relate to people. Mixed with water, they are sympathetic and nurturing but find long-term commitment difficult and are passive-aggressive.

Emotionally, Virgo Moons process emotions like a robot. They organize and categorize their feelings as they come. They prefer to see emotions from a practical perspective, so they tend to be dismissive of feelings they feel are unproductive or irrelevant to the situation. This can leave others feeling like they are too cold, but they are just focused on how to resolve an issue without all the background noise. They also have strong boundaries when it comes to others, so they can be quick to dismiss people altogether but will always opt to do what is morally right should the situation get out of hand.

Virgo Moons talk about their feelings as if they're sitting with a therapist and believe that every emotional situation is a learning experience for both parties. However, if they feel the other party is in the wrong, they will not hesitate to correct or criticize them. They can be quite harsh but not more than they are to themselves. Virgo Moons strive for inner perfection and emotional control. To them, perfection requires constant internal reviews, which in turn creates true self-awareness and emotional discipline.

☀ ☆ ☾

VIRGO ENERGY IN OTHER PLACEMENTS

VIRGO ASCENDANT (RISING)

♍ AC

"I analyze myself."

Virgo Risings project diplomacy, sharpness, detail, and meticulousness in everything they do. Upon first impression, they can come off as respectful yet cold or cautious, but it's only because they like to observe and listen more than talk. It can be hard to break through with just emotions alone, as they do not like to cloud their assessments with biased feelings.

When it comes to physical appearance, Virgo Risings are conservative and prefer timeless looks. They are very nitpicky about what they wear and how they wear it. They are also very critical of how people perceive them, wanting to always project a sense of confidence and perfection into the world.

VIRGO MIDHEAVEN (MC)

♍ MC

"I analyze my career."

Virgo Midheavens pursue careers that allow them to utilize their analytical mindset, so anything complex where they are constantly problem-solving will help them thrive. Although they thrive on routine, they are very restless. If a job is too trivial, they will responsibly put in their two weeks.

Virgo Midheavens are experts in managing and organizing expenses. This makes them outstanding accountants, as they can save companies massive amounts of money through efficient processes and superb negotiation skills.

VIRGO MERCURY

♍ ☿

"I analyze my thoughts."

Virgo Mercurians are fast thinkers who analyze, sometimes overanalyze, every detail in every situation. They have a critical eye and can't help but fix broken things or broken people. Perfecting what they can control will be very important to them. They are also highly methodical, diplomatic, articulate, and communicative. Most will enjoy a good intellectual debate based on facts.

Virgo Mercurians invest a lot of their energy in educating themselves, and the majority of them are mathematical and physical learners. To them, there's a scientific reason for everything. The majority of them like to learn and research independently and do not tolerate any ignorance or misinformation.

VIRGO VENUS

♍ ♀

"I analyze love."

Virgo Venusians are very selective and private when it comes to love and relationships. They try their best to make realistic decisions, straying far away from irrational ones. When they are in a loving relationship, they will work to become the ideal partner and strive for open communication and fairness.

Virgo Venusians take partnerships very seriously, and they will research, interrogate, and scrutinize everyone until they find a perfect match. Most will commit to singledom rather than settle for anyone mediocre. Being extreme perfectionists, they also have a long, detailed list of who they want. They are at their best with those who can carry an intelligent conversation, are adaptable yet organized, and those who prioritize self-improvement.

☀ ☆ ☾

VIRGO MARS

♍ ♂

"I analyze physical power."

Virgo Martians analyze the deeper meaning of physical power, believing that mind over matter is true strength. Yet, they take their physical health seriously and will make a ritual out of diet and exercise. They don't invest a lot of their energy in impressing others with their physical prowess, as they aren't in it to attract others. All they do physically is for their future benefit, especially in old age, so they'll research everything that goes into their bodies.

Virgo Martians are highly diplomatic with every situation. They don't feel the need to assert their dominance in tense situations, as they are confident and secure in their stances. Most are non-violent, rational individuals who like to mediate and communicate until all solutions have been exhausted.

VIRGO JUPITER

♍ ♃

"I analyze expansion."

Virgo Jupiterians expand both mentally and physically. They believe that by working toward inner and outer perfection, you are able to project good intentions into the physical realm. This, in turn, creates ultimate success and wealth, as the majority of them are devoted to creating the perfect lifestyle.

Virgo Jupiterians are technical thinkers when it comes to life's biggest challenges; however, many get hung up on bad decisions, harshly criticizing themselves for things they wish they could have done or said in the past. Fortunately, most are constantly analyzing and reorganizing their thoughts to make more efficient, responsible, and successful decisions.

VIRGO SATURN

♍ ♄

"I analyze restriction."

Virgo Saturnians love the idea of restriction because it is the foundation of discipline and fortitude. They find it most appealing when they are in control of every situation, as this gives them the opportunity to create standards for everyone to abide by. Structured regulations and routines will be important to their everyday living because anything messy or unorganized will bring out the nagging criticizer in them.

Virgo Saturnians work hard to create the perfect environment, career, and family. They see themselves as providers, yet they also want their partners to be equally financially responsible. They believe everyone should play a productive role in the family, so even their children will have chores to teach them better life skills.

VIRGO URANUS

♍ ♅

"I analyze change."

Virgo Uranians believe that change begins with heavy research followed by education, which ends with informed, rational decisions. They are educated advocates who believe that anything and everything can be fixed, and any system that is broken should be prioritized for immediate repair.

Virgo Uranians believe in creating and maintaining productive and highly organized systems, which creates more value and efficiency in communities while also placing higher accountability on individuals to fulfill their personal duty and responsibility as a citizen of the world.

✵ ☆ ☾

VIRGO NEPTUNE

♍ ♆

"I analyze spirituality."

Virgo Neptunians find the occult, supernatural, and spiritual hard to accept, as they place more faith in science and math or anything else man-made. Although they are intrigued by things that are not easily understood or proven, they still require things they can see, touch, and analyze. Otherwise, they are highly critical of things that cannot be backed with factual evidence.

Virgo Neptunians take a realistic approach to life's supernatural mysteries and believe more in physical energy than spiritual energy. Many value natural medicinal methods because they like to know how to purify and purge their bodies through organic herbs, and they will maintain their physical health and energy through holistic and nutritional means.

VIRGO PLUTO

♍ ♇

"I analyze evolution."

Virgo Plutonians research the evolution of all life-forms on Earth, finding it both intriguing and enlightening. Understanding how others live helps them build stronger awareness and purpose in their own life. The majority of them will devote themselves to long-term research and examinations of different cultures and rituals, finding purpose in the study of human behavior.

Virgo Plutonians naturally evolve past their mental and physical limits. During their lifetime, they will pursue everything and anyone who educates them in becoming mentally wiser and physically stronger, and before they depart, they will have reached and mastered true human perfection.

LIBRA

Venusian Scales

♎

September 23 – October 22
Element: Air
Modality: Cardinal
Ruling Planet: Venus
Symbol: The Scales
Motto: I Balance

☀ ☆ ☾

LIBRA SUN

♎ ☉

"I balance."

Libra is a cardinal air sign, guided by the Scales and ruled by Venus. It shares this planet with Taurus. As the seventh star child, second air sign, and third cardinal sign, Librans bring forth balance, justice, and feminine beauty into the world below. Like their air sibling, Gemini, they believe in mental empowerment and require a lot of mental stimulation. However, unlike Gemini, they are more committed to their goals and have stronger mental discipline. They also utilize their mental strengths to push for fairness and equality in everything they do.

Like their cardinal cousins Aries and Cancer, Librans are natural leaders with strong ambitions and are just as aggressive in achieving success. Unlike their cousins, though, they prefer to charm their way to the top of the ladder instead of climb. Like Virgos, the sign before them, Librans strive for total perfection, but they place more value on perfecting their relationships rather than themselves. Since Librans focus more on relationships, they invest most of their energy in balancing them. They also take them very seriously. Because of this, the universe has blessed them with a higher thought process and stronger communication skills, which helps them understand relationships on a much deeper level than the rest of the zodiac.

As the Venusian Scales, Librans are empowered by Venus' energy, which embodies the Greek goddess Aphrodite. Love, physical beauty, vanity, and persuasion are gifts Venus has bestowed to them. You will find many Librans who take great care of their physical and mental well-being and seek long-term relationships. A lot of Librans will also save up for cosmetic surgery to

☀ ☆ ☾

achieve the beauty they envision in themselves. With Venus' insights, they naturally see the inner and outer beauty in someone else and are able to bring it out of someone who is shy, conservative, or insecure. They are masters in inspiring others to show off their hidden beauty in confidence, which they believe is true empowerment.

Since they share Venus with Taureans, Librans also have expensive taste and are lovers of money, material wealth, and ultimate pleasure. Money isn't an issue with this sign, as Librans are highly opportunistic and optimistic about their financial success. They are also resourceful with their money and possessions, either saving up for something expensive or buying inexpensive items then making it look more expensive than what it actually is. It's important to note that their external world must match their internal value, and because they prioritize partnerships of all kinds, you will find that whomever they surround themselves with is how they feel about themselves.

Since Librans love to surround themselves with beautiful art and furniture, aroma and aesthetics will be especially important to them. The majority of them are avid decorators or high-end collectors. The higher the price, the higher the quality, or the more famous the creator, the more attracted they are to it. It's all for the sake of owning beauty from any era they're attracted to. They are also admirers of physical beauty and are true romantics who love to charm the pants off of others. Although they may seem more superficial than most, they are not all beauty and no brain. In fact, they work more on their mentality than they do anything else.

Librans have plenty of mental strengths, which can surprise many suitors who see that they offer more than just a pretty/handsome face. They possess strong beliefs of justice and equality, and they'll fight aggressively to make positive changes in society. Since they are highly intelligent and expressive, they will invest their energy in educating themselves to learn how to better communicate their strong beliefs and strategize their innovative ideas.

⁕☆☾

Librans tend to take on long-term successful careers as lawyers, judges, or motivational speakers or in marketing, sales, acting, writing, or music. And since they love beauty, they can also take on careers as models, photographers, or artists. There are also many famous Libran musicians who are lyrically gifted because they've mastered the art of language. Since they love a good debate, they can also be excellent candidates as legislators, governors, and even president. Librans thrive in any space where they can take on a leadership voice that promotes beauty or justice and usually has to do with popularity so they can reach the masses.

Libra's symbol is the Scales, and like scales, they strive for balance in all aspects of their lives. If they're the rebellious type, they are constantly devising tactics to tip the scales in their favor. They can think more about what pleases them than anybody else. Fortunately, the majority of Librans are concerned with doing what is fair and just. They are also one of the most forgiving zodiac signs, believing that almost every situation can be mediated in some way. If it cannot be mediated, they will balance their thoughts and emotions and create closure with the situation, leaving it behind for good.

The Scales symbolize Libra's swinging moods. They can be social and chatty one day, antisocial and withdrawn the next. When they are withdrawn, they tend to be stuck in their mind, having an internal argument about what they should do next. It's also hard for them to tolerate one-sided conversations. They will zone out and escape reality within their mind if they feel trapped in an unwanted conversation. If you provoke them, they'll argue your ears off, even becoming violent if you refuse to leave.

With their internal scales tilting from side to side, they often require time to process a situation and tend to make decisions based on logic rather than emotions. They are highly philosophical and reasonable and see situations from multiple perspectives, as all air signs do. They are also highly aware that a balance of actions and words can tilt the energy of the room from negative

✲ ☆ ☾

to positive or vice versa. Therefore, they do their best to make more informed decisions and opinions through heavier research, and by collecting as much information as possible, they are able to ensure that their scales of justice are even enough for them to express their findings. If they conclude that the evidence collected is not enough to make a final decision, they will allow the situation to play out naturally without interference.

The motto of Libra is "I balance." Their life challenge is their indecisiveness and spreading themselves too thinly. They are known to change directions impulsively, confusing themselves and being unable to balance work and pleasure. They can also become obsessed with superficial vanity, beauty, and wealth. To overcome this, they must implement a healthy routine that organizes their thoughts and ideas more efficiently. They must also learn that external beauty is not more captivating than internal beauty, so they must focus on building their internal character by adopting self-love practices that have nothing to do with their physical bodies.

Librans balance and foster partnerships and relationships of all kinds and place high importance in nurturing them. They are naturally very loving and supportive, oftentimes adopting younger people who don't have strong parental figures as mentees. They strongly believe that everyone should have a tribe or village to care for them, no matter how different they are. They tend to always see the best in others, believing that showing kindness and providing guidance and education can rehabilitate those who have lost their way. This type of mentality is what makes them the most popular and likeable sign of the zodiac, as they strongly believe that everyone can and will blossom when given the right environment.

Librans are extremely protective of their loved ones, going to great lengths to shelter them from anybody who wishes them harm. Should you mess with someone they love, they will not hesitate to use their words or fists to silence you forever. They are also extremely loyal to friends, siding with them no

✷☆☾

matter if they're wrong or right. If you don't like someone, neither do they. However, if they are in the middle of two loved ones, they will mediate the situation because they believe in sustaining their community.

As one of the most romantic signs in the zodiac, Librans will fight to keep their loved ones close, and they do not give up easily when in a committed relationship. This can lead them into pleasing a loved one for the sake of keeping it, even though the love has died; but once they've decided that the relationship is no longer worth keeping, they will be civil in cutting all emotional ties. However, they are not against remaining friends afterward. That's how important relationships are to them. If the friendship is good, they'll keep it going.

As a cardinal air sign, Librans are one the most progressive signs. They are natural visionaries who focus on the end result of multiple ideas. They welcome their life's journey with open arms, being fully aware of the ups and downs that come with it. Through their reflection and life experiences, they motivate people to strive for total inner and outer balance, sharing both realistic and hypothetical perspectives to persuade others to reach their full potential. As such, Librans instinctively form stronger partnerships and utilize the art of thought and language to their advantage.

Overall, Librans embody strong leadership and partnership from a mental and physical perspective. They teach other zodiac signs the true meaning of inner and outer balance, the balance of work and pleasure, and how to lead with beauty in the heart, mind, and body.

✷ ☆ ☾

UNEVOLVED LIBRA — VAIN CON ARTIST

Unevolved Librans are vain con artists who use their mental strengths to manipulate the mentally weak into doing what they want. Like unevolved Virgo, the sign before them, they are obsessed with perfection, yet their perfection lies more in superficial beauty and material wealth. Like their unevolved air sibling, Gemini, they've learned that words hold power over people. Like their cardinal cousins, unevolved Aries and Cancer, they've learned to focus selfishly on their own desires. This type of negative behavior usually bleeds into their relationships.

Since their motto is "I balance," unevolved Librans do the opposite and create imbalance in other people's lives. They do this without remorse. In most of their relationships, they scheme ways to take advantage of others and use their words to cheapen and devalue people. Many Librans also have issues with being alone, finding balance and comfort in multiple relationships or back-to-back monogamous relationships. They can be highly co-dependent and will use others as a crutch to boost their self-esteem.

As a cardinal air sign, unevolved Librans will do almost anything to get ahead in life. They can be cold and unemotional yet feign love and interest if it benefits them. They utilize their physical beauty or their gift of charm to seduce others into their web of unrealistic fantasies. They can lie and manipulate to get their way. If they meet someone who is mentally strong, they can become verbally abusive and break their spirit into submission. Needless to say, unevolved Librans do a lot of talking to cover up and deflect their ulterior motives or insecurities, all of which only furthers their selfish ambitions.

✲☆☾

EVOLVED LIBRA – CAPTIVATING INNOVATOR

Evolved Librans are charming and captivating innovators who seek social change and public influence. They've learned from Virgo, the evolved sign before them, to uphold and maintain their strong moral beliefs. They've learned from their air sibling, evolved Gemini, to utilize creative communication for the good of people. They've learned from their cardinal cousins, evolved Aries and Cancer, to lead with strength in heart and honest intent. Because of this, evolved Librans are expressive leaders who push for justice and equality in all aspects of everyone's life.

Since their motto is "I balance," evolved Librans have a full understanding of how to balance work and pleasure. They are strong believers of education and will invest their energy in building themselves up mentally. They see the true beauty of people and use their powers of balance and optimism to bring out a person's full potential. As highly communicative signs, they use colorful, thoughtful words to share their ethical beliefs frequently. They don't believe in silencing their thoughts because they strive for maximum transparency and open communication in everything they do. They, in turn, leave an open floor for everyone else to do the same.

As a cardinal air sign, evolved Librans push for social justice and equality on all levels of society. They know how to motivate and inspire a crowd through words alone, yet they are not afraid to partake in any protests or be the first to act on what they preach. They seek widely acceptable solutions with consideration of those who are most affected by their decisions. This makes them highly competent leaders whose only intent is to bring out the inner beauty of the world and restore faith in humanity.

☀ ☆ ☾

LIBRA MOON

♎ ☽

"I balance what I feel."

Individuals with a Libra Moon handle their emotions by weighing all the pros and cons to every emotional situation, but it depends on other celestial factors. Mixed with fire, they are more philosophical and humorous but can be difficult and overly controlling. Mixed with earth, they are organized and logical yet emotionally detached and calculating. Mixed with air, they're communicative and open-minded but are overly opinionated and too talkative. Mixed with water, they are highly imaginative and romantic but can be clingy or unfaithful.

Emotionally, Libra Moons balance both positive and negative emotions. They are constantly resetting the scales, finding their energy too heavy when it's tilted to one side. When confronted with a sensitive issue, they will weigh every perspective, collecting as much information as possible to make a clear and balanced decision. They also prioritize their relationships with others, so they will be considerate of everyone involved and create resolutions that benefit all parties. However, they can play favorites with people they feel can bring more to the table than others.

Libra Moons are extremely optimistic about life and offer philosophical guidance to all who will listen. They are strong believers that one can manifest negative opportunities if they dwell in their own negativity. Yet, they can be completely dismissive of any negative emotions, wanting to only focus on the good of a situation. This, in turn, creates a lot of emotional indecisiveness. Fortunately, most Libra Moons prefer to minimize confusion by assessing all emotions through a masterful balancing act like a tightrope walker.

☀ ☆ ☽

LIBRA ENERGY IN OTHER PLACEMENTS

LIBRA ASCENDANT (RISING)

♎ AC

"I balance myself."

Libra Risings project a sense of unity, justice, beauty, femininity, charm, and grace in everything they do. Upon first impression, they always have a warm and friendly smile. Although they are open to new people, they remain distant as if they are in a different world mentally.

When it comes to physical appearance, Libra Risings love to feel beautiful and are not against cosmetic surgery to obtain a desired look. They also love to adorn themselves with jewelry, and how they dress is usually based on who they're trying to impress or mirror, even if it's just themselves.

LIBRA MIDHEAVEN (MC)

♎ MC

"I balance my career."

Libra Midheavens pursue careers that give them space to talk and persuade freely. They are highly adept in negotiating and selling, so they will naturally excel in rewarding, commission-based careers or businesses. They thrive in any space where they can talk and make money or sell and promote a certain lifestyle while making money. They're also good at team leadership.

Libra Midheavens make balancing work and pleasure look effortless, yet underneath, they are burdened by it. It can be challenging for them to find real friends, as their high status and money can attract the wrong types of people.

LIBRA MERCURY

♎ ☿

"I balance my thoughts."

Libra Mercurians balance their thoughts and ideas by weighing all sides of any and every situation. They are very thoughtful and prolific, and they prefer to take an unbiased perspective to provide more rational and perfectly weighed insights. However, they can also be extremely indecisive, especially if their judgments are clouded by emotions.

The majority of Libra Mercurians are logical, visual, and verbal learners. They love learning about anything and anyone and are adept at finding solutions to complicated situations. They are also the voice of reason and will always stand up for someone who is afraid to express themselves.

LIBRA VENUS

♎ ♀

"I balance love."

Libra Venusians love long-term, committed relationships and partnerships, as they take them seriously and are devoted to growing and nurturing them. They are the most balanced when they have a strong support system of friends and family who love and appreciate them. They are also highly romantic and generous and often surprise loved ones with thoughtful gifts.

Libra Venusians have magnetic personalities and attract different types of lovers throughout their lifetime. Though they may entertain them temporarily, they are always looking for someone to balance their mind and heart. They are at their best with someone who is highly optimistic, ambitious, intelligent, and they are capable of getting along with everyone.

☼☆☾

LIBRA MARS

♎ ♂

"I balance physical power."

Libra Martians balance power through communication, persuasion, mental thought, and physical appearance. They believe that true power requires loyal followers, so they work hard on themselves to be as influential as possible. They can also be extremely aggressive and argumentative, especially since they are highly protective over their beliefs and the people they care for.

Libra Martians understand that beauty helps when reaching certain heights of your career. They believe it makes them more powerful, relatable, and likeable. They may not always gravitate toward physical exercise to obtain their desired figure; instead, most will opt for cosmetic surgery or anything else that gives them fast or instant physical results.

LIBRA JUPITER

♎ ♃

"I balance expansion."

Libra Jupiterians are highly philosophical individuals who see expansion in everyone and everything, especially when it comes to fame and fortune. They can form multiple partnerships to obtain the beauty and wealth they desire. However, these partnerships are not always made in good faith.

Regardless, it's effortless for Libra Jupiterians to accumulate their wealth, as they possess high faith in their skills and talents and people are naturally attracted to them. Therefore, they balance expansion through the use of others they attract. They must then decide if they'll become the used, the useful, or the user. It's up to them to judge which side of the scale tips where.

✸ ☆ ☽

LIBRA SATURN

♎ ♄

"I balance restriction."

Libra Saturnians balance hard work and discipline with ultimate pleasure and relaxation. They can have great spurts of energy that inspire them to work all day and night, yet they can wake up another day and lose all momentum, finding it hard to get back in the zone. They must develop a routine that works with their energy, otherwise they will become completely overwhelmed.

The scales of productive judgments weigh heavy on Libra Saturnians' minds, as they feel the pressure to succeed daily. This can create a lot of mental anxiety and procrastination if they do not learn how to balance work and play. Fortunately, the majority of them are ambitious and intelligent enough to pursue both. They work hard to play hard and vice versa.

LIBRA URANUS

♎ ♅

"I balance change."

Libra Uranians seek justice, fairness, quality, and equality in everything and everyone. They play judge and jury with much ease, and they genuinely believe that people can be rehabilitated from their past mistakes. They feel that change is necessary and voluntary.

Libra Uranians fight for causes that create equality, especially in judicial systems. Many of them become lawyers because they feel so strongly about it, or they may join advocacy groups, where they become the voice for the unheard. Regardless of what they choose, they become leaders of the free world and passionately fight for the balance or rebalance of humanity.

☼ ☆ ☾

Libra Neptune

♎ ♆

"I balance spirituality."

Libra Neptunians have a deep connection with divine femininity. They are completely secure with their sexuality and do not see a division between masculinity and femininity; however, the majority seek to rebalance feminine power in themselves and others. Thus, they seek soul comfort in all things that praise and honor women, fertility, or sisterhood.

Libra Neptunians seek to restore old traditions with modern twists, as they believe there can be a balance between both worlds. They also often join large communities where they are allowed to vocalize their thoughts and feelings without pre-judgment, which usually consists of sister-like members or men who honor, worship, and appreciate matriarchy or women leadership.

Libra Pluto

♎ ♇

"I balance evolution."

Libra Plutonians believe that evolution is formulated when there is an equal union of femininity and masculinity, all of which they strive to balance. During their lifetime, they'll undergo many relationships and commitments that will help enrich, enlighten, and rebalance their perspectives of true unity.

Libra Plutonians take relationships very seriously, and they believe that every person has a role and duty to balance each other's weaknesses. Many devote themselves to marriage and partnerships, believing that life is not fully lived until they have the perfect union. As true romantics, they want to walk away into the next lifetime with someone dedicated to eternal marriage.

✹ ☆ ☾

SCORPIO

Plutonian Scorpion

♏

October 23 – November 21
Element: Water
Modality: Fixed
Ruling Planet: Pluto
Co-Ruling Planet: Mars
Symbol: The Scorpion
Motto: I Desire

SCORPIO SUN

♏ ☉

"I desire."

Scorpio is a fixed water sign, guided by the Scorpion, ruled by Pluto, and co-ruled by Mars. Mars is a planet Scorpio shares with Aries. As the eighth star child, second water sign, and third fixed sign, Scorpios are the type to form deeper emotional and spiritual attachments with everything and everybody. Unlike Taurus and Leo, their fixed cousins who are fixated on present life, Scorpios are fixated on the afterlife, the spiritual realm. They are true believers that death is a part of life that must be accepted for a living soul to reach full enlightenment.

Like their water sibling, Cancer, they are extremely sensitive and intuitive individuals who value and honor emotions and seek strong soul connections. Unlike Cancer, though, they are not as compassionate or empathetic, and they believe that controlling and reflecting on their emotions is much more powerful than expressing them. They also take a higher spiritual approach to life, believing there is a divine reason for everything. As such, the universe has blessed them with the ability to channel spiritual connections with others, becoming the true seekers of soul growth and deliverers of soul karma.

As the Plutonian Scorpion, they are known as the psychics of the zodiac. They possess a strong connection with their third eye, using their extremely strong intuition to make lifelong decisions. This is especially true when they reach their evolved form. With Pluto's influence, Scorpios are constantly transforming themselves internally, and they will regenerate (refresh) their energy when they feel heavy or drained. They also think of death constantly, which proves to be a huge motivating factor in their lives.

✸ ✭ ☾

Scorpios are focused on the soul and how to acquire good karmic value as they prepare for the next lifetime. They are not judgmental per se, but they do hold people's souls accountable based on their actions. Depending on the rest of their planetary placements, they can dive deeper into the true meaning of spirituality and its attachment to karma, but if they are not seekers of the soul, they will be seekers of material desires. It's usually one or the other.

Scorpios are co-ruled by Mars, a planet shared with Aries, and like Aries, Scorpios are seething with wildfire. However, unlike Aries, they tend to internalize it. Still, Scorpios can be as vicious and spiteful as their stinger. This boiling rage usually only comes out when they are provoked or if a situation becomes emotionally charged or trying. Though they can be calm on the outside, underneath they will be thinking of dangerous tactics, which can manifest into vengeance and self-righteousness.

With Mars influencing their aggression, discipline, focus, and dominance, Scorpios love the thrill of a good challenge, whether it's physical, mental, or emotional. It's usually all of the above. They may never express their motives out loud, but they are always predicting their next move in life. Mixed with their Plutonian energy, they are also very cautious when trusting new people. It can take years for them to feel comfortable with someone unless they feel a soul connection. It's not a good idea to make these signs angry or betray their trust and loyalty, as they can hold a grudge for eternity, a trait learned from their fixed cousins, Leo and Taurus.

Scorpios are known for embracing their sexuality, which is a trait that stems from Mars as their co-ruling planet. Thus, you can find many as adult entertainers, believing that sexuality and pleasure can be a healing experience. This doesn't mean they go around wanting to have sex with anybody they see. In fact, they are known to withhold sex and pleasure if they don't feel a soul connection with their partner or potential partner.

Instinctually, Scorpios possess strong self-awareness and are highly alert

☀☆☾

to their surroundings. They observe with the intent to understand things and are able to see people's true value and worth, a trait adopted from the sign before them, Libra. Since Scorpios are so perceptive, they do not take things or people at face value and aren't the gullible types. They are just as patient and tolerant as their fixed cousin, Taurus, and will allow people's true colors to show on their own, no matter how long it takes. They also do not reveal their true colors right away and are very selective when trusting someone.

If Scorpios feel that something is off, especially in their relationship, they will become a super detective and uncover all of the lies and deceit (if any). It would be wise not to undermine their investigative techniques, as they can become obsessed with their research. If and when they do find something, they will drain your soul of all life and, like Cancer, they will overwhelm you with a surge of intense emotions. Go too far and they will completely cut you off in this lifetime and the next.

The symbol of Scorpio is the Scorpion. Their eyes are their stingers, which they are famously known for. They are strong believers that the eyes are the windows to the soul. Upon first impression, they subconsciously search for depth behind a person's physical appearance. Their stare is also described as intimidating even if they don't have the physique to match, and it's because they possess the darkest energy in the zodiac, which can be felt by anybody they look at. However, this doesn't always mean they live in darkness; it means that they know how to embrace their shadow side and believe light and dark energy are married. Thus, it's equally important to accept both.

Scorpios are extremely intense and possess a higher sensitivity to everything and everyone. Emotional manipulation is not out of the realm of possibilities for them. They master this at an early age and will use it to unveil or twist the truth. They believe that if they can get people to their vulnerable state, they are more receptive to the messages given to them, even if they're lies. Ultimately, it's their understanding of karma that decides whether they

☼ ☆ ☾

use this superpower for good or evil.

As intense as they are, Scorpios are just as intensely affectionate with their loved one. Since they are capable of regenerating their own energy, they are the only zodiac sign that will give their loved one all of their energy when they feel down or drained. Although they may not always vocalize how they feel, if someone they love needs encouragement, they will be there to give a powerful speech that uplifts their soul. They will fight for their honor should anyone talk about them behind their back. They will go to great lengths to prove how much they care by giving and doing things that hold more meaning to someone's life.

Scorpio's motto is "I desire." Their life's challenge is their powerful intuition, which can be used to manipulate others for the sake of vengeance and control. Scorpios also strongly desire to fill any dark voids in their life; whether they fill this void with material wealth or emotional wealth is up to them. They can struggle with material desires and superficial possessions, habits passed down from their fixed cousins. This can cloud their intuition, making them believe their karmic worth is based on what they collect. To overcome this, they must learn the true meaning of karma, how to wield their intuition for the good of others, and how to accept that possessions do not hold any spiritual meaning in the afterlife.

Scorpios are naturally possessive, which can be a good or bad thing, as they are one of the most loyal and protective signs of the zodiac. Still, their higher sensitivity doesn't allow them to emotionally detach very easily. They are known to obsess and reflect on their desires constantly, using their psychic intuition to know whether or not something desires them back. When they latch onto their desires, they pursue it with intense energy and dedication. Others may become envious of this, as Scorpios often pursue predictions that manifest much of their success and wealth.

As a fixed water sign, Scorpios are fixated on—you guessed it—the

✸☆☾

afterlife. If Librans are considered the judges of character, then Scorpios are the judges of souls. They have a very strong connection with the spiritual realm, which is where their intuition lies. Many believe in reincarnation and are motivated by death, which they feel creates a stronger sense of urgency. Thus, they work even harder to create a more meaningful existence. Scorpios can also be intensely religious or spiritual. Spiritual entities can be a strong benefactor in their lives, and you will find many Scorpios who take their spirituality seriously, becoming a channel for any kind of spiritual wellness, such as priests, witches, spiritual teachers, energy workers, psychic mediums, astrologers, or anything that has to do with souls or spirits.

Scorpios are an enigma. They value silence in ways that other zodiac signs do not. This is their secret of success. When alone, they are able to recharge their energy and transform their souls into a higher state of enlightenment. They are fixated on having secrecy, extreme privacy, and emotional control and discipline. The majority of them have hidden talents and skills and don't feel the need to share them. They love having and holding secrets, even yours. To them, it's a sign of great discipline and independence to have something all to yourself. It's also a sign of loyalty and devotion to the people they love.

If you betray them by exposing any of their secrets, the majority won't stoop to anybody's low levels and will continue to harbor your secrets; plus, you're now dead to them, so none of what you did exists. It's also just bad karma that they don't want to carry or be burdened by later.

Overall, Scorpios embody soul and karma. They are the true masters of manifestation and spirituality. They achieve this with the ability of psychic intuition, which is a trait that is often overlooked. They teach other zodiac signs to be mindful of their actions, keeping them focused on their soul's purpose in this lifetime and the next.

✲ ☆ ☾

UNEVOLVED SCORPIO – VENGEFUL MANIPULATOR

Unevolved Scorpios curse eternal damnation on every soul that has ever hurt them. They are vengeful manipulators who find it difficult to overcome their traumas, so they project their insecurities, jealousy, and bitterness onto others. From Libra, the unevolved sign before them, they learned that manipulation is the key to success. From their unevolved water sibling, Cancer, they learned that uncontrolled emotions leave a person vulnerable and weak. From their unevolved fixed cousins Taurus and Leo, they've adopted self-preservation and eternal grudges.

Since their motto is "I desire," unevolved Scorpios have uncontrolled desires and malicious intentions, and are intensely jealous and possessive. They can also become overly obsessed with the object of their desire. Unwilling to take no for an answer and driven by madness, they can go above and beyond in stalking or seducing their obsession with colorful promises, only to trap them in an emotionally abusive relationship. They don't see anything wrong with it either and will guilt-trip and gaslight people into staying.

As a fixed water sign, unevolved Scorpios are fixated on their own sick fantasies. They can have severe trust issues, paranoid that people have ulterior motives. They take advantage of silence and listen with the intent to collect ammo on people just in case they need to expose them. They are known to blackmail people and can play cruel emotional games to feel a sense of power over people. If you're on their blacklist, they will obsessively work to hurt you, as they possess a delusional sense of self-righteousness and believe they can play God and become someone else's karma.

✷☆☾

EVOLVED SCORPIO – INTUITIVE PSYCHIC

Evolved Scorpios are intuitive psychics who utilize their spiritual senses to enlighten and empower others. They've learned from Libra, the evolved sign before them, to see the true beauty in people. They've been taught by their evolved water sibling, Cancer, to control and express their emotions in a healthy manner. They've been taught by their evolved fixed cousins Taurus and Leo to hold onto their true beliefs without imposing them on others. Due to this, evolved Scorpios are spiritual mentors who encourage signs to awaken their souls and work toward spiritual enlightenment independently.

Since their motto is "I desire," evolved Scorpios desire soul connections with everything and everyone. Their strong intuition is a superpower they use to maneuver through life's obstacles. They make decisions based on energy and how they feel. Regardless of the outcome, evolved Scorpios take everything as a soul lesson. They possess strong spiritual beliefs, believing there is a reason for every situation and every person who enters or exits their life. They are faithful and loyal to those they love, always offering spiritual insights when a loved one is feeling energetically drained.

As a fixed water sign, evolved Scorpios are fixated on how to utilize their third eye, which provides karmic insights (good and bad). They are highly private signs that internalize their emotions and find energetic and emotional release in deep reflection and meditation. As highly independent signs, they find solace and peace in isolation and are able to resolve situations through spiritual justification. They are sensitive and peaceful souls who always think of the future and are motivated to leave something behind for those who seek the true meaning of spirituality and the afterlife.

☀ ☆ ☾

SCORPIO MOON

♏ ☽

"I desire what I feel."

Individuals with a Scorpio Moon handle their emotions using their strong intuition and justify them through karma, but it depends on other celestial factors. Mixed with fire, they are decisive and instinctual, but they can be intensely controlling and assertive. Mixed with earth, they are realistic and perceptive, but they are more skeptical and emotionally guarded. Mixed with air, they are inventive and prolific, yet they can be detached from reality and paranoid. Mixed with water, they are more intuitive and mysterious but are more possessive and jealous.

Emotionally, Scorpio Moons lead their hearts with strong intuition and a clearer perception of spirituality. They often justify emotional situations as either karmic punishment or divine blessings. They usually do not stray from their intuition, especially when they are feeling out a person's intentions. If they are unsure of a person's intent, they will patiently observe their actions and words before making a final judge of their character. They are known to guard their vulnerability well, finding privacy and solitude more peaceful, and can even enjoy possessing others' secrets.

Scorpio Moons are emotionally intense and are either-or types of people. They need to feel a soul connection with others to feel safe. They have strong emotional desires that require a lot of trust to reveal them. They tend to internalize a lot of their feelings, often obsessing over them in private. Since darkness is their natural habitat, Scorpio Moons are fully aware that people hide behind their light façade, where true colors can only be revealed in the dark, the only space where they trust what they feel and sense.

✺ ✫ ☾

SCORPIO ENERGY IN OTHER PLACEMENTS

SCORPIO ASCENDANT (RISING)

♏ AC

"I desire myself."

Scorpio Risings project a sense of sincerity, allure, secrecy, and intimacy in everything they do. Upon first impression, they can come off emotionally unbothered or intense. With their high sensitivity, they are very cautious when meeting new people, and stranger danger is a thing for them, so although they may be cordial, they often keep to themselves until they are comfortable.

When it comes to physical appearance, they often dress classy or dress to impress or be desirable. However, the more secretive types will invest in more lingerie or underwear, wearing it under very conservative styles, as they prefer a more hidden type of sex appeal.

SCORPIO MIDHEAVEN (MC)

♏ MC

"I desire my career."

Scorpio Midheavens pursue strict, challenging, yet stable careers, or they choose careers that allow them to heal people emotionally or spiritually. They like a sense of emotional freedom and extreme independence, so they work best when they're unsupervised with mutual trust and loyalty.

Scorpio Midheavens are highly focused and resilient, and they excel in intensely energized careers. They can also become obsessed and possessive of their work, investing a lot of their energy into perfecting masterpieces.

SCORPIO MERCURY

♏ ☿

"I desire what I think."

Scorpio Mercurians are bright, sharp, and intuitive. They can be extremely private, sensitive, and possessive of their thoughts and beliefs, having many hidden secrets, talents, and skills that they keep to themselves. They can have many hidden obsessions that turn into massive collections of stuff, and they do not easily detach themselves from it.

The majority of Scorpio Mercurians are visual, auditory, and solitary learners. They can absorb an intense amount of data when they're alone and in the zone. They often have intense thoughts and desires, strong likes and dislikes, and a majority rely on their intuition to feel their way around. They are also fascinated by death, spirits, spirituality, the occult, or religion.

SCORPIO VENUS

♏ ♀

"I desire love."

Scorpio Venusians do not trust every easily and are cautious and selective of people they let in. However, they have such a hypnotic allure that people are naturally attracted to them, even when they're trying. Many detest unwanted attention and are not afraid to get hostile if they need space.

Scorpio Venusians take love and relationships very personal. They don't love easily, as they are not the type to settle for anybody less than a soulmate. They desire nothing else. They can withhold any feelings or sex, as they feel it takes much trust to become vulnerable or intimate. Once they're committed, they're intensely affectionate, possessive, loyal, and faithful to their lover.

✹ ☆ ☾

SCORPIO MARS

♏ ♂

"I desire physical power."

Scorpio Martians are intense and intimidating, and they like it that way. They desire physical power in all aspects of their lives, and many of them use seduction or sexual dominance to get it. Manipulation and insinuation are also not out of the realm of possibilities since it comes so naturally to them.

Fortunately, the majority of Scorpio Martians would rather be direct with what they want. Their unstoppable energy, high perseverance, and strong intuition harbor their true power. Inevitably, they learn that there is nothing they cannot manifest, so they spend their lifetime collecting material possessions and wealth that showcases how powerful they've become.

SCORPIO JUPITER

♏ ♃

"I desire expansion."

Scorpio Jupiterians desire soul and karmic expansion. They have a strong connection to the spiritual realm, and they believe there is a divine reason for everything that happens in life (good or bad). Much of their expansion is based in internalized reflections of life and death, and because they believe in karma, they are more inspired to stay on the path of good.

Scorpio Jupiterians are manifestors of spiritual wealth, energy awareness, and spiritual knowledge, which, to them, is more desirable than anything or anyone superficial. They seek true enlightenment of the mind, heart, and soul and will travel to the ends of the world to find revelations in their life. This, in turn, helps to keep their soul weightless and optimistic.

☀ ☆ ☾

Scorpio Saturn

♏ ♄

"I desire restriction."

Scorpio Saturnians are emotionally and physically strict on themselves, especially when it comes to things or people they care about. The majority are family-oriented and value time spent with loved ones, finding it hard to be apart from them for long periods of time. They can also be very protective when they are parents, becoming very involved in their children's lives and laying out strict rules to shelter them from danger.

Scorpio Saturnians are intensely ambitious and invest a lot of their energy in their careers. It can be hard for them to part with their money or wealth. They are also extremely responsible, so control and prevention of temptation or distractions will be important to their overall success and stability.

Scorpio Uranus

♏ ♅

"I desire change."

Scorpio Uranians find it challenging to get involved in their communities because they do not like to be in emotionally charged situations, especially ones that lack stable leadership. It can take a personal traumatic situation for them to join a cause or become an advocate. They have to feel it to fight for it. Otherwise, they prefer to be isolated and away from anything they have not felt, seen, or experienced.

Although Scorpio Uranians desire change and intensely fight for justice, they possess a more self-righteous stance in it and would rather make positive changes in themselves so they are not part of society's bigger problem.

☀ ☆ ☽

SCORPIO NEPTUNE

♏ ♆

"I desire spirituality."

Scorpio Neptunians are extremely spiritual signs and take their spiritual wellness very seriously. They will invest a lot of time and energy in learning how to manage their thoughts and actions because they are heavy believers of karma. The majority will intentionally make good and honest decisions based on spiritual consequences. They desire nothing more than to be enlightened by good deeds and empowered by good karma.

Scorpio Neptunians are fascinated by the afterlife and the supernatural. The majority of them possess psychic medium gifts and use them to predict events or channel messages from the spiritual realm. If they are strictly religious, they will be heavily involved and devoted to church activities.

SCORPIO PLUTO

♏ ♇

"I desire evolution."

Scorpio Plutonians are true manifestors of emotional evolution. They seek richness of the soul. During their lifetime, they will undergo intense spiritual and emotional transformations. They naturally have regenerative energy, so they are constantly refreshing and reinventing their outlooks on life.

Scorpio Plutonians are highly progressive and productive when working on themselves. They are driven to accomplish and learn as much as they can before their time runs out. This includes diving deep into work, money, and lots of pleasure. Thus, their goal in one lifetime is to absorb every meaningful moment so they can carry it into the next.

☀ ☆ ☾

SAGITTARIUS

Jupiterian Centaur

November 22 – December 21
Element: Fire
Modality: Mutable
Ruling Planet: Jupiter
Symbol: The Archer/Centaur
Motto: I See

☼☆☾

SAGITTARIUS SUN

"I see."

Sagittarius is a mutable fire dual sign, guided by the Centaur and ruled by Jupiter. It shares this planet with its mutable cousin Pisces. As the ninth star child, last fire sign, and third mutable sign, Sagittarians are the mindful, sometimes mindless, philosophical archers and gamblers of the zodiac. Like their fire siblings, Aries and Leo, they are aggressive, passionate, impulsive, and impatient. Unlike their fire siblings, they are more reasonable, expressive, and outspoken; their opinions and ideas shoot out in a hail of arrows. Like their mutable cousins, Gemini and Virgo, they believe in mental awareness and fulfillment. Unlike their mutable cousins, they do not focus on the smaller details, preferring to always see the bigger picture.

Like Scorpio, the sign before them, Sagittarians prefer to reflect before they react. Unlike Scorpio, however, Sagittarians have instant reflexes and quick-witted insights. Due to this, the universe has blessed them with alertness and hunter's hindsight, allowing them to aim their arrows of truth, dreams, hopes, and philosophies into the atmosphere with more precision and faith.

As the Jupiterian Centaur, Sagittarians base most of their decisions on luck and faith. Being ruled by the biggest planet of the solar system also has major benefits. With Jupiter's guidance, Sagittarians take negative experiences and philosophize them into positive learning experiences. They have the gift of seeing situations with great tact and strategy, pointing their arrows with true aim and confidence that it will pierce the root of the issue. Since they are the playful type, shooting their arrows can also be more of a sport or a test of their mental and physical strengths rather than anything serious. They are forever

✦ ✩ ☾

hunting down greater life experiences, choosing never to settle or fully commit until they find something that provides a long-term challenge or greater fortune.

With Jupiter's guidance, Sagittarians seek optimism and transparency in everything and everyone, and the faith they have in themselves is unlike any other sign. Communication will also be extremely important to them, as they want to discover the ins and outs of any given topic. Since they always stand by their truth, they absolutely hate when someone makes false accusations on their character. Like Scorpio, the sign before them, they abhor lies of any kind and will uncover the truth obsessively. Should a false accusation come about, Sagittarians will defend themselves until they die, and they would rather die than live with a lie.

Sagittarians have a strong connection with the universe. You will find many Sagittarians who have trouble sleeping at night because they are always dreaming of reaching the stars (literally or figuratively). With so many thoughts racing around their horse track, Sagittarians are constantly galloping toward the finish line. They want to know what it feels like to win in life, and this feeling is only heightened by Jupiter's exuberant energy.

As creative and resourceful individuals, Sagittarians can turn nothing into something. Thanks to Jupiter, they have massive amounts of energy and drive to tackle just about any project they choose. Because of Jupiter's endless supply of self-improvement and superior knowledge, most are born with a strong creative talent or two and can master any skill they pick up. However, they often shoot their energy into multiple directions, and indecisiveness and procrastination can hinder their progression. Since commitment is also not their greatest ally, they can shoot their arrows and abandon them at will if something or someone else offers a greater reward or challenge.

To Sagittarians, commitment and restraint is like taming a wild horse. They're always ready to kick their way to freedom, and they absolutely abhor

✦☆☾

domestication, preferring to live unsaddled and unridden. Many arguments happen when they feel fenced in, so it's good to remember that they require space to roam and experience life without constraints or high expectations. If they're unbound, they're bubbly and carefree. Needless to say, the majority of them prioritize movement and travel, even if it's forced on them. If they cannot afford to travel or are forced to stay put, they will escape into their greater imagination and create stories that offer a traveling experience.

The Sagittarius' symbol is the Centaur. As a dual sign, they are half-human and half-beast (horse). The horse side possesses dark energy, while the human side possesses light energy. Their horse side is rooted in the physical realm, which provides them with greater physical strength and stamina, whereas their human side provides them with wisdom and intellect to see past the horizon. Because of their duality, they feel strongly about equality in everything and everyone. Both sides give them incredible foresight, a trait also given to them by the sign before them, Scorpio. Though they value direction and purpose, they are not always thinking of present times. They can get stuck in their future goals and dreams, never allowing their hooves to set a realistic path toward it. Fortunately, most Sagittarians do not like mental confusion, so they will reset their purpose when they feel they've lost their direction.

As the centaur, Sagittarians love wild experiences. They can party like there's no tomorrow, and they can throw a grand party where anything goes. If they're feeling lucky, they'll gamble it in casinos or a thrilling game of poker. Even if they lose money, they still have faith that they'll get it all back. This can be a double-edged sword if they're not careful, as they can gamble all their savings for instant gratification. Fortunately, most are aware of their addictive behaviors and will practice prevention by riding far away from anything or anyone they have no willpower to fight.

Since Sagittarians are mainly focused on their mental, physical, and spiritual growth, they can be inconsiderate to other people's emotions. Like

✷ ☆ ☾

their fire siblings, they can be boastful, arrogant, and self-centered. However, they believe in resolving issues right away and don't like to dwell in tension. So if you have an issue, they are not too proud to apologize and acknowledge any hurt or wrongdoing. They also feel that if they apologize, you should take it and never bring it up again. This can come off as dismissive, but they believe that time is more valuable when you're moving forward.

Sagittarians have an infectious laugh and enjoy entertaining others with clever sarcasm and humor. They see the light in every situation, a trait given to them by their fire sibling, Aries; and they always try to laugh everything off even if it hurts. They also find it hard to stay angry for too long, but if they are angry, they unleash it as fast as a gunshot to the heart. They aim to hurt, but they'll try not to kill you. It's always just enough pain to disable you until they can get the hell out of there. Escape plans for life.

Sagittarians' motto is "I see." Their life's challenge is gambling with luck, love, and life. Their high co-dependence on faith and hope can lead them down dark paths if they're not fully alert. Unfortunately, their rebellious horse side causes them to push past their limitations, relying on luck to catch them if they fall. Fortunately for them, though, luck is their greatest ally, thanks to Jupiter. This planet can also teach the biggest and harshest lessons to those who take advantage of it. This type of mentality can make them feel invincible, and because they focus too much on the future, they can push their luck until it runs dry. To overcome this, they must learn that life is more about greater strategy and tact than impulsive risk-taking.

Because Sagittarians are gifted with sight, they become seekers of truth and honesty. The power of words and optimistic ideals are something they pride themselves in. They believe in vocalizing and expressing their honest insights with the world, though sometimes their honesty can be too brutal for people to accept. Sagittarians love to share their experiences through animated storytelling, which is a special talent they have. Philosophy will also become

✵ ☆ ☾

a priority for them, as they like to justify their experiences through higher thought and deeper reflection, and they will share their philosophical insights to uplift and empower others.

Sagittarians love to develop and expand their strengths and talents, even if those talents are not always used for the greater good, meaning they can be reckless with their intentions and intelligence, gambling their luck and their talents in criminal activities. Yet, regardless of whether they have good or bad intentions, they are always hustling and working toward reaching their full potential and possessing high faith in their own abilities (good or bad).

As a mutable fire sign, Sagittarians constantly adapt to their surroundings. Like their mutable cousins, Gemini and Virgo, they are witty and intelligent, possessing fast reflexes and instincts to solve issues as they arise. Unlike their mutable cousins, though, they don't get caught up in things they cannot or do not care to control. As free-spirited travelers of the mind and body, they prefer to go with what is most flexible. This isn't to say that they won't do hard work; they just prefer the option of choosing it rather than being forced into it. They must also feel extremely passionate about a subject to commit to it.

Freedom to choose and roam is everything to a Sagittarius. They are extremely independent. Like their mutable cousins, they are curious students who take their education and careers very seriously. Most prefer self-education rather than organized education because it's less confining. Since they can adapt and excel in almost any flexible and challenging career, you will find many who are freelancers, novelists, journalists, pro gamblers, pro athletes, or any career that involves freedom to do what they want in any place they dream of moving or traveling to.

Overall, Sagittarians embody luck, philosophy, and vision. They are built for truth in mind, heart, and spirit. They teach other signs to use their physical and mental strengths to elevate themselves past the horizons, reaching places nobody has ever dared to go before.

☼ ☆ ☾

UNEVOLVED SAGITTARIUS – RECKLESS GAMBLER

Unevolved Sagittarians are reckless gamblers who find it very difficult to commit to anything or anybody. They have no self-control, only doing what they feel like at any given moment. They learned from the unevolved sign before them, Scorpio, that pleasure and desires are a priority in fulfilling happiness. From their unevolved fire siblings, Aries and Leo, they learned that aggression and power is more important than forming long-lasting relationships. From their unevolved mutable cousins, Gemini and Virgo, they learned not to get distracted by thoughts, dismissing all reason and logic to pursue only what fulfills their ginormous ego.

Since their motto is "I see," unevolved Sagittarians only see and believe in their perspectives, even if their views are exaggerated or unrealistic. They are known to invent experiences to alter their way of life or prove a baseless point. They have permanent hoof-in-mouth disease, always preaching things even they cannot live up to. They say things without consideration of others, then try to justify any hurt feelings with unreasonable philosophies that only benefit them. They can also be boastful and arrogant, always saying things that make them appear more superior than others.

As a mutable fire sign, unevolved Sagittarians do not feel the need to set goals or make commitments. They are party-hard animals with roving eyes who wander around aimlessly, and they are known to break obligations and promises without remorse. Most of their traveling consists of searching for escape routes from any major responsibility. If they're not careful, their careless and reckless gambling in life can lead them into dark, even criminal, paths where their luck runs out as fast as their mouth.

✵ ✩ ☾

EVOLVED SAGITTARIUS — ENLIGHTENED TRAVELER

Evolved Sagittarians are enlightened travelers who philosophize the meaning of life and the experiences that come with it. They've been taught by the evolved sign before them, Scorpio, to leave something behind after death. They've been taught by their evolved fire siblings, Aries and Leo, to pursue their greatest passions fearlessly while alive. And they've been taught by their evolved mutable cousins, Gemini and Virgo, to be adaptable and think freely without restraint. Due to this, evolved Sagittarians are free-spirited explorers who pursue truth and deeper meaning in all aspects of life.

Since their motto is "I see," evolved Sagittarians are voyagers of the mind, heart, and soul. They yearn to see and experience the world in any way they can, even if they can't afford to do so. To them, the journey is more important than the money invested. Wherever they go, they soak in every opportunity to learn and create. They are always up for any challenge, having high faith in themselves and their abilities to overcome any obstacle. They see luck more as blessings for their good deeds and good karma. They also prefer to see situations from a philosophical perspective, believing there's always a deeper truth for everything and everyone to discover.

As a mutable fire sign, evolved Sagittarians are highly adaptable and often strategize ways to educate, experience, and elevate themselves. This type of mentality allows them to pursue long-term spiritual journeys where they become truly enlightened and energetically free. Wherever they travel, they respect and honor culture, sacred spaces, and boundaries, adapting to the world as they experience it. They often leave behind trails of inspirational stories of self-discovery for future travelers of the mind, heart, and spirit.

✹ ☆ ☾

SAGITTARIUS MOON

♐ ☽

"I see what I feel."

Individuals with a Sagittarius Moon process their emotions through reason and philosophical thought, but it depends on other celestial factors. Mixed with fire, they are extremely driven and ambitious but can be more reckless and boastful. Mixed with earth, they are strategic and resourceful yet lack compassion and are arrogant. Mixed with air, they are open-minded and free-spirited but non-committed and combative. Mixed with water, they are wise and spiritual but can be overbearing and insecure.

Emotionally, Sagittarius Moons prefer to see the bright side of every issue but will fight to the death if someone accuses them of something they didn't do. They live by honesty and transparency, so lying is a huge trigger for them. They are straightforward types who like to shoot their arrows of truth and heart one topic at a time. Although they can sympathize with people, they also tend to keep emotions off their radar. Should someone stray into the realm of irrelevant emotions, they will become frustrated and either ride away never to be seen again or emotionally snap into the point of no return.

Sagittarius Moons tend to live day by day as if it's their last, so they aren't really paying attention to how their actions affect others. If they've wronged someone, they will always try to make it right because they hate to feel guilt and regret. Sagittarius Moons are mostly focused on how to overcome themselves and find truth in why they feel what they feel. With bow in hand, their philosophical mindset seeks out far destinations that target enlightenment and emotional freedom. Should someone try to silence or invalidate their feelings, they will buck until they let go.

✴ ☆ ☾

SAGITTARIUS ENERGY IN OTHER PLACEMENTS

SAGITTARIUS ASCENDANT (RISING)

♐ AC

"I see who I am."

Sagittarius Risings project tact, spontaneity, charisma, free-spiritedness, and foresight in everything they do. Upon first impression, they are direct, humorous, and sarcastic. They may even be aggressive and impersonal, but it depends on the rest of their cosmic aspects. If they're on a mission to get shit done, they will be hyper-focused on hitting targets and nothing else.

When it comes to physical appearance, they are more tomboyish and like to dress for comfort. They may like a few flashy things, but they like to keep it simple and travel-safe. Most carry bags with everything they need.

SAGITTARIUS MIDHEAVEN (MC)

♐ MC

"I see my career."

Sagittarius Midheavens need to feel passionate about their job to keep it. They also need to have a flexible schedule that allows them space to roam. They're best in careers that are never routine and are constantly giving them new challenges to pursue. Anything strict or confining will cause them to be out the door in the blink of an eye.

Sagittarius Midheavens are ambitious racehorses who just want to win in life. Once they set their sight on a career they love, they become a rocket ship, racing faster and blasting further than any other sign.

SAGITTARIUS MERCURY

↗ ☿

"I see what I think."

Sagittarius Mercurians always see the cup half full. They are optimistic, lively, humorous, sarcastic, and bubbly, a self-improving, carefree traveler who always envisions their future with confidence, hope, and faith in their abilities to succeed. They have a huge mouthpiece on them, though, and you will find many who love to talk and share their explicit stories unfiltered.

Sagittarius Mercurians are visual, physical, and verbal learners. They need to see it, write it, talk about it, and experience it in order to adopt it. With their flexible mindset, they are always willing to try something once, no matter the consequence. This can get them into trouble if they gamble too much on luck.

SAGITTARIUS VENUS

↗ ♀

"I see love."

Sagittarius Venusians see love as a sport, where the top contender is one who gives them enough of a challenge to stay put. They categorize people into family, friend, lover, or soulmate. Once you're in a category, you most likely will never move from it. They're also the type who don't feel a need to be too close to family, preferring to love them from a distance.

When Sagittarius Venusians do fall in love, it's as if Cupid himself came down, caught them off guard, and shot them in the heart. Once their heart is tamed, they submit to their forever jockey and will ride with them to the ends of the world. They are at their best with someone who is willing to explore mentally and physically without limitations, expectations, or restraints.

☀ ☆ ☾

SAGITTARIUS MARS

↗ ♂

"I see physical power."

Sagittarius Martians are passionate about their physical prowess, placing much focus on their legs and arms. Exercise will be important in their life as it provides them with the energy and stamina to keep running, literally and figuratively. With their hooves ready, they race through life, their eyes set on winning and rewarding themselves. Their energy is always ready to go, never willing to stop until they've reached their destination.

Sagittarius Martians are highly strategic and like to empower themselves both mentally and physically. With their incredible foresight, they are able to point their bow toward the stars, shooting down and collecting opportunities as they land. However, if they don't pace themselves, they'll burn out and become just another falling star, never to shine again.

SAGITTARIUS JUPITER

↗ ♃

"I see expansion."

Sagittarius Jupiterians are curious philosophers who justify every outcome with enlightened wisdom and awareness. They strongly believe in expanding the mind, spirit, and energy, so they often research and test various methods that allow them to discover new perspectives and solutions.

When it comes to fortune and wealth, Sagittarius Jupiterians are made of luck, faith, and manifestation. Instinctually, they are opportunistic and often take risks when pursuing success. Magically, it seems that they always land on their feet and money continues to circulate when they need it the most.

SAGITTARIUS SATURN

♐ ♄

"I see restriction."

Sagittarius Saturnians struggle with discipline and excel in procrastination. It's not to say they are lazy, but they require more effort when trying to stick to routines. They don't like to be restricted by anything or anyone because it makes them feel trapped and suffocated. They prefer to roam freely with the option of being tied down to responsibilities or obligations.

When Sagittarius Saturnians are inspired to commit to goals, they become hyper-focused in shooting them down. Yet, once they do, they can toss it aside for other, more worthwhile goals. However, once they have their own families, they willingly settle down and put on the reins for good, becoming invested in the growth of their ponies and teaching them to run wild and free.

SAGITTARIUS URANUS

♐ ♅

"I see change."

Sagittarius Uranians are passionate advocates who see positive outcomes for every challenging situation, especially when it comes to social injustice. They often join causes and protests that create freedom and equality for all communities, and they also make sure not to follow blindly and ignorantly.

Sagittarius Uranians strongly believe that change can come, so long as you fight for it. Since they love freedom in all aspects of their lives, they are not afraid to rebel against hierarchy and authority to obtain it. They are devoted to researching information that keeps them educated, informed, and away from the reins of tyrants, manipulators, and dictators.

✵☆☾

SAGITTARIUS NEPTUNE

↗ ♆

"I see spirituality."

Sagittarius Neptunians love the idea of spirituality, as it often goes hand in hand with philosophy. However, they do not always commit to one belief. They feel as they go and adopt whatever they see, so their spiritual beliefs can change and adapt to their present environment or wherever they travel to.

Sagittarius Neptunians come up with their own set of spiritual rules to live by, which are often loosely based on various myths, traditions, and cultural beliefs. The majority of them do not like to conform, so they will stay away from religious organizations, yet they can be devoted to the idea of religion if it proves to benefit and energize their spirit.

SAGITTARIUS PLUTO

↗ ♇

"I see evolution."

Sagittarius Plutonians evolve mentally and physically, most if it having to do with their traveling experiences. If they are not the type to travel or cannot afford to, they will travel far and wide in their minds. In one lifetime, they will explore unknown worlds to discover the deeper meaning of life in others. This, in turn, helps them philosophize their own life's meaning.

Before Sagittarius Plutonians depart into the afterlife, they want to leave without any regrets, and they want to live a life full of traveling experiences and stories for people to read, enjoy, and be inspired by. If they can help one person evolve past their bad circumstances, they'll leave knowing all their efforts in life were not in vain.

CAPRICORN

Saturnian Sea Goat

♑

December 22 – January 19
Element: Earth
Modality: Cardinal
Ruling Planet: Saturn
Symbol: The Sea Goat (half-fish/half-goat)
Motto: I Use

CAPRICORN SUN

♑ ☉

"I use."

Capricorn is a cardinal earth sign, guided by the Sea Goat and ruled by the planet Saturn. It shares this planet with Aquarius. As the 10th star child, last cardinal sign, and last earth sign of the zodiac, Capricorns harness the deeper meaning of status, labor, discipline, solidity, and responsibility. Like their earth siblings, Taurus and Virgo, they are grounded in realistic perspectives. Unlike their earth siblings, they are more aggressive in pursuing their goals, love recognition, and work for reputation. Like their cardinal cousins, Aries, Cancer, and Libra, Capricorns are natural leaders who yearn to stand above the rest. Unlike their cardinal cousins, they build and climb their mountain of gold with more discipline and realism.

Capricorns have learned from the previous sign, Sagittarius, to prioritize self-improvement, but unlike Sagittarians, who require absolute freedom and run away from strict commitments, Capricorns require absolute restraint and are in charge of commitments. Due to this, the universe has blessed them with higher resilience, self-discipline, and ambition.

As the Saturnian Sea Goat, Capricorns are guided by Saturn's brightly focused energy and are surrounded by its rings of abundant dreams of prosperity. These rings represent Capricorn's goals of being encircled by wealth, worldly possessions, and lifetime achievements. Since Saturn is the second biggest planet next to Jupiter, Capricorns are resourceful visionaries who ground and nurture their big dreams into reality. Being that Saturn represents restriction, Capricorns will naturally be strict on themselves and everyone else around them, especially family. They are also strict believers in

☼ ☆ ☾

respecting authority, abiding the laws of man, following rules of hierarchy, and honoring parents and ancestors. It only makes sense for them to do so because they work hard to be respected and honored for all their superior knowledge, experience, status, and accolades.

Capricorns invest their energy wisely and believe in higher education, pursuing the things that make them more skilled, wealthy, knowledgeable, experienced, marketable, and reputable. They are highly independent and live by strict rules and timelines. To them, every year is an opportunity to gain a new achievement in life. They believe in working hard when you're young and playing hard when you're old. They also believe the older you get, the more wealth you should accumulate; if you have a family, you should be able to provide for them, and when parents are old or sick, children should honor them by taking care of them.

With Saturn dictating limitations, there will be very limited tolerance and acceptance with Capricorns, and they refuse to tolerate any kind of disrespect, stupidity, or impracticality. They're not intimidated by people or challenging situations and will assert their dominance when necessary. You'll also hear the word "respect" a lot from them. It's one of their favorite trigger words, and they enforce it at will. If they feel like someone isn't respecting their authority or credibility, they will not hesitate to remind them of their lower rank or belittle them until they no longer respect themselves.

Being ruled by the second biggest planet can create much pressure for Capricorns. However, they thrive and master the art of pressure. Nothing is too big or too small for them to handle. They strongly believe that everyone has a role or a status to fulfill, and if you can't handle the pressure of reality or responsibilities then you should quit while you're behind. It sounds cold, but they don't want to waste time coddling your feelings.

With time moving against them, Capricorns are not the type to waste it. Like Sagittarians before them, Capricorns are built to improve themselves no

☼☆☾

matter the cost. Unbeknownst to many, they love to research history and are inspired by major historical events, especially when they involve a great leader. They love the idea of being the underdog who triumphs and proves their worth in some grand battle. They also love the idea of people doubting them, as they know that their skills and intelligence will overcome any type of obstacle. At the end of the day, the joke is on everyone else.

When building their ladder of success, Capricorns usually start at a very early age. Family will be very important to them, so they will do everything they can to honor them. Since Capricorns' success is built on their upbringing with their parents or older siblings, they tend to follow in their footsteps. One of their first goals is to become a responsible adult who makes their parent(s) proud. If they come from humble, or less than humble, beginnings, they will work to have the things they never could as a child.

If their family consists of good role models, they will flourish and thrive in their careers, making sure their family members are provided for later on. If their family members are not ideal role models, their resolve will harden and they will push past their families by becoming what they could not be. Underneath their hard exterior, they are sensitive and work hard for acceptance and appreciation, which can add a lot of pressure and weight on their shoulders. They yearn for their loved one(s) to say, "I'm proud of you." They can also be dismissive of this pain, choosing to work it off and ignore it, so it's highly encouraged that they seek therapy for the things they have trouble expressing.

Capricorns have a difficult time relating to the youth. This is even more apparent if they've had a rough childhood. Once they've elevated in society, either through age, wealth, or status, they become absorbed with their current responsibilities. They strongly believe that there is a strict hierarchy that those below them should follow; and if they're higher than you, you should follow and trust their guidance without question. After all, they worked hard to get

☼ ☆ ☾

there, so why wouldn't you listen? This isn't to say that they cannot empathize with others. When they've taken a step back from being a provider, they become a full-time caretaker for their loved ones, but they will not pamper the weak-willed and they cannot sympathize with those who dwell on things they cannot control. Victim mentalities are considered weak to them, so they will instill strength in their children and expect them to mature sooner so they can have an advantage in life.

Even though Capricorns can be extremely sensitive, they are still rock-hard individuals who want nothing more than to be the ideal parent, provider, or leader. The highly ambitious types will sacrifice a temporary pain, such as romantic abstinence or the absence of family and friends. They are realists, so they are aware that love cannot feed a family and will prioritize responsibility, stability, and financial security before they commit to having one. However, if they are void of love after they've reached financial success, they will fill that void with material possessions. You'll find many Capricorn hoarders or shopping addicts due to a lack of love and emotional support.

Capricorn's symbol is the Sea Goat, a sign that swims in water and walks on land. Although they are not technically a dual sign in astrology, they still possess both dark and light energy because of their two halves. Their dark half internalizes and suppresses their feelings under water, while their light half concentrates in building grand sandcastles under the sun. The dark side is sensitive and intuitive, and the light side is resourceful and pragmatic. They are more than capable of utilizing their intuition to seek and manifest realistic opportunities that provide long-term benefits, yet it will take both sides to provide the energy needed to balance what the other half desires.

Capricorn's motto is "I use." Their life's challenge is mastering discipline, opportunity, resourcefulness, and usefulness, which can cause the love of wealth and success to be prioritized above everything and everyone. They are also prone to using others selfishly for monetary gain and temporary pleasure.

✹ ☆ ☾

To overcome this, they must learn that people are not tools and that money can't buy true love and loyalty. When they can combat these urges, they become a powerful and unstoppable leader, teaching people to follow their dreams with integrity, restraint, and strong moral principles.

As a cardinal earth sign, they are one of the only zodiac signs that can put their emotions aside to climb further than any sign before them. They are hyper-focused in finding their own path in life and pace themselves with calculated steps toward success. Like their earth sibling, Taurus, they are sternly regimental. They build foundations for themselves early so they have something to stand on in their later years, and when they are older or have reached ultimate security, they become the opposite of stern and strict. Their watery side will take over and they will become playful, completely relaxed, and focused in creating meaningful and pleasurable memories.

Since Capricorns require a career that allows stable financial growth and hierarchal organization to climb, you will find many who become investors, realtors, military officers, politicians, entrepreneurs, stockbrokers, athletes, or any other career that provides them with recognition, titles, and awards while also expanding their savings.

Capricorns are diamonds in the rough who are built on strong traditional values. They shine and thrive under pressure, can spin air into gold, and are always competing with themselves to reach their maximum potential. They believe that everyone should see themselves more realistically, having the strength and common sense to grow from their failures and weaknesses. If you are unable to do so, you are not meant to be successful.

Overall, Capricorns embody true discipline, responsibility, family, and resourcefulness. They are the ultimate provider, never stopping themselves from reaching the next step in life. They teach other signs to follow their lead, always encouraging them to look ahead and never backward, for failure is guaranteed but success is not.

✵ ✰ ☾

UNEVOLVED CAPRICORN — ABUSIVE CAPITALIST

Unevolved Capricorns are abusive capitalists who want nothing more than to be obeyed and respected. They've learned from the unevolved sign before them, Sagittarius, not to take risks on a whim, so they do their best to carefully calculate every move they make. From their unevolved earth siblings, Taurus and Virgo, they've learned to prioritize and perfect authority and status. From their unevolved cardinal cousins, Aries, Cancer, and Libra, they've learned that controlling others is the ultimate power.

Since their motto is "I use," unevolved Capricorns do just that. They can use and restrict others unapologetically and abuse their status and power. If they are in a powerless position, they will challenge those who are in power or scheme to get to the top while using others at scapegoats. If they feel that you've fulfilled your role and are no longer useful to them, they will toss you aside without remorse. They consume money and material possessions, investing in whatever portrays them as a successful role model. To top it off, they can be extremely judgmental, always using their status in life to shame others who they feel are less superior or less educated.

As a cardinal earth sign, unevolved Capricorns do not care to lead others; they care to manage and use others. Emotions to them are frivolous and get in the way of their selfish decisions. They are in favor of capitalism, wanting more money to feed their materialistic desires. If anybody challenges them, they become overly defensive, aggressive, and unwilling to see their wrongdoings. Their superiority complex leaves them loathed by many, but so long as they have money and status, they could not care less.

�֍ ✰ ☾

EVOLVED CAPRICORN – RESOURCEFUL PROVIDER

Evolved Capricorns are resourceful providers who are focused on building a strong foundation for their families. They've learned from the evolved sign before them, Sagittarius, to travel and experience all that life has to offer. They've learned from their evolved earth siblings, Taurus and Virgo, to create stability and nurture their environment. They've learned from their evolved cardinal cousins, Aries, Cancer, and Libra, to be a compassionate sign who listens and reciprocates energy. Due to this, evolved Capricorns become true leaders who construct change, strength, and financial security in society.

Since their motto is "I use," evolved Capricorns utilize their skills and high intellect to create grand plans or pursue long-term careers that involve and help entire communities. They know how to resource funds and manage others for maximum productivity without abusing their power or status. They invest wisely in the energy of others and listen to the economic needs of every social class. They often stand up for the lower class, as they are fully aware of their economic importance.

As a cardinal earth sign, evolved Capricorns are opportunistic signs that strive to be financial independent. They tend to be mentally, physically, and emotionally strong. They possess highly realistic views in life but aren't against spirituality. Although they lean more on strict traditional values that encourage unity and non-violence, they aren't against aggressive protesting that challenges old traditions. To them, everything must evolve with the new norms of society. To go against it is considered an injustice to humanity. Therefore, everything and everyone in life must reconstruct their mentality to maintain a more solid foundation for everyone to stand on.

☼ ☆ ☾

CAPRICORN MOON

♑ ☽

"I use what I feel."

Individuals with Capricorn Moons process their emotions realistically and responsibly, but it depends on other celestial factors. Mixed with fire, they are innovative and dominant but lack acceptance and deep understanding of others. Mixed with earth, they are more rational and disciplined but are highly dismissive and judgmental. Mixed with air, they are engaging and clever but can be idle and rebellious. Mixed with water, they are insightful and idealistic, yet they can be naïve and too lenient.

Emotionally, Capricorn Moons tend to use the feelings of others to better understand their emotions. It's not to say that they don't have any; they just don't find them to be useful. This can come off as unbothered, but it's natural for them to restrict how they feel. They value emotional control and find it hard to express how they feel because they hate showing vulnerability. They strongly believe that having emotional discipline creates a type of strength that others don't have. If caught in a stressful or emotional situation, they will walk out until all parties have had enough time to cool down and be civil.

Capricorn Moons like to work on their feelings independently or work through them with a credible professional. They require a lot of structure, financial security, and career expansion to feel happiness. They tend to dislike anything that gets in the way of their professional life. They value traditional goals, such as a marriage, family, career, retirement, etc. When Capricorn Moons are feeling down, they will dismiss their negative emotions by keeping themselves mentally and physically busy. To them, there's no better feeling than overcoming painful experiences through their own success.

☼ ☆ ☾

CAPRICORN ENERGY IN OTHER PLACEMENTS

CAPRICORN ASCENDANT (RISING)

♑ AC

"I use myself."

Capricorn Risings project seriousness, calmness, responsibility, and duty in everything they do. Upon first impression, they're professional, polite, and cautious. It's important for them to guard their vulnerability, so they can come off very private and guarded.

When it comes to physical appearance, they like to dress conservatively, professionally, classy, or anything else that makes them look respectable or important. It can be difficult for them to dress provocatively because they do not want to be subjected to unwanted sexual advances or negative judgment.

CAPRICORN MIDHEAVEN (MC)

♑ MC

"I use my career."

Capricorn Midheavens take their careers and education very seriously and invest a lot of time and energy in nurturing them, and they are always willing to work on self-improvement. Since they are money-motivated, resourceful, organized, and value hierarchy, they excel in climbing the corporate ladder.

Capricorn Midheavens possess much dignity and self-respect. If they feel they are not valued in their workplace, they will not hesitate to leave and take their talents elsewhere. They work best when they're guaranteed growth.

CAPRICORN MERCURY

♑ ☿

"I use my thoughts."

Capricorn Mercurians are decisive in their ideas and actions because they always take and use opportunities to climb higher. Most of them are logical or physical learners who like to get their hands dirty because it allows them the opportunity to use their skills and resolve complex situations.

Capricorn Mercurians possess productive and useful thoughts, and they are focused on doing things the right way once, which means they can be quite narrow-minded. They also do not entertain multiple perspectives because they hate mental confusion. This type of clarity and focus allows their ideas to climb without any distractions, which ultimately propels them to success.

CAPRICORN VENUS

♑ ♀

"I use love."

Capricorn Venusians seek out useful and beneficial relationships and take commitment very seriously. They want to be in long-lasting partnerships, and they are extremely family-oriented and traditional, so courting, marriage, and children (in that order) will take priority in their life.

Capricorn Venusians are best in relationships where they take the lead and remain financially independent. They want to be with a partner who doesn't use them, can carry their own weight, is capable of managing their finances, and is heavily involved with family responsibilities. When in love, they work to become the ideal and responsible partner and parent, as they believe fulfilling their duties shows how much they care and love their families.

☀☆☾

CAPRICORN MARS

♑ ♂

"I use physical power."

Capricorn Martians love using what they know to obtain power and status. They are highly intelligent and practical signs who work long and hard in building themselves up. They are their own worst enemy at times, as their ego and arrogance can get the better of them.

Capricorn Martians remove emotions when making decisions. They feel that emotions are irrelevant factors when it comes to making money. They can be very aggressive when they want something or someone and are prone to using others to get ahead in life. However, their determination for success and even fame is more resilient than diamonds, and there is nothing they won't sacrifice to reach their mountain of success and even fame.

CAPRICORN JUPITER

♑ ♃

"I use expansion."

Capricorn Jupiterians use money and material wealth to expand their direct environment. They want the houses, cars, family, and career to represent their status in the community. If they own businesses, they are driven to expand them across the world. The more their money expands, the more they expand.

Capricorn Jupiterians are one-sided scholars. They are extremely realistic and grounded in their thoughts and ideas, finding it challenging to fantasize about things that can never come true or do not exist. They don't like to fix things that are not broken, but if they have to, they are highly resourceful and can invent or reinvent things out of necessity.

☼ ☆ ☾

CAPRICORN SATURN

♑ ♄

"I use restriction."

Capricorn Saturnians are extremely focused and disciplined. They restrict themselves from getting distracted from their lifelong goals. They strongly believe in staying productive, reasonable, and progressive. They believe that responsibility of self and family is important to their well-being. If they feel that something or someone gets in the way of their progress or success, they will remove themselves from the equation altogether.

Capricorn Saturnians have strict boundaries and rules, and they'll restrict others from overstepping them. They believe in respecting authority and will take disciplinary actions should someone disrespect theirs. The majority put their work ahead of everyone else, sternly believing that accumulating resources and wealth creates a stable and safe environment for their families.

CAPRICORN URANUS

♑ ♅

"I use change."

Capricorn Uranians are fascinated by politics and government. They see the usefulness in it, and many believe in following hierarchy and man-made laws to the T. The majority stay away from any type of protest or riots, as they feel there are other respectable ways to get your point across.

Capricorn Uranians believe that change should come from a higher power, and people who follow that higher power should abide by it. However, they are not all mindless sheep. They will rebel if they feel they are being used, especially financially. You'll get overthrown if you mess with their money.

☼ ☆ ☾

CAPRICORN NEPTUNE

℩ ♆

"I use spirituality."

Capricorn Neptunians use spirituality to manifest good fortune and status in their lives, and as realistic as they are, one would think they stay away from the occult, yet that isn't always the case. Whatever spiritual channel they use, they become devoted to performing consistent rituals and daily mantras—whatever helps alleviate any energetic pressure or stress.

Capricorn Neptunians will have a fascination with religious organizations because they like the idea of any hierarchy. However, many do not like the idea of being used for someone else's greed or power. Then, there are some who don't believe in spirituality at all, believing only in themselves and using their own energy to manifest opportunities of growth and abundance.

CAPRICORN PLUTO

℩ ♇

"I use evolution."

Capricorn Plutonians evolve financially and environmentally. During their lifetime, they will do everything humanly possible to achieve greater heights of success. As one of the most resourceful signs, they empower themselves by evolving their skills, talents, and tools. They are also generous with their wealth and will create foundations for others; this can include charity.

Before Capricorn Plutonians depart from this world, they want to be able to leave behind a solid financial footprint for their families to live off. If their children become more successful than them, they can leave this life with great pride knowing they were useful to the people they loved.

AQUARIUS

Uranusian Water Bearer

♒

January 20 – February 18
Element: Air
Modality: Fixed
Ruling Planet: Uranus
Co-Ruling Planet: Saturn
Symbol: The Water Bearer
Motto: I Know

AQUARIUS SUN

♒ ☉

"I know."

Aquarius is a fixed air sign, guided by the Water Bearer and ruled by Uranus and Saturn. It shares Saturn with Capricorn. As the 11th star child, last fixed sign, and last air sign, Aquarians were created to redefine order and regulation, bringing forth absolute mental, emotional, and physical freedom. Unlike Capricorn, who is built on strict rules of conformity and hierarchy, Aquarians are built on rebellion, non-conformity, and anarchy. Like their fellow air siblings, Gemini and Libra, they utilize their mental strengths to observe situations and people from multiple perspectives. Unlike their air siblings, they're not as indecisive and are more optimistic and hopeful that there can be good in everything and everyone.

Aquarians are the true humanitarians of the zodiac and strive for positive reformation in the world. Like their fixed cousins, Taurus, Leo, and Scorpio, they are extremely stubborn when it comes to their beliefs. Unlike their fixed cousins, though, they are more accepting and understanding of different beliefs, so long as it serves the greater good. Due to this, the universe has blessed them with higher mental resolve and expansive thinking power.

As the Uranusian Water Bearer, Aquarians collect and absorb the waters of worldly information and are in charge of distributing it evenly to everyone. With guidance from both Uranus and Saturn, they learn to sort and decipher information with both instinct and logic. With Uranus guiding their mental energy, they understand that great change is based on our moral compasses, which place good intentions into the great void of silence. With Saturn co-piloting their willpower, they believe that change must be empowered and

☼ ☆ ☾

organized through strict boundaries as well as emotional and mental control. In turn, they believe that change cannot be possible without the support of various communities, thus making them true advocates who support and encourage others to fight for what is fair and just, a trait they adopted from their air sibling, Libra.

Aquarians do not like to follow traditional societal norms, yet they also believe in following strict humanitarian rules. It's as if there are two sides of them, which there is because they are guided by two planets. Uranus pushes them to challenge giants (tyrants and dictators), whereas Saturn challenges them to push moral standards for everyone to follow. It's often a conflict of interest, as they struggle to define and balance what they can or cannot conform to.

Aquarians possess very firm beliefs that abide by the universal laws of free will and natural evolution. They abhor those who attempt to gain control through mental and emotional manipulation. Though they are strict with their beliefs, they still rebel against the strict rules of government and hierarchy, believing that everyone has the willpower and intelligence to rule and guide themselves as long as they have the information and willpower to do so. This can be counterintuitive, however, as they can be too reluctant and rebellious to trust any kind of authority, even if an authoritative figure has proven to be trustworthy and credible in their field of expertise.

Guided by the Water Bearer, Aquarians learn what it means to give and take. However, they can be overly helpful and self-sacrificing, forgoing their needs to help sustain the life of others. This type of mentality can fill their bucket with disappointment, especially when their needs are not being reciprocated or if they realize a trusted person turns out to be different from who they claimed to be. Honesty and transparency are highly important to them, and they tend to give people the benefit of the doubt because they believe people are inherently good. However, if a person proves to be

✵ ☆ ☽

untrustworthy or disloyal, they will be gone like the wind or create a never-ending storm of mental chaos in their life.

Like their fixed cousins, Taurus, Leo, and Scorpio, Aquarians have a difficult time fully trusting anybody. Because they see all perspectives, both good and bad, they can have a hard time deciding a person's true intentions. They also believe that people put up a façade before they reveal their true selves, so they take things and people at face value. For example, if someone is being flirty, they will think they are just being friendly. If someone talks badly about them, they will think that maybe they did or said something to accidentally offend them. If someone is in love with them, they will think it's the same kind of love you can give to anybody. Like Gemini, their air sibling, they have difficulty fully understanding, trusting, and accepting complex emotions, as they are not guaranteed to last.

This type of behavior is more apparent when Aquarians have experienced something traumatic in their lives, in which they will start to distrust people's intentions and can even become paranoid by them. This is the main reason why most Aquarians choose to stay away from all the noise and find comfort in their isolation. Though they are not as social as their air siblings, they are always respectful, friendly, and well-mannered in every social situation. They love to learn about other people as they meet them, but they will still feel that they cannot relate to most of them. It's a tricky situation to say the least.

Like the water they pour, Aquarians don't believe in holding anything or anybody hostage, and just like their air siblings, Gemini and Libra, balance, equality, mental stimulation, transparency, and communication are extremely important to them in any relationship. Jealousy and control are suffocating to them. They like having the option to come and go as they please without any obligations or expectations to stay. The freedom of choice is something they give freely to others, but in all fairness, they expect it in return. And even though the majority of them are passive-aggressive, they will, surprisingly,

✸☆☾

fight fiercely if you corner them.

Aquarians are naturally inquisitive signs, especially at a young age. They can be heard questioning everything in existence. Their favorite words are "why" and "how." Regardless of the topic, they question and research every perspective because it allows them to draw their own informed conclusions. They are also known to play devil's advocate in any given situation, wanting to choose an alternative method or solution because they hate to conform and are not capable of trusting word of mouth. This ultimately makes them one of the most rational yet unpredictable and opinionated signs, as they can easily and quickly change their beliefs, actions, or feelings without notice.

Aquarian's motto is "I know." Their life's challenge is overcoming their rebellious self-righteous beliefs, unpredictable actions, and endless non-sensical opinions, which can lead to a severe case of "know-it-all ego." To overcome this, they must be willing to listen, learn, and grow from other people's experiences, not just their own. Depending on the situation, they must also learn that they can trust and follow someone's authority and expertise without having to question or criticize everything they do.

Fortunately, as a fixed air sign, Aquarians are fixed on the evolution of their knowledge, so they are not against reinventing their thoughts and actions, especially if it serves the greater good or if there is good reasoning behind it. Unlike any other zodiac sign, Aquarians can distance and detach themselves emotionally from anything and anybody, even from old ideals or bad habits that no longer benefit them. Because they like their information to be uncontaminated, they become a well of refreshing information for anybody to draw from; and they will ensure that everyone, no matter who, has an equal share of information to sip on.

As a fixed sign, Aquarians can withhold information when it comes to their personal life but will expect others to divulge their own lives like a public book. It may seem hypocritical, but they are aware that people can and will

✸☆☾

judge them, and judgment is one of the things they hate the most in life. It's only when they can fully trust someone that they are capable of sharing more of their vulnerable side. Like their fixed cousins, Taurus, Leo, and Scorpio, Aquarians value and enforce their privacy, so distancing themselves and maintaining strong boundaries for mental peace is a requirement.

As emotionally distant as Aquarians may seem, they genuinely care about humanity and will fight against injustice and oppression. They also seek to advance or heal society through scientific research. Since they devote themselves to knowledge, they often choose careers in forensic science, health care, astrophysics, archaeology, or any other career that helps humanity through investigative research. Regardless of their career, many Aquarians, especially in their later life, dedicate themselves to causes that help reform society for the better.

As one of the most enigmatic signs of the zodiac, Aquarians love a good mystery and love to be a mystery; and they like to harbor very dark curiosities. They are not easily squeamish and will entertain any type of research no matter how odd, morbid, or dark the topic is. It is hard to imagine that this friendly, smiling advocate who seems so unbothered and detached is so fascinated by grotesque or unimaginable subjects. Needless to say, if something or someone can be thoroughly investigated by an Aquarius then it will without anybody else knowing. However, there is one thing that they can find too scary to research and that's usually anything that can't be outright explained, such as the supernatural or paranormal. If they have braver signs in their chart, then there is nothing that can't be mentally explored.

Overall, Aquarians embody absolute change, knowledge, and perception. They master multiple perspectives without prejudgments, and they fill the void of silence with flowing information that allows other zodiac signs to free themselves from mental manipulation.

✸ ✰ ☽

Unevolved Aquarius – Opinionated Rebel

Unevolved Aquarians are opinionated rebels that strive to win every argument and create mental chaos in people's lives. From the unevolved sign before them, Capricorn, they've learned to rebel against restrictions and authority, believing that they are mentally superior. From their unevolved air siblings, Gemini and Libra, they have learned to use the power of mental thought and influence for evil. From their unevolved fixed cousins, Taurus, Leo, and Scorpio, they've learned to stubbornly hold onto their perspectives and beliefs without consideration of others.

Since their motto is "I know," unevolved Aquarians are the biggest know-it-alls of the zodiac. They strongly believe they are more educated, intelligent, and wiser than everyone else. They force their unwanted opinions and beliefs down the throats of others, believing their views are more superior. When a person shares their perspective, they can play devil's advocate on purpose, choosing to share opposing perspectives for the sake of arguing or deflecting. They also seem to never have a sure stance on anything, always giving contradicting views to different people. They can also jump to wild conclusions, never trusting verifiable sources because they hate to be wrong.

As a fixed air sign, unevolved Aquarians tend to be one-sided. They can be difficult to work with because they rebel against everyone. They are also known to instigate situations for their own entertainment, wanting to see how far they can mentally push someone over the edge. They strive so hard to be different and distant but cannot accept that they are the reason why nobody wants to be around them in the first place.

✳︎☆☾

Evolved Aquarius — World Advocate

Evolved Aquarians are world advocates who partake in organizations that fight for justice and equality. These are values they've learned from the evolved sign before them, Capricorn. They've learned from their evolved air siblings, Gemini and Libra, to educate themselves in the fight for justice and equality. They've learned from their evolved fixed cousins, Taurus, Leo, and Scorpio, to be resilient and relentlessly pursue their life goals. Due to this, evolved Aquarians willfully educate, advocate, and enforce moral obligations into humanity.

Since their motto is "I know," evolved Aquarians invest wisely in their education and are fully aware that knowledge is the key to erasing ignorance. They are diverse in their thinking and consider all perspectives to find clear and thoughtful resolutions for every situation. They focus on humanitarian endeavors that can be achieved through global efforts. They understand and accept that change starts with one person, and they also believe that it is the civil duty of that person to educate those around them. Once they pass on their wise knowledge, they will leave it up to the individual to do whatever they please with it rather than forcing their will upon them.

As a fixed air sign, evolved Aquarians are fixated on changing their environment and the people around them for the better. They strongly believe that all issues are case-by-case scenarios that require different resolutions, and every issue must be addressed with consideration of all parties involved. They honor and respect everyone's decisions, never judging or correcting others unless it is absolutely necessary to erase their ignorance. As a true advocate to society, they always stand up against society's bullies, showing others that positive changes can be made when people are held accountable for their wrongful actions and the oppressed rebel against evil as one.

☀ ☆ ☾

AQUARIUS MOON

♒ ☽

"I know what I feel."

Individuals with Aquarius Moons find detachment and solitude easier to deal with than their emotions, but it depends on other celestial factors. Mixed with fire, they are highly outgoing and playful but can be more confrontational and thoughtless. Mixed with earth, they are reasonable and tolerant yet are more emotionally detached and stubborn. Mixed with air, they are more hopeful and knowledgeable but are also more aloof, whimsical, and non-committal. Mixed with water, they are very helpful and attentive, yet they are more guarded and defensive.

Emotionally, Aquarius Moons try to distance themselves from emotionally charged situations to gain an unbiased perspective. They tend to see things more rationally than others and try to mediate and resolve issues in a calm manner. However, if they feel that a conversation is going nowhere or if the person is incapable of having an adult conversation, they will walk out and vanish. They're also not the type to dwell on their emotions, so when they walk out, they never look back.

Aquarius Moons often know and understand their feelings and will enforce their strict boundaries if necessary. They can be very private and unwilling to share their vulnerability with people they feel will judge them or persuade them into changing their minds. Aquarius Moons try to maintain an unbiased, optimistic, and honest perspective in any emotional situation. They do not have a fragile ego, as they believe everyone is entitled to self-expression and freedom of choice and every situation can be mediated through civil conversation. If it can't, then it's perfectly fine to detach yourself altogether.

☼ ☆ ☾

AQUARIUS ENERGY IN OTHER PLACEMENTS

AQUARIUS ASCENDANT (RISING)

♒ AC

"I know myself."

Aquarius Risings project curiosity, transparency, advocacy, kindness, and unpredictability in everything they do. Upon first impression, they are either friendly, inquisitive, genuine, and talkative, or if they don't care to interact, they're in their own bubble, completely absent, quiet, and distant.

When it comes to their physical appearance, Aquarius Risings are very unpredictable. However, the majority do not care to follow trends and are low maintenance, finding clothes and accessories an unnecessary investment. Yet, they are able to switch it up and dress to the nines to surprise people.

AQUARIUS MIDHEAVEN (MC)

♒ MC

"I know my career."

Aquarius Midheavens love to conduct a lot of research and want to utilize their knowledge in advancing their communities. The majority will go into careers that make a difference in humanity, especially with the help of technology or science. If they feel mentally trapped by a job, they will vanish into thin air.

Aquarius Midheavens will invest heavily in their education and career. They are extremely focused on having their freedom and independence, so they will distance themselves from all distractions until they obtain it.

☀ ☆ ☽

AQUARIUS MERCURY

♒ ☿

"I know my thoughts."

Aquarius Mercurians take knowledge very seriously, so they will invest a lot of their time into researching any and every topic. They abhor ignorance of any kind and love intellectual debates with others. They see life unbiasedly and from multiple perspectives because they like to collect and assess as much information as possible to make informed decisions.

The majority of Aquarius Mercurians are solitary, logical, auditory, and visual learners. They take information in through almost all of their senses because they take learning to a new level. This makes them incredible teachers because they know so much, and they are capable of articulating and sharing their knowledge efficiently.

AQUARIUS VENUS

♒ ♀

"I know love."

Aquarius Venusians see love from a much higher and logical perspective than any other sign. They can be quite unpredictable when they date, choosing to date different types of people before they commit. Yet, they can also be highly selective, private, guarded, and distant from people they like, making it challenging for others to get to know them on a deeper level.

Aquarius Venusians reflect on love and all that comes with it, good and bad. They prefer to have a strong friendship first before they commit, as they feel love is not guaranteed to last. When they are in love, they are completely devoted to a forever friendship, which they feel is the true foundation of love.

✺ ☆ ☾

AQUARIUS MARS

♒ ♂

"I know physical power."

Aquarius Martians believe that knowledge is true power. However, they understand the importance of both mental and physical well-being, so they will research nutrition and exercise to balance it. They are also not the type to start fights or disrupt others physically, as they do not feel the need to constantly assert their dominance. In fact, most will walk away if things get too heated, or they'll agree to disagree after they've stated their facts.

Aquarius Martians are meditators of the mind and body, and they believe more in giving power to people rather than to themselves. They strongly feel that if they can empower people's minds with useful information, it's their choice to empower themselves with it.

AQUARIUS JUPITER

♒ ♃

"I know expansion."

Aquarius Jupiterians expand mentally at faster rates than any other sign. They are the keepers of superior knowledge and unique perspectives, and people often come to them for their wise counsel. There is nothing they won't learn, as they love to be enlightened in every topic known to man and beyond.

Aquarius Jupiterians believe in possessing a wealth of knowledge, as this helps them gain true awareness of humanity as a whole. To them, the fortune of educating others takes precedence over anything else superficial. Thus, they spend most of their lives as astute hermits who want nothing more than to observe humanity from God's eyes.

☀ ☆ ☾

AQUARIUS SATURN

♒ ♄

"I know restriction."

Aquarius Saturnians have extreme boundaries with others, and they don't believe in entertaining others with small talk or superficial parties, not even lunch or dinner. They master in distance and don't like to lose focus on their responsibility to self. It's not to say that they won't socialize. They will, but they also know that their mental well-being takes priority.

Aquarius Saturnians take their responsibilities very seriously, and most find comfort in isolation from others. It's in this way they are able to focus solely on themselves, never losing their independence through the influence of others. However, once they have achieved all that they needed to, especially in their later years, they become childlike and playful, wanting to catch up on the life they sacrificed long ago.

AQUARIUS URANUS

♒ ♅

"I know change."

Aquarius Uranians are the true humanitarians and advocates of the world. They embody it, are born into it, and embrace all that comes with it. They are kind, wise, and compassionate, especially to the oppressed and impoverished. Often rebellious to tyranny, they are passionate when expressing their beliefs and will go above and beyond to fight it.

Aquarius Uranians can be self-sacrificing and can become martyrs of their time. So, as long as justice and equality serve the greater good, they will fight for it with more aggression, influence, and knowledge than any other sign.

✷ ☆ ☾

AQUARIUS NEPTUNE

♒ ♆

"I know spirituality."

Aquarius Neptunians are curious about spirituality, but they also lean more on scientific or technological studies. If they are into spirituality, they stay away from religious organizations because they don't like to be controlled mentally. If they are not into spirituality, they will dismiss it completely. However, most will feel that anything is possible, and if it cannot be disproven, there is a need to investigate it further.

Aquarius Neptunians are strong believers of alien life-forms and can be obsessed with researching conspiracy theories. They are genuinely fascinated with anything not of this world, and if they're spiritual, they will also gravitate toward anything supernatural. They can even believe in zombies and lizard people, anything dark, obscure, or downright impossible.

AQUARIUS PLUTO

♒ ♇

"I know evolution."

Aquarius Plutonians take their time evolving mentally, as they are aware that mental awareness requires a lifetime of education and experience. During their lifetime, they will pursue the evolution of mankind, especially anything involving the elevation and well-being of those who need it the most.

Before Aquarius Plutonians depart from this world, they want to know that they made a difference in society. Because of this, they will devote their lives to finding solutions that advance communities, big or small.

☼ ☆ ☽

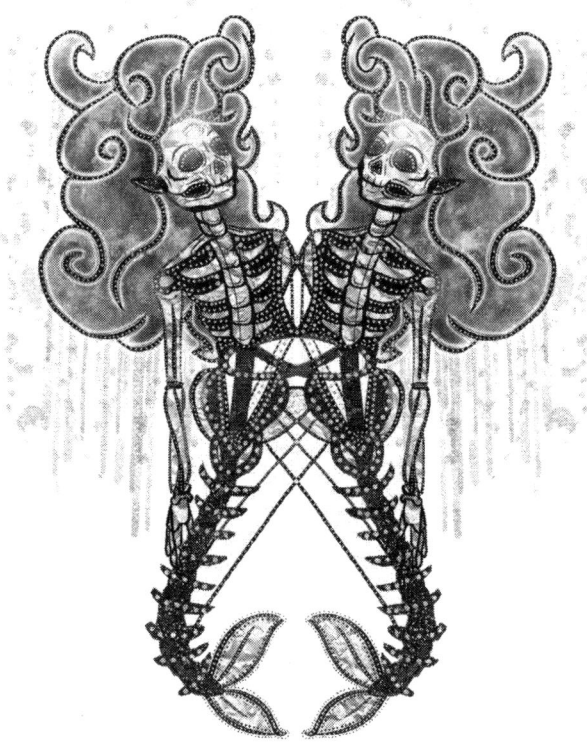

PISCES

Neptunian Koi Shark

♓

February 19 – March 20
Element: Water
Modality: Mutable
Ruling Planet: Neptune
Co-Ruling Planet: Jupiter
Symbol: Two Fish
Motto: I Believe

PISCES SUN

♓ ☉

"I believe."

Pisces is a mutable water sign, guided by the two fish and ruled by Neptune and Jupiter. It shares Jupiter with Sagittarius. As the last star child, last mutable sign, and last water sign, Pisceans are the youngest but the wisest. As the last zodiac sign, Pisceans have learned all there is to know from every sign before them, taking only what they deem is valuable for emotional and spiritual growth. Anything superficial or confining is usually out the door, as this deters them from finding true emotional fulfillment.

Like Aquarius, the sign before them, Pisceans are inquisitive, rebellious, and aloof. Unlike Aquarians, who are distant with their emotions and value mental expression and evolution, Pisceans embrace their emotions and value emotional expression and evolution. Like their water siblings, Cancer and Scorpio, they are extremely intuitive and are constantly internalizing and reflecting on their thoughts and emotions. Unlike their water siblings, they are highly adaptable and tend to swim away from suffocating commitments like their mutable cousins, Gemini, Virgo, and Sagittarius.

Pisceans flow further and dive deeper into the meaning of life than any other sign, and they are the only ones who swim in a constant flow of whimsical fantasies, lucid daydreams, and vivid prophecies, their mind and emotions moving together as one current or against one another in a battle of dominance. Due to this, the universe has blessed them with the highest receptivity, intuition, empathy, and imagination.

As the Neptunian Koi Shark, Pisceans swim up and down the paths of light and dark energies. With the guidance of both Neptune and Jupiter, they dive

✦ ✧ ☾

deep into the abyss of their subconscious to find the meaning of spirituality and soul purpose then float up to catch the waves of philosophical truth and mental awareness. With that said, Pisceans have a challenging time striking a balance between reality and imagination. Since being grounded is not a trait Pisceans absorbed well, they will rebel and swim free without restraint.

With Neptune as their main ruling planet, Pisceans receive compassionate and sensitive energy. Their intuition is also doubled, as they prefer to utilize spirituality to connect the dots. They feel everything and everyone on a much deeper level but can have trouble guarding and controlling the amount of energy and emotions they absorb, traits learned from their water sibling, Cancer. However, like their other water sibling, Scorpio, they find self-preservation and emotional control more appealing. They instinctually swim away from emotionally vulnerable situations. It often takes a very patient and kind person to draw their emotions out, but even then, it can be too scary for Pisceans because once they do, they will no longer have emotional control.

With Jupiter as their co-ruling planet, Pisceans receive higher imagination, spirituality, and foresight to justify their reality. They share these traits with Sagittarians. However, Pisceans do not have the gift of gab or philosophical perceptions like their mutable cousin. Instead, Jupiter gifts them with abstract, animated, and artistic views when expressing themselves. When processing their emotions, they fully embrace them, but they are also aware that words alone cannot fully explain them. This is the reason why so many are drawn to art, dance, and music, which allows them to project what cannot be said but can be felt. It's really a sad day when their voices are being silenced or kept hidden, as creative emotional expression is their strongest trait.

Unbeknownst to many people, Pisceans are very good at mimicking others. They have a wonderful talent of adapting to tones, sounds, and behaviors. This isn't to say that they will purposely try to be someone else; they won't. They just acknowledge the noise that nobody else wants to tune into. This

✹☆☾

provides them with a creative library for them to be inspired by. Like ripples of water, they are so in tune with life and the vibration of others, that they become vibration itself.

Most Pisceans gravitate toward a career that allows them to express their inner voice or connect deeply with others spiritually and emotionally. You will find many Pisceans who are professional healers, artists, musicians, and writers. However, many will flow into health care or any other career that allows them to feel people out, such as human resources. Not all of them do well in management positions, as they do not feel the need to constantly assert themselves, and most do not like the feeling of being in charge of a team of people. It's too stressful on their energy. They also like the freedom to move without obligations and do not like to be fish tanked in boring, meaningless routines. It compresses and depresses their spirit.

The Pisceans' symbol is the double fish. They are the last dual sign of the zodiac. One fish is guided by Neptune (swimming downward), which invigorates their spirit and emotions and allows them to utilize their intuition for the betterment of themselves. And the other fish is guided by Jupiter (swimming upward), which enlightens their mentality and allows them to utilize their intelligence to bring forth the knowledge from the abyss below. They master in taking people's souls on a journey of true self-discovery, soaking in all that is good and bad and making sense out of it through spiritual justification.

Pisceans take a spiritual and sensible approach to everything and everyone. They believe everything happens for a reason, even if that reason is traumatic. However, it can take them a while to process their emotions. The unevolved ones often turn to self-medication, self-abuse, or self-sabotage because they can't handle the reality of their current situation. However, when Pisceans can overcome and evolve, they learn to instill faith and hope in their lost souls, which in turn gives them the energy to swim forward and start fresh.

☀ ☆ ☽

The Pisces motto is "I believe." Their life's challenge is being an ungrounded dreamer who finds reality too hard to accept. They are prone to running away and playing victim rather than confronting it and becoming a survivor. To overcome this, they must learn they're much stronger than they believe they are and appear to be. They must learn to be proud of their strengths in order to confront past trauma and overcome their insecurities, using their stories of survival to inspire others to also believe in themselves.

Unlike Scorpio, who is a strong advocate for death and the afterlife, Pisceans are all about life and the living. There are many Pisceans who don't even like to think of death at all. It terrifies them. They would much rather fantasize of everything light, frothy, and blissful. Even their fantasy of heaven and hell are skewed to their optimistic ideals. Nothing can be as bad as it seems. However, if they reach a dark side of themselves, they can become so depressed and so overwhelmed with darkness that they cannot seem to swim out of it. Yet, like the fish in the abyss, some love to dwell in it.

Like Aquarius, the sign before them, Pisceans are enthralled with the idea of helping others. However, unlike Aquarians, they have a hard time enforcing their boundaries because they find constraint suffocating. They want everything and everyone to flow freely like water. Thus, the guilt of suffocating others will be a natural part of their watery senses, which can deter them from making decisions that involve their own happiness.

Fortunately, the majority of Pisceans are true believers of faith and spirit. They use both to rise above any negative circumstance. They always believe there will be better days ahead, but first, you have to embrace and ride out the dark storms. Although they are believers of living in the moment, they are capable of adapting to any future current. They also have otherworldly ideas and fantasies only they comprehend. Like their mutable cousin, Gemini, they are often misunderstood, and they can find it challenging to find a school of fish that truly appreciates their mental and emotional perspectives.

※☆☾

As a mutable water sign, Pisceans are highly sensitive signs who naturally take a more passive approach to life. It's not to say they cannot assert themselves, overreact, or lash out because they will definitely tear into you like a shark when provoked. However, when fully evolved, they're able to tap into their higher intuition and lessen any tension by adapting and empathizing with a person's deeper pain. They truly believe that anger comes more from a space of hurt and frustration, all of which they embrace and have learned to tolerate and heal. This is why people believe they are passive, when in fact they are just an enlightened and worldly sign that doesn't believe in reacting without genuine provocation.

Pisceans keep their souls bound in euphoric dreams, envisioning a world where everything and everyone is immortal and eternally at peace. With their heads in the cloud, people may feel like they're not fully interested, which is false. They're just not the type to pry into your personal life unless you open up about it. They respect people's personal boundaries and are great listeners who only give advice when given permission to connect energetically and emotionally. Even if they don't always say things out loud, you can tell how they feel by their facial expressions. If they feel provoked or threatened, they will absorb that person's negative energy and throw it back at them like a boomerang or bite your head off with their shark-like jaws.

Overall, Pisceans embody spirituality and emotional expression. They teach other zodiac signs to dig deep within their soul, utilize their intuition to heal trauma and pain, always believe in their dreams, and always express themselves emotionally through their greater imagination.

�✩☾

UNEVOLVED PISCES – PETTY SIREN

Unevolved Pisceans are petty mermaids that swim in and out of people's lives. They've learned from Aquarius, the unevolved sign before them, that distance and rebellion is the only way to live. They've learned from their unevolved water siblings, Cancer and Scorpio, to play victim and overreact with spite and vengeance. They've learned from their unevolved mutable cousins, Gemini, Virgo, and Sagittarius, that commitment is non-existent and self-expression has no filter. This, in turn, creates obsessive emotional attachments or detachments and an unfiltered and unchecked mouthpiece.

Since their motto is "I believe," unevolved Pisceans believe that nothing good can come into their life. They can be stuck in the abyss of their fragile emotions, which is fully projected when they reach the surface to interact with others. Unevolved Pisceans strongly believe they are permanent targets and that people go out of their way to personally attack them. They will always choose to play the helpless victim, even when they're in the wrong. They can drown themselves in their own sorrow, choosing to self-medicate or drink their insecurities away. They are also known to overreact and overwhelm others with their emotions, especially when loved ones try to get them help. If they feel threatened, they can be petty, spiteful, and jealous.

As a mutable water sign, unevolved Pisceans have a vicious mouthpiece. They hurt people whenever they feel like it, especially when they're in self-defense mode. Their distance and rebelliousness are mostly a façade that guards their deeper insecurities. They will flee at the thought of commitment, especially if it's getting professional help. Even though they are guided by two fish, both are constantly swimming downward and away from reality. They can live in a world of fantasy and delusion, luring in helping hands only to grab them and sink into the dark void below.

✹✫☾

EVOLVED PISCES – COMPASSIONATE MERMAID

Evolved Pisceans are compassionate mermaids who know how to wield their intuition for the betterment of themselves and everyone around them. They were taught by the evolved sign before them, Aquarius, to advocate for causes that help society. They've learned from their evolved water siblings, Cancer and Scorpio, to trust their intuition and embrace emotions. They've learned from their mutable cousins, Gemini, Virgo, and Sagittarius, to adapt to their environment and be flexible in their thinking. Due to this, evolved Pisceans courageously pursue the elevation and evolution of spirituality and emotional connectivity within all communities.

Since their motto is "I believe," evolved Pisceans possess high spiritual beliefs that promote true self-awareness and enlightenment. They encourage others to find their true meaning in life and believe that everyone's life path is unique. They don't believe in timetables, allowing life to flow naturally without stress or tension. They internalize and reflect on the pros and cons of every situation, which allows them to gain a deeper understanding of their beliefs and values. They have a strong understanding of both the physical and spiritual realms and believe in maintaining their spiritual and emotional well-being, oftentimes joining causes that promote it.

As a mutable water sign, evolved Pisceans swim upward and into their higher selves, a space that is full of imagination and creativity. They express themselves from a sacred space, oftentimes spilling poetry and music into the world as a source of healing. They are truly enchanting, compassionate, and sensitive beings that feel every painful and happy moment with the world around them. Though they find it hard to control how they feel, they will always do what is right and put aside their selfish desires, especially if it helps the world become a more peaceful and serene place.

☀ ☆ ☾

PISCES MOON

♓ ☽

"I believe what I feel."

Individuals with a Pisces Moon process their emotions passively and intuitively, but it depends on other celestial factors. Mixed with fire, they are blunt and brave yet lack empathy and can be hostile. Mixed with earth, they are tranquil and nurturing but are too tolerant and forgiving. Mixed with air, they are highly imaginative and expressive but impractical and verbally abusive. Mixed with water, they are more insightful and receptive but can be extremely insecure and overly possessive.

Emotionally, Pisces Moons are highly sensitive to the energies of people, animals, and nature. They are constantly recycling good and bad energy, which also means they can shift between these moods very frequently. They can be sweet and hopeless romantics one day but distant and depressed the next day. They are also susceptible to soaking in other people's energies and adopting them as their own. They are free-flowing spiritual types who feed off the energy of others (good or bad). As highly sensitive signs, they feel for others when they're down, and they will always do their best to console your spirit with words and affection that are catered to just you.

Pisces Moons are believers of all emotions: love, hate, and anything in between. They are a very forgiving sign who utilizes their strong intuition to guide their emotions. However, they can fall for their own illusions and overreact or shut down in very stressful situations. Since they are so sensitive to energy and emotions, Pisces Moons have very vivid and spiritual dreams of life and love, which creates a powerful imagination that can be used in creative work that helps enlighten others who forgot how to dream.

☀ ☆ ☾

PISCES ENERGY IN OTHER PLACEMENTS

PISCES ASCENDANT (RISING)

♓ AC

"I believe in myself."

Pisces Risings project wisdom, compassion, imagination, idealism, and fantasy in everything they do. Upon first impression, it can seem as if their minds are wandering off, unaware or unbothered with present circumstances. It probably is. Most times, they would rather be in some distant world doing something fun and enchanting with other people.

When it comes to their physical appearance, Pisces Risings are bohemian, free-flowing dressers, meaning they like to wear anything loose-fitting yet stylish and even sexy. The less clothes they wear, the freer their spirits feel.

PISCES MIDHEAVEN (MC)

♓ MC

"I believe in my career."

Pisces Midheavens require peaceful environments in order to excel in their careers, otherwise they will become easily frustrated and overwhelmed. Many of them prefer careers in which they are constantly expressing their emotions, such as music, dance, or art. It's both free-flowing and serene.

Since Pisces Midheavens value peace and serenity, they do best in careers where they can provide it for themselves and others. You'll find many who like to heal others through sound and motion. They also gravitate toward any type of design, such as graphic design, interior design, photography, etc.

PISCES MERCURY

♓ ☿

"I believe in my thoughts."

Pisces Mercurians possess very whimsical and thoughtful ideas. They are extremely creative and imaginative. They constantly reflect on their feelings and live within a trance of daydreams. They are sensitive to the world around them, yet they can remain guarded and aloof because their minds are dancing in their own bubble of fantasies.

Pisces Mercurians are often solitary, audio, and verbal learners. They like to take their time when processing information, though they can be obsessive in their research. They also need to be away from others because they can be easily distracted. Words and audio will have a powerful effect, as they like to envision situations as they are reading or hearing them.

PISCES VENUS

♓ ♀

"I believe in love."

Pisces Venusians love to fantasize love and romance but are very selective when choosing a forever swimming partner. Like fish, they don't want to be an easy catch. They will be slippery in love because they are always unsure if someone is baiting them with false dreams or if they're in it forever.

When Pisces Venusians are in love, they become devoted to love and can be vulnerable, emotional, and submissive, which scares them. However, they are strong believers that their one true soulmate will whisk them away like a fairy tale come true. Until that day comes, they will hold out for as long as they can while dismissing anyone who isn't a soul connection.

✴ ☆ ☾

PISCES MARS

♓ ♂

"I believe in physical power."

Pisces Martians are spiritually and intuitively powerful. Although they are fully aware that people can and will use physical power, they are not the type to tolerate it. They don't believe in using violence, and they don't condone physical abuse of any kind. To them, if a person is unable to express their feelings without asserting their dominance, they are internally weak.

Pisces Martians may not push or bully others, but that doesn't mean they won't defend themselves. They'll charge at you like a great white shark if you provoke them far enough, especially if you bring up anything personal. Still, they will give you a few warnings before they attack you. It may be wise for you to listen.

PISCES JUPITER

♓ ♃

"I believe in expansion."

Pisces Jupiterians expand spiritually, mentally, and emotionally. They find wealth and success in possessing meaningful information, as this brings them closer to true emotional awareness and mental enlightenment. They are also highly intuitive, artistic, and imaginative. Creative freedom and emotional expression will be especially important to their overall well-being.

Pisces Jupiterians believe in having faith in everything you do, say, and think. They love to inspire others to do the same. Money doesn't play a big role when it comes to their success because all they dream of doing is living an expansive life full of freedom, creativity, and storytelling.

PISCES SATURN

♓ ♄

"I believe in restriction."

Pisces Saturnians believe in restricting their emotions when it comes to career and money. They don't believe in restricting their emotions when it comes to family and friends. However, if they sense something fishy or if someone tries to ensnare them with false dreams, they will immediately guard themselves and enforce strict boundaries.

Pisces Saturnians use their intuition to set meaningful and realistic goals. Money is just a bonus to them, as they often pursue careers they have a special emotional attachment to. This sign has two fish with opposing sides: one is extremely professional and the other is extremely sensitive. If this sign is able to balance their energy, they will be able to provide one of the most ideal loving and stable environments for themselves and their families.

PISCES URANUS

♓ ♅

"I believe in change."

Pisces Uranians are believers of adapting and adopting change. They have high faith and hope in obtaining world peace, and they don't believe in being aggressive or violent to get it. The majority of them believe that positive change can happen if and when people are open to love and not hate.

As one of the most compassionate signs, Pisces Uranians take healing and advocacy very seriously, and they refuse to tolerate any kind of injustice, hate, or oppression. They may not take up arms or join protests, but they will join peaceful charitable events and express their feelings through multiple outlets.

✸ ✰ ☾

PISCES NEPTUNE

♓ ♆

"I believe in spirituality."

Pisces Neptunians embody spirituality, so believing in it is second nature to them. When fully evolved, they become the ultimate spiritual teachers and healers of the world. The majority of them possess vivid clairvoyant dreams and have a strong connection with the spiritual realm. Like all water signs, they are in tune with their emotions and are natural empaths who feel and absorb the energy of others. This, in turn, helps them heal the pain in others.

Pisces Neptunians can be heavily involved in religion or any sacred space that provides a positive and uplifting atmosphere, especially if it was part of their upbringing. They also love joining a school of fish that eats, prays, performs rituals, and protects one another. The more, the merrier.

PISCES PLUTO

♓ ♇

"I believe in evolution."

Pisces Plutonians believe in evolving emotionally and spiritually, and they will have visions of a heavenly, weightless afterlife. During their lifetime, they will soak in everything meaningful, spitting out anything superficial. They will endure many emotional trials in life, but because they are adaptable, they remain optimistic and hopeful even in their darkest moments.

Before Pisces Plutonians depart from this world, they will work to have a peaceful, serene, and creative life. It may not be full of achievements, but it will be filled with special memories of happiness and love with others. And that's all they want: to be surrounded by fishies who love and appreciate them.

☼ ☆ ☾

CUSPS

Cusps symbolize the evolution (transition) of one zodiac sign to the next. Just like the zodiac, there are 12 cusps. Each cusp pulls energy from the last sign into the new one. These transitional phases from one zodiac sign to the next are usually made up of 10 days/10 degrees, five days in one zodiac sign and five days in the next, including the date of transition.

Some astrologers have different time lengths for cusps; they can go by three days or six days. The reason I go up to 10 days is because I intuitively feel that transitions take much longer than three or six, and I use the pattern of 10° each, which is approximately 10 days. Ultimately, do what feels right for you. If you feel it's shorter than 10 days, then go with that.

Cusp babies are born during these times. If you were not born within these date ranges, you are not considered a cusp baby.

GLYPHS	CUSPS	CUSP DATES
♈ ♉	Aries – Taurus	April 15 – April 24
♉ ♊	Taurus – Gemini	May 16 – May 25
♊ ♋	Gemini – Cancer	June 16 – June 25
♋ ♌	Cancer – Leo	July 18 – July 27
♌ ♍	Leo – Virgo	August 18 – August 27
♍ ♎	Virgo – Libra	September 18 – September 27
♎ ♏	Libra – Scorpio	October 18 – October 27
♏ ♐	Scorpio – Sagittarius	November 17 – November 26
♐ ♑	Sagittarius – Capricorn	December 17 – December 26
♑ ♒	Capricorn – Aquarius	January 15 – January 24
♒ ♓	Aquarius – Pisces	February 14 – February 23
♓ ♈	Pisces – Aries	March 16 – March 25

ARIES – TAURUS CUSP

APRIL 15ᵀᴴ – APRIL 24ᵀᴴ

♈ ♉

"I am and I have."

You have both the fiery aggression of Aries and the earth-like tough exterior of Taurus. Stability will be important to your livelihood, but you are impulsive and impatient with decisions. You are what you have, and having a powerful status and financial security takes priority in life. You won't settle for mediocrity; you want it all. You burn and build with such vigor that those who cannot keep up are left in dust and ashes. You tend to focus on what needs to get done and are a natural survivor and warrior in this world. Nobody can stand in your way because you'll ram or bulldoze them out of the way.

TAURUS – GEMINI CUSP

MAY 16ᵀᴴ – MAY 25ᵀᴴ

♉ ♊

"I have and I think."

You have both the earth-like tough exterior of Taurus and the flighty and airy personality of Gemini. The freedom to express your ideas and creativity is important to you, and you won't let anybody stop you from doing it. You are also family-oriented, though you love better from a distance. You have both a friendly and serious demeanor, depending on whether or not you can trust a person. Your keen insights keep you organized, though you like to take your time to process your thoughts and ideas. You possess very stubborn, even dogmatic, views and are always up for a good debate but can become argumentative because you don't like to be proven wrong.

GEMINI – CANCER CUSP

JUNE 16TH – JUNE 25TH

Ⅱ ♋

"I think and I feel."

You have both the flighty and airy personality of Gemini and the high emotional sensitivity of Cancer. You are highly intuitive and thoughtful, and you feel what you think and think what you feel. You prioritize open communication and share your feelings and ideas openly without fear. You are a great and loyal lover who wants to nurture relationships, whether they be friends, family, or lovers. You are funny, observant, and in sync with all of your creative efforts. Be careful of your high mood swings and energy, though. It can be challenging for you to control your mental and emotional shifts because you don't believe in holding anything back.

CANCER – LEO CUSP

JULY 18TH – JULY 27TH

♋ ♌

"I feel and I will."

You have the sensitivity of Cancer's moody water and the aggression and affections of Leo. You feel your willpower and are highly affectionate and passionate, so taking care of your heart's desires will always be a priority. You are prone to dramatic displays of just about anything. You tend to live life like a movie and aren't afraid to shine brighter than anybody else, day or night. To you, there are no limitations. You are very determined, which gives you the willpower to make all of your dreams come true. However, you get upset if things don't come to fruition and are known to have temper tantrums.

☀ ★ ☾

LEO – VIRGO CUSP

AUGUST 18TH – AUGUST 27TH

♌ ♍

"I will and I analyze."

You have the aggression of Leo and the logical sense and self-maintenance of Virgo. Your earth-like senses make you cool and calm, but underneath is a lava of passion and drive. You analyze your willpower often, as you are a professional, hardworking person who invests a lot of time in dreaming and grounding your bigger-than-life goals. You value privacy, loyalty, and honor. You can be hard on yourself when you're not productive. You also abhor unnecessary drama or confrontations, so you do your best to mediate tense situations, taking a more logical approach to fan out the flames.

VIRGO – LIBRA CUSP

SEPTEMBER 18TH – SEPTEMBER 27TH

♍ ♎

"I analyze and I balance."

You have the intellectual mindset of a Virgo and the charming personality of a Libra. Partnerships and community will take priority in your life, and without this, you feel incomplete. You also balance what you analyze. This makes for a great combination, as you have the ability to teach and motivate people around you to reach their maximum potential. To you, perfection is a goal that can be reached, so long as you are constantly working on it. You often strive for the ideal lifestyle, as well as ideal physical beauty. However, you are highly critical of yourself, wanting to perfect everything and anything you do. Be careful not to overthink your doom.

LIBRA – SCORPIO CUSP

OCTOBER 18TH – OCTOBER 27TH

♎ ♏

"I balance and I desire."

You have the charming magnetism of Libra and the hypnotic energy of Scorpio. You tend to have the sexual appeal most people wish they had, even when you're not trying. People are drawn to you like a moth to a flame and are in awe of all your intuitive insights. You balance what and who you desire the most. You know what to say, when to say it, and how to say it. However, you can be very petty and vengeful, finding it easy to tear someone down whenever you feel like it. This can lead you to having difficult relations with others, especially those who envy all of your beauty or intelligence.

SCORPIO – SAGITTARIUS CUSP

NOVEMBER 17TH – NOVEMBER 26TH

♏ ♐

"I desire and I see."

You have the hypnotic and intense energy of Scorpio and the awe-inspiring and bubbly personality of Sagittarius. People are attracted to your dark humor as well as your sexual confidence. However, you rarely pay attention to what others see because seeking the truth and the deeper meaning of life is your only priority. You are an expert strategist who masters intuition, gaining more accuracy when you shoot your arrows out into the world. What you see is what you desire, and you can become overly attached to things or people after you've invested your energy. Love and hate have the same intensity levels to you. People are either an ally or an enemy; there's no in between.

☼ ✫ ☾

SAGITTARIUS – CAPRICORN CUSP

DECEMBER 17TH – DECEMBER 26TH

♐ ♑

"I see and I use."

You have the free-spirited energy of Sagittarius and the earthy demeanor and perseverance of Capricorn. What you see is what you use (good or bad), as you are highly resourceful and tactical. It's a struggle to balance your pace, as you like to go either really fast or really slow. Regardless of which pace you're in the mood for, you're always down to take a risk to gain higher rewards. Respect for yourself and from others is also high on your list, and you like to present yourself as an honorable and respectable professional. If you are disrespected, the animal in you will take over, ready to stomp out any threats.

CAPRICORN – AQUARIUS CUSP

JANUARY 15TH – JANUARY 24TH

♑ ♒

"I use and I know."

You have the earthy determination of Capricorn and the open-minded and friendliness of Aquarius. What you use is what you know, so you will invest a lot of your time and energy in education and self-awareness. You believe strongly in helping others, and to make a difference, you are willing to rebel against tradition. You like meeting and learning about different cultures and beliefs, which helps you gain a deeper understanding of how the world operates. There's nothing in this world that you can't see yourself accomplishing, as you are focused on realistic perspectives with strong goals.

☼ ☆ ☾

AQUARIUS – PISCES CUSP

FEBRUARY 14ᵀᴴ – FEBRUARY 23ᴿᴰ

♒ ♓

"I know and I believe."

You have the friendliness and humanitarian strengths of Aquarius and the compassion and non-judgmental side of Pisces. What you know is what you believe. You are an intuitive friend of the world who likes to see things from all perspectives, making sure every side is considered. You tend to be very sensitive and will debate and fight for a cause you are passionate about. You are also very aloof, enigmatic, and detached yet will somehow always be there for a good friend. Draining situations are really not worth your time and energy, and you dislike confrontation, so you tend to remove yourself from it altogether. You'd rather do something more positive than negative.

PISCES – ARIES CUSP

MARCH 16ᵀᴴ – MARCH 25ᵀᴴ

♓ ♈

"I believe and I am."

You have the sensitive and intuitive side of Pisces and the brave and fiery energy of Aries. You tend to be a boiling pot of water at times because you can be highly aggressive and will vocalize your feelings fearlessly, yet you are also highly optimistic, social, playful, and outgoing. You also have a blistering mouthpiece on you, which may get you into more trouble than necessary. As quick as you are to heat up, it's just as easy for you to cool it. You prefer to have more positive experiences than negative and will search for opportunities of self-growth and worldly success.

✸✦☾

✵☆☾

DECANATES

ZODIAC SIGN	1st DECAN 0°–10°	2ND DECAN 10°–20°	3RD DECAN 20°–30°
♈	MARS	SUN	JUPITER
♉	VENUS	MERCURY	SATURN
♊	MERCURY	VENUS	URANUS
♋	MOON	PLUTO	NEPTUNE
♌	SUN	JUPITER	MARS
♍	MERCURY	SATURN	VENUS
♎	VENUS	URANUS	MERCURY
♏	PLUTO	NEPTUNE	MOON
♐	JUPITER	MARS	SUN
♑	SATURN	VENUS	MERCURY
♒	URANUS	MERCURY	VENUS
♓	NEPTUNE	MOON	PLUTO

Your chart is made up of 360 degrees. Divide that by 12 signs and you'll get 30 degrees each. Within these 30 degrees are 10-degree slices called decanates, aka decans. You will also notice that decans have cusps in between their transitions, where the next decan starts at the end of the last one.

In total, each zodiac sign is split into three decans (10°, 20°, and 30°), and each decan is co-ruled by their elemental siblings' ruling planets. Their dates can last between nine to ten days, depending on the solar calendar. The ones shown in this chapter are based on traditional dates.

For example, Sagittarius' first decan is ruled by Jupiter, its second decan is co-ruled by Mars (Aries' ruling planet), and its third decan is co-ruled by the Sun (Leo's ruling planet).

✸ ✰ ☾

BREAKING DOWN DECANATES

★ There is a total of 36 decans, which equal 360 degrees.

★ Each zodiac sign's season lasts for approximately 30 days, or 30 degrees.

★ Each decan is 10 degrees, with each degree being approximately one day. So 10 degrees equals 10 days.

AUTHOR NOTES

Decans can be a major or minor influence, depending on how you want to interpret them into your reading. If you're more of a technical reader, meaning you are extremely detailed and analytical, then you can add them. There's nothing wrong with being more detailed. It's up to you to decide what resonates with your readings and what doesn't. Personally, I do not use them for any of my readings because celestial aspects have a stronger influence when it comes to a person's overall character. However, I do believe there is a reason for decans, as they are part of a zodiac sign's natural evolution.

Keep in mind that the dates listed in the next sections are from traditional dates not solar dates.

☼ ☆ ☾

ARIES DECANATES

1ST DECANATE
MARCH 21 – MARCH 31 | 0° – 10° DEGREES: MARS (ARIES)

♈ ♂

You are full of intense and dominant warrior energy. You inspire others to overcome their fears, believing that anything can be conquered with pure strength or force, whichever comes first. Regardless, you're built on innovation and creation and strive to be more than what you're born into.

2ND DECANATE
APRIL 1 – APRIL 10 | 10° – 20° DEGREES: SUN (LEO)

♈ ☉

You don't believe in limitations, and you possess dreams bigger than the Sun. You were made to entertain and be entertained, which allows you to climb the ambitious ladder of success through many creative endeavors. You want to own the spotlight, and sharing it is out of the question.

3RD DECANATE
APRIL 11 – APRIL 19 | 20° – 30° DEGREES: JUPITER (SAGITTARIUS)

♈ ♃

You are a free-spirited and independent individual. You look to expand your horizons by taking up many skills. You have a strong sense of adventure and yearn to travel for greater experiences. You are always moving and find it challenging to be still for fear of missing out on something memorable.

✲✲☾

TAURUS DECANATES

1ST DECANATE
APRIL 20 – APRIL 30 | 0° – 10° DEGREES: VENUS (TAURUS)

♉ ♀

You value beauty, loyalty, and nurturement. You observe natural beauty in everything and everyone, finding superficiality distasteful. You are a lover of great work, especially art and music. You are also possessive when you find the object of all your desires, choosing to stow it away from prying eyes.

2ND DECANATE
MAY 1 – MAY 10 | 10° – 20° DEGREES: MERCURY (VIRGO)

♉ ☿

You love the solitude of your thoughts and privacy. You are a creative thinker, yet you are fixed on your beliefs and perspectives. You have strong likes and dislikes and aren't afraid to vocalize them. You base your decisions on logic and facts and strive for maximum efficiency.

3RD DECANATE
MAY 11 – MAY 20 | 20° – 30° DEGREES: SATURN (CAPRICORN)

♉ ♄

You are a lover of material wealth and success. You possess realistic views and are disciplined, structured, and responsible. You are more conservative and traditional, believing there is a hierarchy of which everyone plays a significant role. Your love of money knows no bound.

GEMINI DECANATES

1ST DECANATE
MAY 21 – MAY 31 | 0° – 10° DEGREES: MERCURY (GEMINI)

Ⅱ ☿

You value freedom of choice and expression and hate the idea of being mentally manipulated or controlled. You act and adapt quickly to situations with logical and creative precision. You are an out-of-the-box thinker, and your genius matches your unfiltered wit but can also get you in trouble.

2ND DECANATE
JUNE 1 – JUNE 10 | 10° – 20° DEGREES: VENUS (LIBRA)

Ⅱ ♀

You love the idea of love but hate the idea of commitment for fear of losing your independence. You prefer to experience life with others, and you like to learn about different cultures. You are more rational than the other decans but are also a friend of the world who finds it challenging to balance love.

3RD DECANATE
JUNE 11 – JUNE 20 | 20° – 30° DEGREES: URANUS (AQUARIUS)

Ⅱ ♅

You love education and research, even if the topics are trivial to others. You are a keeper of the mind and advocate of the world, and finding justice and equality for all is important. You are an intellectual who strives to be part of the community and create change.

✵ ✫ ☽

CANCER DECANATES

1ST DECANATE
JUNE 21 – JUNE 30 | 0° – 10° DEGREES: MOON (CANCER)

♋ ☽

You are receptive and sensitive. You wear your heart on your sleeve and are not afraid to express your feelings. Your moods can shift because you are more sensitive than others, but you are a compassionate person who works toward having true emotional fulfillment no matter the cost.

2ND DECANATE
JULY 1 – JULY 11 | 10° – 20° DEGREES: PLUTO (SCORPIO)

♋ ♇

You love the idea of privacy and internalizing your emotions. You have a higher intuition than the other decans, finding it easy to predict outcomes and judge characters. You are fixed in disciplining your emotions, yet you are also sentimental and possessive in relationships.

3RD DECANATE
JULY 12 – JULY 22 | 20° – 30° DEGREES: NEPTUNE (PISCES)

♋ ♆

You love to dream of romance and love, diving deep in your creativity and imagination. You utilize your intuition to help others, but you also find it hard to enforce personal boundaries. You love to socialize with others because you enjoy observing and accepting different characters.

LEO DECANATES

1ST DECANATE
JULY 23 – AUGUST 1 | 0° – 10° DEGREES: SUN (LEO)

♌ ☉

You love the spotlight and aren't afraid to shine. You always follow your heart, even if it seems selfish to others. You have strong boundaries and aren't afraid to say no. You are a lover of compliments and passionate moments but can't stand ingenuine people who try to take advantage of your shine.

2ND DECANATE
AUGUST 2 – AUGUST 12 | 10° – 20° DEGREES: JUPITER (SAGITTARIUS)

♌ ♃

You are a visionary who yearns to experience life without restrictions. You take your dreams and ambitions seriously, yet you have a hard time sticking to one project. You like to constantly dream of your future and believe you are fated to accomplish something others cannot.

3RD DECANATE
AUGUST 13 – AUGUST 22 | 20° – 30° DEGREES: MARS (ARIES)

♌ ♂

You are a determined person who doesn't involve themselves in drama. You need new and exciting challenges in your life, otherwise you get restless. You believe in investing in your skills and talents, believing that success can't be obtained without first being the strongest you can be.

✵ ⭐ ☾

VIRGO DECANATES

1ST DECANATE
AUGUST 23 – SEPTEMBER 1 | 0° – 10° DEGREES: MERCURY (VIRGO)

♍ ☿

You are highly analytical and perceptive. You pride yourself in your wit and logic, finding it easy to source solutions for every situation. You believe in having the perfect mind and invest a lot of your energy in education. You take a more realistic approach to life, but that's what makes you successful.

2ND DECANATE
SEPTEMBER 2 – SEPTEMBER 12 | 10° – 20° DEGREES: SATURN (CAPRICORN)

♍ ♄

You take your career seriously and are a very detailed person. You believe there is a right and wrong way to do things. You can be hard on yourself when you're not progressing in life but can easily adapt to any situation. You also believe in having material wealth and status to showcase your hard work.

3RD DECANATE
SEPTEMBER 13 – SEPTEMBER 22 | 20° – 30° DEGREES: VENUS (TAURUS)

♍ ♀

You focus more on physical well-being and nutrition. Being part of a community will be important. You can be a lover of good food and pleasure, but you also believe in physical control. Though you can be critical of others, you believe in helping everyone reach their type of perfection.

LIBRA DECANATES

1ST DECANATE
SEPTEMBER 23 – OCTOBER 2 | 0° – 10° DEGREES: VENUS (LIBRA)

♎ ♀

You live for love, beauty, pleasure, and luxury. Your persona is charming and magnetic, so people are naturally attracted to you. You are a generous person who loves to be in relationships, finding it challenging to be alone for too long because there are so many options.

2ND DECANATE
OCTOBER 3 – OCTOBER 13 | 10° – 20° DEGREES: URANUS (AQUARIUS)

♎ ♅

You are highly opinionated and are a strong believer of expression. You tend to aggressively fight for justice and rebel against the norm. You believe in hard work and perseverance, focusing most of your efforts on your career. You also possess strong boundaries that you enforce at will.

3RD DECANATE
OCTOBER 14 – OCTOBER 22 | 20° – 30° DEGREES: MERCURY (GEMINI)

♎ ☿

You are open-minded, intelligent, and productive. You are the innovative type who believes in having open communication with everyone. You like to learn the psychology of people, either using it for or against them. You tend to work best when dealing with the masses, finding it easy to persuade them.

☀ ✦ ☽

SCORPIO DECANATES

1ST DECANATE
OCTOBER 23 – NOVEMBER 1 | 0° – 10° DEGREES: PLUTO (SCORPIO)

♏ ♇

You have intense psychic intuition and tend to have good judgments, but trusting others is extremely challenging for you. You are fixated on having self-control and emotional discipline, and it's hard for you to break rituals. You are the keeper of secrets and value privacy, trust, and loyalty.

2ND DECANATE
NOVEMBER 2 – NOVEMBER 11 | 10° – 20° DEGREES: NEPTUNE (PISCES)

♏ ♆

You are sensitive, playful, and imaginative. You value good friends and family, wanting to be surrounded by love and appreciation. You like to dive deep in your emotions, finding it soothing to your soul to release negativity. You also like to find creative outlets to emotionally express yourself.

3RD DECANATE
NOVEMBER 12 – NOVEMBER 21 | 20° – 30° DEGREES: MOON (CANCER)

♏ ☽

You are highly sensitive to the energies of the people around you, which can cause some very intense mood swings. You are direct, possessing a stronger sense of righteousness. You don't mess around when it comes to your feelings and aren't afraid to say what needs to be said.

SAGITTARIUS DECANATES

1ST DECANATE
NOVEMBER 22 – DECEMBER 1 | 0° – 10° DEGREES: JUPITER (SAGITTARIUS)

♐ ♃

You are a vibrant and carefree person who takes a philosophical approach to life. You seek the truth in all aspects of your life and always give an honest and open answer to everything. Though you miss the smaller details, you are a strong believer of faith and embrace the bigger picture of every situation.

2ND DECANATE
DECEMBER 2 – DECEMBER 11 | 10° – 20° DEGREES: MARS (ARIES)

♐ ♂

You are a highly independent and courageous person but can often get into a lot of trouble for cheap, exciting thrills. You like to live in the now and find the humor in everything and everyone. You also like to feel empowered and will invest your energy in things that make you feel physically stronger.

3RD DECANATE
DECEMBER 12 – DECEMBER 21 | 20° – 30° DEGREES: SUN (LEO)

♐ ☉

You are full of vitality and live life to the fullest without limitations. You make a wonderful host/hostess and love entertaining others. You are very passionate and even dramatic, but you love sharing stories and experiences. You live to have a good time and tend to be lucky with money.

✵☆☾

Capricorn Decanates

1st Decanate
December 22 – December 31 | 0° – 10° degrees: Saturn (Capricorn)

♑ ♄

You are a highly responsible and disciplined person. You devote yourself to being successful and take your career and education seriously. You are a goal-oriented person who never deters from their aspirations. You focus on having assets, status, and savings, as this helps you retire earlier.

2nd Decanate
January 1 – January 10 | 10° – 20° degrees: Venus (Taurus)

♑ ♀

You are family-oriented and dedicate yourself to having and maintaining one. You have an interest in beauty and art and are focused on having material wealth. You like to move at your own pace and tend to have more patience and tolerance toward others. You also find it hard to be without a partner.

3rd Decanate
January 11 – January 19 | 20° – 30° degrees: Mercury (Virgo)

♑ ☿

You are a trustworthy, fair, and respectful person. You like to invest most of your time in education and research and will pursue projects that dedicate time to learning or improving life. You are also a highly rational person who finds emotional expression challenging.

AQUARIUS DECANATES

1ST DECANATE
JANUARY 20 – JANUARY 29 | 0° – 10° DEGREES: URANUS (AQUARIUS)

♒ ♅

You like to be original and innovative with your ideas. You like to see situations from an unbiased perspective, and you are not afraid to judge people fairly. You like to problem-solve and can tolerate others, but you prefer to be distant and independent.

2ND DECANATE
JANUARY 30 – FEBRUARY 8 | 10° – 20° DEGREES: MERCURY (GEMINI)

♒ ☿

You are an educated and highly opinionated person who likes to vocalize and express themselves without restriction. You don't like to be controlled or manipulated by others, believing that you have the right to judge for yourself. You are also more unpredictable and irrational in certain situations.

3RD DECANATE
FEBRUARY 9 – FEBRUARY 18 | 20° – 30° DEGREES: VENUS (LIBRA)

♒ ♀

You are a kind friend to the world who likes to be involved in humanitarian causes that fight for justice and peace. You seek to have balance, peace, and harmony in all aspects of life. However, you tend to be indecisive and struggle with seeing people's true intent.

✶✫☾

PISCES DECANATES

1ST DECANATE
FEBRUARY 19 – FEBRUARY 29 | 0° – 10° DEGREES: NEPTUNE (PISCES)

♓ ♆

You are a highly imaginative and intuitive person who likes to daydream. You like to go with the flow of everything and everyone, believing that no one should live in a fish tank. You can have a challenging time dealing with reality, choosing to escape mentally and emotionally to another dimension.

2ND DECANATE
MARCH 1 – MARCH 10 | 10° – 20° DEGREES: MOON (CANCER)

♓ ☽

You are a compassionate and highly sensitive person who tends to give more than they receive. You have a hard time enforcing boundaries because you believe in loving freely and unconditionally. You are a healer at heart who always finds ways to make others feel special and loved.

3RD DECANATE
MARCH 11 – MARCH 20 | 20° – 30° DEGREES: PLUTO (SCORPIO)

♓ ♇

You are a soulful person whose emotions run deep and intensely. You are a strong believer of spirituality and faith and are devoted to learning the deeper meaning of life and love. You constantly reflect on your emotions but find it challenging to express them without coming off aggressive/passionate.

✸ ✩ ☾

POLAR OPPOSITES

GLYPHS	SIGN	MODALITY	ELEMENT	HOUSES
♈ ♎	ARIES & LIBRA	CARDINAL	FIRE & AIR	1 & 7
♉ ♏	TAURUS & SCORPIO	FIXED	EARTH & WATER	2 & 8
♊ ♐	GEMINI & SAGITTARIUS	MUTABLE	AIR & FIRE	3 & 9
♋ ♑	CANCER & CAPRICORN	CARDINAL	WATER & EARTH	4 & 10
♌ ♒	LEO & AQUARIUS	FIXED	FIRE & AIR	5 & 11
♍ ♓	VIRGO & PISCES	MUTABLE	EARTH & WATER	6 & 12

Polar opposites are zodiac signs that are 180° apart, a direct line from one end of the horoscope to the other. These opposite signs create a yin and yang synergy, where one sign's greatest weaknesses are the other one's greatest strengths.

Polar opposites share the same modality, have compatible elements, and are in opposite houses. Although they share many similar traits, they still remain independent from one another. How they react and handle certain situations will differ. However, their energies will vibe, unlike other zodiac signs, and they will either create an effortless friendship or become the worst of enemies.

How they see one another is based on other celestial factors, but for the most part, these opposite signs will act more as half-siblings who can love and respect each other in ways they can't with others.

Opposite signs share a divine connection between their houses, where one resides in the lower/inner hemisphere and the other resides in the upper/outer hemisphere. The sign that lives in the lower hemisphere creates energy that influences our inner strengths and skills, which then helps the sign in the upper hemisphere create experiences that react to those strengths and skills.

☼ ✦ ☾

ARIES & LIBRA

♈ ♎

"I am and I balance."

Aries is a cardinal fire sign from the 1st House of Self, whereas Libra is a cardinal air sign from the 7th House of Partnerships. They match each other's ambition for social status and self-empowerment. Aries will be more focused on their own well-being, whereas Libra will be more concerned with how their actions affect others. Although both are in it to dominate and control, their natural instincts and judgments will differ when managing others.

Aries will weed out the weak and reward the strong without a second thought, while Libra will take a chance on weaker potentials to build them into stronger beings. Aries will use fear and strength to control. Libra will use persuasion and inspiration to build loyalty for control. Both will use strategy to create a team of people that will follow their lead willing or unwillingly.

Negatively, they will find it challenging to communicate with one another, as Aries is more about authority and Libra is more about equality. Both want to take the lead, as one will feel they have more experience or skills than the other. This can lead to a battle of who is right or wrong, creating petty arguments where Aries will not back down physically and Libra will not back down mentally.

Positively, they possess the same aggressively high energy, optimism, and love of life. They often take pleasure and fun to the next level, hardly saying no to new experiences. Their need for power and worldly success helps them build and uplift one another, as they both feel compelled to become a pillar in society. They will travel and reap the rewards of their success together.

☀ ☆ ☾

TAURUS & SCORPIO

♉ ♏

"I have and I desire."

Taurus is a fixed earth sign from the 2nd House of Possession, whereas Scorpio is a fixed water sign from the 8th House of Regeneration. They match each other's need for possessing the comforts of life. Taurus will be focused on what they can possess realistically and materially, while Scorpio will focus on what they can possess spiritually and emotionally. Both will have a desire to obtain wealth in their lifetime, yet they differ when it comes to its definition.

Taurus possesses more realistic views, wanting to own what they can see, feel, and touch. They focus on higher-quality products and long-term benefits from anything or anyone. Scorpio possesses more abstract views, where wealth comes from within, so they will have stronger emotional attachments. Scorpios will want to possess things or people they deeply desire or have soul connections with.

Negatively, both will have a challenging time expressing themselves, as both value privacy and internalize their emotions. Both will also struggle to fully understand one another when it comes to possession, especially because they are both equally stubborn and find it hard to change their views. Taurus will dream of being surrounded by the comfort of material wealth, whereas Scorpio will dream of being surrounded by spiritual and emotional wealth.

Positively, they require a deep, unbreakable bond built on trust and loyalty. They prove to have the most telepathic union, as they seem to innately understand each other's intentions. They balance one another's desires, making it easy for them to accumulate both material and immaterial wealth.

✹☆☾

GEMINI & SAGITTARIUS

♊ ♐

"I think and I see."

Gemini is a mutable air sign from the 3rd House of Communication, whereas Sagittarius is a mutable fire sign from the 9th House of Mental Exploration. They match each other's wit and intelligence. Gemini will be focused on their creative endeavors and engagements with others, while Sagittarius will be focused on how to move their ideas and strategies forward. Both will invest a lot of their time in building their mentality through personal experiences.

Gemini leads with their head and constantly thinks of innovative and creative ways to live their best life. Sagittarius leads with their spirit and will think of ingenious ways to escape a stagnant life. Both prefer to live a life of freedom, and they hate feeling constrained, wanting to immerse themselves in any experience that allows them the freedom of choice and unrestricted progress.

Negatively, they have a challenging time fully understanding each other's perspectives and ideas, as they both vocalize their unfiltered thoughts without emotional consideration. Since there's no restraint on their expression, these debates can quickly turn into heated arguments or a full-on fight. Gemini will think of details that Sagittarius will find irrelevant, whereas Sagittarius will see the overall grander picture, which Gemini will find irrelevant. Gemini focuses on the now. Sagittarius focuses on the future.

Positively, their willingness to problem-solve and understand different perspectives, as well as their adaptability, keeps their energy flowing more optimistically than pessimistically. After all is said and done, they strongly believe in embracing new ideals, even if adopting it takes an argument or two.

✺ ✯ ☽

CANCER & CAPRICORN

♋ ♑

"I feel and I use."

Cancer is a cardinal water sign from the 4th House of Home, whereas Capricorn is a cardinal earth sign from the 10th House of Career. They match each other's need for family, home, and financial security. Cancer will be focused on how to build a loving nest filled with the emotional support of family, while Capricorn will be focused on how to support a family through financial means. Both will think of ways to build a solid structure for their families, yet they differ in how they obtain it.

Cancer finds family as a motivation to progress. They require an emotional attachment in anything they do, otherwise they won't commit. Capricorn, on the other hand, finds money as a motivation to keep a family and doesn't feel that emotions play a part in providing. Cancer takes a more sensitive approach to their life, whereas Capricorn takes a more logical approach to theirs. Both strongly believe that without the responsibility of family or money, happiness cannot be fully achieved.

Negatively, they will find the balance of work and life challenging. Cancer likes to feel emotionally needed. Capricorn likes to feel financially needed. Capricorn can become so obsessed with their career that they unintentionally neglect their family. Cancer will then respond with overwhelming emotions, creating a rift between them that seems impossible to overcome.

Positively, they balance one another in and out of home. They are strong believers in providing for family and maintaining a home that is built on love and dependence. Both will share the same family values and will honor and respect each other's devotion to long-term sustainability.

✶ ☆ ☾

LEO & AQUARIUS

♌ ♒

"I will and I know."

Leo is a fixed fire sign from the 5th House of Creativity, whereas Aquarius is a fixed air sign from the 11th House of Friendship. They match each other's self-discipline and self-worth and have an influential power. Leo will focus on building their talents and utilizing them for the world to experience, whereas Aquarius will focus on building their intelligence and utilizing it to educate the world. Both are devoted to their life-long goals and will stubbornly hold onto their beliefs without distraction or negotiation.

Leo sees themselves as important beings who were created to shine light in places that are dim and dark. Aquarius sees themselves as knowledgeable beings who shine light in people who are dim and dark. Their motives for change are opposite yet similar. Leo believes that change must be led by a powerful leader who inspires it. Aquarius believes change comes from educated individuals who are willing to create it together.

Negatively, they both will be challenged to see and accept each other's perspectives, even though they both have the same intent. Leo will push living without fear, as this helps people reach their full potential. Aquarius will push rebellion against those you fear, as this will help unify and fulfill people's full potential. Both will struggle to take one another's lead, as they both are dominant and obstinate in their own right.

Positively, when they work alongside one another through independent means, they will balance humanity as a whole. Both are determined to create a difference in their community, with Leo being the leader they're destined to be and Aquarius being the educator they strive to be.

✵ ✵ ☾

VIRGO & PISCES

♍ ♓

"I analyze and I believe."

Virgo is a mutable earth sign from the 6th House of Service, whereas Pisces is a mutable water sign from the 12th House of Self-Undoing. They match each other's self-awareness, imagination, and observations. Virgo focuses on how to better communities through efficient processing and invention, whereas Pisces focuses on how to utilize their intuition to better heal themselves and others through spirituality. Both will be focused on how to promote an ideal lifestyle that is built on mental and emotional wellness.

Virgo likes to analyze everything and everyone and sees life from a more logical, realistic, and pessimistic view. They instinctually see imperfections and will strengthen them into their idea of perfection. Pisces likes to dream of everything and everyone and sees life more abstractly, romantically, and spiritually. They believe there is a divine reason to all flaws and imperfections and they should be embraced to reach true perfection.

Negatively, they will have a difficult time understanding what the other believes. Virgo will only believe in perspectives that have studies or evidence to back them up. Pisces, on the other hand, will believe in what they intuitively feel, with or without proof. Virgo tends to criticize topics that Pisces finds too sensitive. Pisces will combat this behavior with passive-aggressive pettiness, throwing the negative energy back at Virgo and creating further confusion.

Positively, they are willing to work through any issues, as they strongly believe in expressing and understanding their perceptions. This, in turn, creates a perfectly balanced emotional and mental bond. They eventually become the perfection the other has been seeking.

✹ ☆ ☾

☀☆☽

NATAL CHART FORMULA

Now that you've gotten as much information as possible, you can start reading your natal chart. So, let's put everything we've learned together. Using the formula below, fill in the blanks for every planet and aspect in your natal chart. You can get as detailed as you want.

Sign/Planet 1: _____ in the _____ house of _____.

Sign/Planet 2: _____ in the _____ house of _____.

Sign/Planet 1 & 2 create the following aspect: _____.

Sign/Planet 1 means:

_____

_____

_____

Sign/Planet 1 in the _____ house means:

_____

_____

_____

Sign/Planet 2 means:

_____

_____

_____

Sign/Planet 2 in the _____ house means:

_____

_____

_____

Sign 1 & Sign 2 are energetically incompatible/compatible (circle one). Describe the incompatibilities/compatibilities between the two.

_____

_____

_____

The aspect and compatibility of the signs and planets describes this person more accurately as (interpret all the information collected):

_____

_____

_____

_____

_____

AUTHOR NOTES

If you get lost, don't worry. You can always come back to it when you have a better understanding. Success is the act of not giving up, so take your time and be kind to yourself. You can also summarize a lot of these parts or create your own formula!

Remember, different astrologers have different interpretations. You do not have to follow "the rules." Follow your intuition and do what feels good to you. You can't go wrong if your heart and soul are one.

✵ ☆ ☾

SAMPLE FORMULA

Sign/Planet 1: Sagittarius Sun in the 10th House of Career

Sign/Planet 2: Virgo Moon in the 8th House of Regeneration

Sign/Planet 1 & 2 create the following aspect: Square

Sign/Planet 1 means:

The Sun is described as the base energy, and it resides in the zodiac sign Sagittarius, meaning this person will have Sagittarius traits. Sagittarius is a mutable fire sign, known for its fast reflexes, keen foresight, philosophical mindset, risk-taking/reckless behavior, wandering thoughts, free spirit (commitment-phobic), and blunt and vocal expressions.

Sign/Planet 1 in the 10th house means:

A Sun in the 10th house means this person is extremely ambitious, finding value in their achievements and worldly success. Borrowing energy from Sagittarius means this person pursues success aggressively, yet they have trouble committing to anything too routine, tedious, or dull.

They need to feel inspired to achieve success. They may do better as an entrepreneur, where they must take accountability for themselves lest they suffer poverty and shame. It's in this way they will be able to gauge their own sense of worth and achieve financial independence.

Sign/Planet 2 means:

The Moon influences emotional energy, and it resides in the zodiac sign Virgo. Virgo is a mutable earth sign that's known for its analytical and perfectionist mindset. It prides itself on being timely, reasonable, and logistical. Since the Moon is borrowing energy from Virgo, it means this person likes to overanalyze emotions, can come off cold and detached, and likes to be productive with their emotions. They abhor overly emotional

☀☆☾

situations, always wanting to resolve and compromise as quickly as possible.

Sign/Planet 2 in the 8th house means:

The Moon in the 8th House of Regeneration means that a person prefers deep reflection and making use of their intuition when handling strong emotions. They tend to internalize their feelings, wanting to make a spiritual connection with the situation (good or bad).

Borrowing energy from Virgo, we find that this person analyzes with the intent to reflect spiritually before they act. They are also prone to being judgmental and overly critical of themselves and others. There is a strong sense of moral ethics and integrity. They understand that actions must match words, and people who do not follow this rule will be ruled out of their circle.

Sign 1 & Sign 2 are energetically (incompatible)/compatible (circle one). Describe the incompatibilities/compatibilities between the two.

Virgo and Sagittarius are mutable signs, but Virgo is earth and Sagittarius is fire. Elementally, they are incompatible. They form an incompatible hard aspect: square. Naturally, these two zodiac signs are also incompatible.

The aspect and compatibility of signs and planets describes this person more accurately as (interpret all the information collected):

The Sun and Moon form a hard aspect, square, which creates tension between the planets. Virgo and Sagittarius are energetically and elementally incompatible. However, they are both mutable signs, which creates a small amount of compatibility. On the surface, this person is bubbly and vocal, especially when they're in their element of the 10th house, meaning they are comfortable, expressive, and open when they're showcasing their skills and knowledge, and they find it beneficial to open up to get ahead in their career.

However, their Virgo Moon resides in the 8th house, creating distance and tension between their public and private self. This person can experience

✵☆☾

extreme phases of tension, pressure, anxiety, or depression. Self-expression and vulnerability will also be very challenging.

This person requires a lot of deep reflection, where they can take their time in processing or analyzing how they feel before their Sagittarius mouth starts to burn bridges of career opportunities. They may overthink, over-assume, or jump to conclusions, having a more worrisome mentality toward anything unplanned. Where Sagittarius can be spontaneous, Virgo Moons will reduce this craving. Where Virgo is more routine and organized, a Sagittarius Sun will fight against this through procrastination.

FINAL THOUGHTS

You can deviate from this formula as time goes on. The point is to teach you how to break down the information, making it easier to understand and put together. When you have a stronger understanding of all the components, your interpretations will become more accurate and detailed.

Remember to take your time and don't get frustrated. Commit to learning everything and gain experience by reading your friends' and family members' natal charts. You can even Google celebrity birth charts if you don't feel comfortable asking for people's personal information. It's not certain how accurate celebrity charts are, but it can give you a general starting point in developing your abilities.

✿☆☾

☀☆☽

ACKNOWLEDGEMENT

I would like to firstly thank God, our creator. It is a blessing to know that God has blessed, protected, and guided me in my life. Some may feel that God has no place in astrology, but we won't get political here. There were many rough times in my life, and I experienced such a dark depression masked by severe drug addiction when I was young. If it weren't for spirituality, astrology, and God, I wouldn't be here today. Without their sweet words of encouragement and compassion for little ol' me, I wouldn't have had the courage to pick myself up and live my life. For that, I am forever indebted to God, Jesus, and the Archangels, especially Archangel Gabriel.

I would like to thank all of my clients and fans, all of whom I consider friends and family. Without your support for my work, I do not believe I would have gotten this far in my spiritual career. Learning from your experiences, reading your charts, and engaging with you has helped me grow as a person and a professional. It is truly amazing and emotional to me that so many of you have resonated with my work. It is both meaningful and inspiring to have an audience that understands what it means to learn, accept, and love strangers with like-minded beliefs and values. I love you with all my being.

I would like to thank my Taurus grandmother. She helped raise me and introduced me to astrology as a child. She shaped my beliefs, thoughts, and spirituality. She always keeps it real, and I value her guidance, even if it is just repeated stories. I don't mind because I love her for everything she has ever done for my sister and me. She always tells me over the phone that I was the sweetest child, and anytime she corrected me, I would just do it. She vibes with my Virgo Moon and my Taurus IC. I will always cherish and remember the times we had from when I was a child until today. She taught me how to refine my reading and writing. As a former teacher in the Philippines, she is a writer and poet herself. I remember she won a poetry contest and it inspired

☀☆☽

me to continue writing. I love her so much. There isn't anything I wouldn't do to keep her around for the rest of my life.

I would like to thank my Virgo grandmother. Though I didn't grow up with her, I learned so much when we were living together in San Diego with my mother. She is the reason why I have learned and accepted my spiritual gifts. She passed away November 16, 2020. God rest her soul. She was a shining light I will never forget. I wish I had given more time to her when she was alive, but I will always cherish and value our time together. I remember she would predict events through white candle magic, which she always did on a certain night. She loved when I made her wontons, and she loved to gamble in life, literally! I will miss her dearly, but now, she has become one of my great ancestors and a part of my altar and soul.

I would like to thank my husband, my patient and loving Taurus. Without your support, love, and encouragement, I wouldn't have been able to fulfill my wildest dreams. You accept me for who I am and have listened to all my worries, pain, happiness, and success. You always want the best for me. I love and appreciate your unwavering loyalty, stability, and wise advice. Your words and actions have helped shaped me into who I am today. You are more than a lover; you are my friend, partner, and soul. You have shown me that a person *can* love unconditionally. You allow me to be myself and are my favorite shoulder to cry on. The love I have for you is more than I have ever felt for anybody else romantically.

I would like to thank my Aquarius best friend whose natal chart completes my own. We are complimentary in every way. We have remained friends for well over 11 years now, and I have nothing but eternal love for you. You have seen my growth as a person, you have been there for all my ups and downs, and we have always remained connected no matter the distance. When I was young, I had a dark and tragic phase in my life. I prayed to God for just one friend, and I believe that friend is you. I see you as a true blessing from God,

☼☆☾

a soul friend I've met in many lifetimes. You complete me, and I will always be thankful for your wise advice in helping me see life from different perspectives. You have helped me see all the good in humanity, and I love and appreciate you and all the time we've shared in person and our hours of conversations when we are apart.

I would like to thank my Gemini mother. Though in my younger years, we weren't always on the same path, I still love you and thank you for all that you've done for me when I was a young adult. I remember when you took me in when I had nowhere else to go, how you lent me your car to go to school, and how you never once complained because you believed in my dreams. You helped me get back on my feet and made up for all the lost time. I remember you bought us tickets to a show, and we went to the theater. We walked around for so long until we finally asked someone where it was. He told us the show wasn't until the next weekend. We laughed about it on the way home, and it's a memory that I cherish to this day. You also helped me with my wedding and walked me down the aisle and held my hand. These are memories that can never be replaced. I promise I will do whatever I can to give you the best memories in your later years. I love you.

Last, but definitely not least, I would like to thank my Leo sister. You are the shining star of this family. You have the confidence I wish I had, yet it inspires me to always do my best. You have my back no matter what. Your loyalty and protection over me are things I will always cherish. We have been through so much together, but knowing I can always turn to you brings me a happiness and peace I will never find in anybody else. You and I are star twins, destined to move as one until the end of time. There is nobody else I would rather spend my time with. I hope God allows us more lifetimes together as siblings. I love you even when our fiery selves get on each other's nerves. No matter what, I will always be there for you. I know you will always be there for me. Let us light up the world together!

✺ ☆ ☾

☼ ☆ ☾

SPIRITUAL RESOURCES

SPIRITUAL GUIDANCE

Book a spiritual session with Joan Zodianz at **zodianz.com**. She is only available for seasonal work from May to June and November to December.

ONLINE COURSES

Take Joan Zodianz's online courses for spirituality, tarot, and astrology on **zodianz.com**. Take your time and develop your spiritual gifts.

CANVAS ART

If you love the zodiac images by Joan Zodianz in this book or if you are interested in goddess art, you can buy colored canvasses on **zodianz.com**.

SOCIAL MEDIA

Follow Joan Zodianz on Instagram **@zodianz** for the latest updates and subscribe to her YouTube channel **Zodianz** for the latest astrology videos.

SPIRITUAL ZUNDAYZ (PODCAST)

Tune in every Sunday to Joan's weekly horoscope on iTunes, Podbean, Spotify, or Google Play.

✺ ☆ ☾

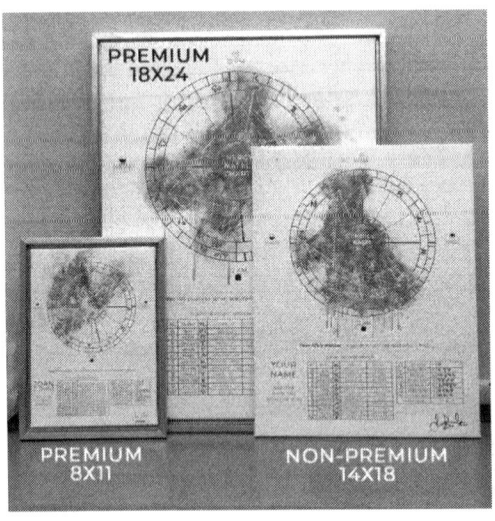

ENERGY NATAL CHARTS

Joan Zodianz provides unique intuitive canvassed artwork based on your personal horoscope (natal chart). Check out her work, fully colored, on **zodianz.com**.

GODDESS PORTRAITS

Joan Zodianz offers digitally painted fantasy portraits based on your image and the Goddess or Archangel of your choice. Check out her work, fully colored, on **zodianz.com**.

*Prices, products, and services are subject to change. Please visit Zodianz.com for any updates.

☼ ☆ ☾

Remember to be kind and humble,
love freely without fear or shame, and
always do your best when nobody is looking.

Love xoxo,
Joan Zodianz

☀☆☾

Printed in Great Britain
by Amazon

349R00181